My Books My Life

OTHER BOOKS by ALMA FLOR ADA

MEMOIRES
Vivir en dos idiomas
Cartas desde Napoli
Tesoros de mi isla. Una infancia cubana

NOVELS
A pesar del amor
En clave de sol

POETRY
Cuando el amor vive en la mirada
Minuto eterno. Poemas, canciones y una fábula poética

LITERARY STUDY
Pedro Salinas: El diálogo creador

PEDAGOGICAL
with F. Isabel Campoy
A Magical Encounter: Latino Literature in the Class. Mariposa.
Alegría: Poesía cada día. National Geographic
Authors in the Classroom: A Transformative Education Experience.
Pearson.
Ayudando a nuestros hijos. Mariposa.
Está linda la mar: Para comprender y utilizar la poesía en la clase.
Santillana. Vista Higher Learning.
Guía para padres y maestros de niños bilingües. Multilingual Matters.
La fascinante historia de la lengua española. Velázquez Press.
Música amiga: Aprender cantando. Mariposa.
Palabra amiga. Domina el idioma. Velázquez Press.
Spanish Literacy Strategies for Young Learners. Frog Street.

A complete list of my published work at the end of this book.

Alma Flor Ada

My Books My Life

Foreword and final essay by
Janet Hill and Anthony L. Manna

With collaborations from
F. Isabel Campoy, Suni Paz, Leslie Tryon,
Gabriel Zubizarreta-Ada and Rosalma Zubizarreta-Ada

MARIPOSA. Transformative Education.
San Rafael, California

COVER:

ODALISCA
Martha Jiménez, 2016

To my grandchildren
Timothy, Samantha, Victoria and *Nicholas, Daniel* and *Dougie,*
Camille, Jessica and *Collette Zubizarreta*

my great-nieces and nephews:
Julian, Emily Flor, Ethan and *Robert Pettit,*
Via, Aidan, Sky and *Harmony Rohde*
Ivy *Grace* and *Paul [Hoke] Fellers*
Elva Gladys, Faye Modesta and *Delphine Beverly Fellers*

and all the new generations of the
Lafuente Salvador Family

Acknowledgements

My gratitude to the generous editors and publishers
who helped turn my manuscripts into books:

Dámaso Alonso, *Editorial Gredos, Spain*
Donna Bray, *Hyperion*
Rosemary Brosnan, *HarperCollins*
Susan Burke, *Atheneum*
Ana Cerro, *Atheneum*
Arthur Chou, *Velázquez Press*
Sharon Coatney, *Libraries Unlimited*
Anne Davies, *Harcourt Children's Books*
Kristy Domenech Miller - *Houghton Mifflin Harcourt*
Amaya Elezcano Tolosa, *Alfaguara, Spain*
Nuria Esteban, *Editorial Espasa-Calpe, Spain*
Karen Kotyjla, *Dell*
Jonathan Lanman, *Atheneum*
Sam Laredo, *Santillana, Laredo Publishing*
Emma Ledbetter, *Atheneum*
Arthur Levine, *Putnam*
Donna Dombroski Locki, *Harcourt School Publishers*
Tony Locki, *Harcourt School Publishers*
Sherry Long, *Hampton-Brown*
Aurora Martínez, *Allyn & Bacon*
Emiliano Martínez, *Santillana, Spain*
Silvia Matute, *Alfaguara/SantillanaUSA*
Isabel Mendoza, *Alfaguara/SantillanaUSA*
Luisa Noguera - *Panamericana, Colombia*
Felicidad Orquín, *Editorial Espasa-Calpe, Spain*
Susan Pearson, *Lothrop*
Kristy Raffensberger, *Atheneum*
Antonio Ramos, *Santillana, Spain*
Lousie Roberts, *Aladdin*
Boris Romero, *Editorial Arica/Editorial Brasa, Perú*
Lucas Rodríguez Plaza, *Hijos de Santiago Rodríguez, Spain*
Diane Thomas Pittari, *Harcourt School Publishers*
Liz VanDoren, *Harcourt*
Patricia Vásquez, *Cengage*

And with deep appreciation to the memory of Bernice Randall, editor extraordinary, creative translator, and dear friend, from whom I learned about the care that is needed to produce a book that makes us proud.

With much gratefulness to the illustrators whose talent
and creativity have given visual life to my stories and poems:
María de Jesús Álvarez
Reg Cartwright
Felipe Dávalos
David Díaz
Viví Escrivá
Susan Gaber
Stephanie García
Leonid Gore
Susan Guevara
Kim Howard
G. Brian Karas
Barry Koch
Kathleen Kuchera
Claudia Legnazzi
Lori Lohstoeter
Ana López Escrivá
Sandra López Escrivá
Antonio Martorell
Jacobo Muñiz
Abigail Pizer
Larry Ramond
Frank Remkiewicz
Lizzy Rockwell
Edel Rodríguez
Enrique O. Sánchez
José Ramón Sánchez
Louise Bates Satterfield
Elivia Savadier
Simón Silva
Maribel Suárez
K. Dyble Thompson
Pablo Torrecilla
Leslie Tryon
Gabhor Utomo
Neill Waldman
Ulises Wensell
Terry Ybáñez
and to Suni Paz for the beautiful music she has created
for my poetry and for the unique voice with which
she sings these poems turned into songs.

Contents

WELCOME

Authors are frequently asked for information about their lives as they relate to their writing as well as the process of creating their book. Providing answers to those questions motivated Libraries Unlimited to develop the series *The Author and You.* This book is an outgrowth of the two volumes of *Alma Flor Ada and You,* published in that series. It consolidates and upgrades significantly the previous content, and brings it up to date. I am deeply grateful to Libraries Unlimited, and in particular to Sharon Coatney, for the opportunity to create the original books and for the many new insights about my own work and its connections with my life that I discovered in the process of writing them.

An intensely lived long life of prolific production provides ample information. Since I do not anticipate any reader going through this book all at once I have occasionally repeated some information in different chapters to facilitate their consistency.

As I revisited those pages to bring them up to date and to include information on my writings for adults readers I could not but feel immense gratitude for life's generosity in granting me the opportunity to work with such talented illustrators, musicians, translators, editors and co-authors, as well as for the support that I have always received from my family, as I engaged on these activities. .

I am also indebted to F. Isabel Campoy, Leslie Tryon, Suni Paz, Rosalma Zubizarreta and Gabriel Zubizarreta for the chapters they wrote to share the extent of their collaboration in the creative process and to Janet Hill and Anthony L. Manna, for the generous texts that open and close this book. I am also grateful to my granddaughter Camille Zubizarreta for her help in the revising and publishing process.

Foreword: A Promise for a Better World

Janet Hill and Anthony L. Manna

For many years, Alma Flor Ada's books have delighted audiences of all ages while they have also given voice to the experiences of parallel cultures. Her books have been appreciated for the social issues they uncover, for the way they celebrate the basic goodness of people, and for how they motivate readers to take action for democratic change and liberation.

The more we spend time in her world, the more we see that Alma Flor Ada's vision is informed by a deeply rooted commitment to social change and reform. As a disciple of the educational philosopher Paulo Freire, she has adopted Freire's legacy that calls for the social transformation of our world through the liberation of mind and spirit. Freire's theory promotes an educational system that liberates underrepresented populations, through claiming and reclaiming their own voices and their dignity, from the dominance of power structures and individuals who oppress others. Freire spent his life working for people's liberation, awakening them to a profound quest in which they experience a transformation of consciousness and recognition of their true voices and their newfound freedom. Through this experience, marginalized people are able to realize that their situation is limiting rather than hopeless and that they can take action to transform their situations as a way of making them more equitable and giving them power over their own lives. Freire offers people liberation through their own personal narratives. In a sense, then, giving them the words is the beginning of their empowerment.

Freire's presence is felt in Ada's books as her characters work against oppression and liberate themselves through positive action within the community, an action that supports an

awakening to personal rights, personal freedom, social consciousness, and responsibility to self and others. Her books echo Freire's statement, "Men (and women) are not built in silence but in word, in work, in action-reflection."[1] In Alma Flor Ada's works, this sense of community is evident in the adventures of a little field mouse in *Friend Frog,* the delightful fairy-tale characters in *Dear Peter Rabbit* and its sequels, and in the lives of contemporary children, as in *I Love Saturdays y domingos.*

Freire tells us that in "order to read the word we must read the world."[2] What he implies here is that language can dispel the myths that are controlled by the dominant culture. By this he means that we must read the word in the context of the cultural, social, and political practices of those in power and control. Yet, reading the world is not only developing a critical awareness of this dominance, it is also taking action by working within the culture and among the people to effect the kind of understanding that will lead to social change and personal transformation. Alma Flor Ada's life and work bring to reality this humanization in books that addresses the search for companionship, the recognition of humanity in others, the construction of community through solidarity, and the challenge of working toward the common good. Our task in this chapter is to take the social worlds Ada constructs in her critically celebrated picture books and bring to light their significance in the context of their social commentary. In a sense, we are reading **her** reading of the world as it is manifested in her picture books.

MOVING FROM ISOLATION TO COMMUNITY

In many of her picture books, Ada explores the transition from isolation to community. Her characters are often incomplete until they develop relationships with others and begin thinking outside themselves. In the picture book *Friend Frog,* this incompleteness is felt by Field Mouse as he sets out to find a friend, only to discover that this is no easy task. When he finally meets Frog, Field Mouse is disheartened because he cannot croak, jump, or swim like her. But Field Mouse persists and, one day, literally saves Frog's life by  alerting her with a quick warning that allows her to jump away from the clutches of a hungry falcon. Although Field Mouse wishes he could be like Frog so they could be friends, he also appreciates Frog's skills and admires her charming ways. What makes this delightful fable so outstanding, in addition to the surprising role reversals, is the feeling that the unassuming Field Mouse does not have to compromise his identity to form a friendship, although he cannot jump, croak, hop, or swim. In other words, he doesn't have to assimilate in order to be accepted. Instead, he is able to hold on to his individuality.

Ada has spoken about the loss of individuality when a person wants to be accepted by others. She believes that assimilation drains self-esteem, a sense of cultural pride, and a close communication with family members.[3] The story of *Friend Frog* plays out this tension of choosing between individuality and change for the sake of friendship. Field Mouse's persistence is the key to securing a satisfying relationship. All it takes, sometimes, is the discovery of a common bond for companionship to develop. In the case of Field Mouse and Frog, the  falcon's threat and the need for survival are what eventually bring the two together.

 In *The Malachite Palace,* another picture book, a sheltered princess moves from her lonely existence into the outside world where she joins a group of children playing beyond the palace gates. The princess, bound by the class bigotry of her elders, is forced to live without friends. Her mother, governess, and lady-in-waiting forbid her to play with the local children whom they perceive as being "rude,"

"ignorant," and "common." What gives the adults' attitude an ironic twist is that they are thwarting the development and happiness of the child they are supposed to be nurturing. One day, tough, a golden bird enters the palace, filling the girl's dreary room with music. The adults immediately and symbolically capture and cage the intruder who then ceases to sing. When the princess sets the bird free and transforms the cage from a confined space to an open feeder, her bird returns with other birds and awakens her own need for companionship. Defying her elders, she takes responsibility for her own freedom and at last joins the children that she has wanted to be with for so long.

In *The Malachite Palace,* the catalyst for change is nature. It is nature that motivates the princess to take responsibility for her freedom and remove her from the forces that hold her down. Alma Flor Ada once told us about her own deep spiritual connection with nature. As a child, she gained comfort from nature, especially when she sought solace in a particular large tree near her house. "I felt like the tree was embracing me. I would just hold on to those smooth roots and feel that I was being caressed. It's very difficult to explain, but if I had a sorrow or a pain I would go and tell it to the tree . . . and I felt totally heard, understood, supported."

Jordi in *Jordi's Star* also has a special relationship with nature that gives him comfort and later transforms him. While changing the land from a barren, desolate hillside that has been stripped by loggers to a lush countryside filled with plants and trees, Jordi, himself, changes radically from a sad and lonely hermit to a man in love with nature and with the people around him. For Jordi, it all starts when a star appears in a pool of water that was formed during a storm. Hypnotized by the star's power, Jordi cultivates the area around the pond to make a more pleasant home for his new friend the star, whom Jordi believes lives in the pond. Over time, he transforms the entire countryside.

Through this process of caring, he begins to see how beauty and friendship can enrich his life as he reaches out to the local farmers. Jordi awakens to the world around him and becomes a man filled with joy because he is able to touch the lives of others through beauty. This original folktale employs a true blend of text and image. In the beginning, the illustrator, Gaber, emphasizes his desolation by showing Jordi bent over as he makes his way home. At one point, she positions him at the bottom of a vast, barren hillside, which gives the impression that Jordi is very small and insignificant when, in fact, as later illustrations show, he is a burly giant of a man. And once Jordi discovers his star, Gaber juxtaposes the delicate features of nature against this large, but gentle soul.

Macedo has said, "People and their cultures perish in isolation, but they are born or reborn in contact with other men and women, with men and women of another culture, another creed, another race."⁴ Ada's tale of the princess caged in *The Malachite Palace* echoes Macedo's sentiments of the need for the individual to become fully realized through contact with others, particularly with others who are unlike us. This is exactly what the

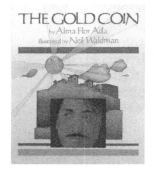

princess has come to, a place where she has the potential to grow through her experiences with children of a different class. And this is Ada's gift to her readers, that through our renewed relationship with the world, we come to know those different from us and thereby enlarge our understanding of human possibility. Similarly, Jordi has come into contact with others through his own spiritual reawakening. His personal transformation is set into motion by his desperate loneliness. He discovers he has inside him all the power that he needs to overcome his isolation.

Loneliness also serves as a vehicle for personal change in *The Gold Coin*. It is through work on the land that Juan, a miserable thief, breaks through his loneliness and begins to understand the true meaning of wealth. Juan ransacks an old woman's hut, intent on stealing her gold. When his search is unsuccessful, he follows her as she travels the countryside, caring for the

sick. At each destination, he arrives too late and learns that the healer has already gone to help another. Juan is obliged to work for the farmers he meets along the way in exchange for help in finding her. While he is harvesting potatoes, corn, beans, squash, and coffee, he experiences an evolutionary process of self-discovery. At each farm, Juan is reacquainted with life's simple gifts: the beauty in nature, a home-cooked meal, a handshake, and a smile. Along the way he learns of the generosity and special powers of the healer, Doña Josefa. By the time he meets with her, all his good work has changed him from a greedy thief to a more caring human being. But it isn't until he discovers that each of his helpers refused Doña Josefa's gold that the transformation is complete. In the end, Juan also refuses the gold coin and offers to repair the damages he made to Doña Josefa's house so that she may leave to heal others.

Freire has said, 'The pursuit of full humanity . . . cannot be carried out in isolation or individualism, but only in fellowship and solidarity."[5] About Juan's transformation, Freire might say

that Juan's journey is the process of becoming authentically human, of moving out of his self-absorbed misery into relationships with others. As a thief, Juan is not fully human and considers his victims, particularly Doña Josefa, as objects that exist only to help him survive. Doña Josefa's mysterious power and her altruistic spirit serve as Juan's spiritual guide. And it is the self-fulfillment brought about by good, collaborative work that serves as a conduit to connect him to others and brings him outside himself.

At the heart of this story, there is a tension between Doña Josefa's acts of love and Juan's acts of "violence." Happily, this tension is resolved as Juan's respect for humanity grows when he recognizes her goodness. Juan grows to appreciate Doña Josefa's goodness as he develops a respect for humanity, or in the words of Macedo, "If we do not recognize our humanity in others, we shall not recognize it in ourselves."[6]

Field Mouse in *Friend Frog,* the Princess in *The Malachite Palace,* Jordi in *Jordi's Star,* and Juan in *The Gold Coin* live solitary lives until their worlds are reopened through their contact with others. They are lifted out of their isolation once they have touched community.

THE BEST OF ALL WORLDS

In several of Ada's other picture books, community is the bond for the help, support, validation, and mobilization around a cause. The Hidden Forest books bring these elements of community to life. Ada blends characters from several well-known European children's tales in a format that allows for a delightfully diverse community of animals and humans. The inhabitants of the Hidden Forest interact, solve problems, ward off the common threat, and celebrate accomplishments and milestones. Told in the form of letters, each of the three books explores different aspects of community. In the first, *Dear Peter Rabbit,* a supportive community is established. In *Yours Truly, Goldilocks,* the threats of two wolves become a community responsibility. In the third book in the series, *With Love, Little Red Hen,* the characters work together to help a new resident, a single mother hen, establish herself. In all three books, the illustrations create a playful and imaginative natural setting that vividly interprets the idyllic world of the hidden forest. The illustrator of the books, Leslie Tryon's charming characters, clever details, and dramatic scenes strengthen the emerging solidarity that develops further with each new book.

In *Dear Peter Rabbit,* Goldilocks is given the role of Mr. McGregor's daughter who serves as a catalyst to bring diverse characters together by inviting them all to her birthday party. This is a new, reformed Goldilocks who, after her apology, makes friends with Baby Bear and revisits the Bears' house, this time by invitation. She also gets to know Little Red Riding Hood whom she first meets in the woods after seeing her talking to a seemingly friendly wolf. She even tries to correspond with Peter Rabbit, although he is eating her father's

vegetables. Also taking center stage are the Three Pigs whose famous efforts to secure a home are related within this story. Lurking in the background is the constant threat of the wolves whose plans to get a meal are always thwarted.

It has been said that Ada's work, "deftly balances a celebration of the uniqueness."[7] The first of the Hidden Forest books does just that. In this story, there are no dominant groups. The female voices are strong; females and males have an equal say. The characters work out difficulties, such as Goldilocks apologizing for her entry into the Bears' house, and embrace differences, such as Red

Riding Hood's enjoyment of the company of Goldilocks's interesting animal friends at the party. There is no class or caste hierarchy and everybody looks out for the good of everyone else in cordial, but not smothering, ways. The characters maintain their individuality within a community where respect and admiration are the norms.

If ever there were a series that could help children hone their inferential skills, it is the Hidden Forest books. In other words, Ada leaves many gaps for readers to fill based upon their understanding of the stories and the structures and motifs of children's traditional literature. For example, the two wolves, aptly named Wolfy Lupus and Fer O'Cious, are predictably devious and hungry, enjoying the task of preying on the innocent even though they are defeated at every turn by those more clever than they. One can count on them to act and blunder exactly as they do. It is Ada's skill as a storyteller that prevents these stories from becoming predictable. She embellishes the tales with clever turns, playing with the relationships among the characters and creating humorous twists to events.

In *Yours Truly, Goldilocks,* the second book in the Hidden Forest series, the community is once again brought together for a celebration; this time it's a housewarming party for the pigs' new brick house. Meanwhile, those incorrigible wolves are plotting another attack. When the friends return home from the party, the wolves' plan goes awry, thanks to Mother Bear's valiant rescue. The friends are then united by their mutual need for self-protection. In the last letter in the book, Goldilocks is not only the catalyst for bringing the forest inhabitants together, but she also serves as an organizer for the cause. She calls her friends to action by asking them to join her and Red Riding Hood in planning "how to make sure those ugly wolves cannot hurt us." She continues by encouraging them to mobilize when she says, "Please begin thinking of wonderful ideas. When we decide a time and place to meet, we will let you know."[8] Here, once again, we see the Freirian notion that individuals must join forces and recognize their need to work together for freedom.

With Love, Little Red Hen is the third of the Hidden Forest books. This time, the citizens come together as concerned and caring neighbors. The center of their attention is the delightfully industrious Little Red Hen, a single mom taking care of her seven young chicks. In contrast to Red Hen's industriousness are her three neighbors, Mr. Cat, Mr. Goose, and Mr. Dog who, when asked to help, can only come up with the familiar, "Not I, Not I, Not I." In this story, Goldilocks returns in her role as organizer. She writes to Little Red Riding Hood suggesting that they all become good neighbors and help Red Hen with her farming. Red Riding Hood, Goldilocks, and the Bears, Rabbits, and Pigs secretly hoe, weed, and water Red Hen's crops. The wolves join forces with the lazy Mr. Cat, who lets them down in the end, leaving the wolves without their planned chicken dinner.

Each of the Hidden Forest books highlights a particular aspect of the dynamics of an ideal democratic community where the citizens develop friendships, unite against threats, and work for the common good. In the delightful picture-book medium, Ada is bringing to light a liberatory, transformative process of discovery that illuminates for her readers an ordered world of respect, shared values, support, camaraderie, and celebration.

In a more realistic vein, some of the same sentiments that emerge in the Hidden Forest series can be found in *I Love Saturdays y domingos* in which two cultures are explored on opposing pages until they finally come together on the same page in a grand celebration as a blended family. The idea is that they do exist side by side or, as Virginia Hamilton has said, as parallel cultures.[9] The grandparents—both European-American and Mexican-American—share rich language and life experiences through the stories they lovingly tell their granddaughter, the narrator. The final move in this warmhearted tribute to different family cultures is a special occasion that brings together this diverse group of people. This is truly the best of all possible worlds: parallel cultures existing harmoniously.

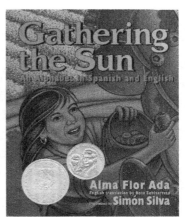

Throughout her children's books, there are echoes of the vision that Alma Flor Ada and her colleague, F. Isabel Campoy, have practiced and shared with communities around the world. The creative literacy process that they have named *Transformative Education* takes its participants on a journey of self-discovery by helping them "to find the tools to act on their own already established values and goals."[10] As with many of her characters, the participants are motivated to realize their own strength and power and to develop a strong social consciousness. Here again is the pursuit of the ideal democratic community as it is manifested in the real world. This Freirian vision of participatory democracy in a world in which diversity is respected and social justice is the norm is at the heart of Alma Flor Ada's life's work.

RESPONSIBILITY

In the movement for liberation envisioned by Freire and his followers, hope is sustained when people are responsible to one another. This type of solidarity encourages people to embrace the same dream about the same social concerns and social ideals.

In Alma Flor Ada's books we see people demonstrating this type of social accountability through their genuine interactions with each other, through good work, and through their resistance to oppression. We believe that her books generate an awareness of the kind of responsibility that is needed to improve society so that three goals can be accomplished: 1) to preserve humanness, 2) to care for and help one another, and 3) to work for the greater good.

These three social themes emerge through the diverse situations, conflicts, and relationships that Alma Flor Ada explores in her books. In *The Gold Coin,* for example, Doña Josefa's humane compassion directs Juan on a circular path that moves from one household to another and which ultimately leads to his transformation. *The Gold Coin* also puts the value of community at the heart of Doña Josefa's life's

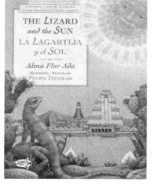

work. Her commitment is founded on the satisfaction of seeing people healed, healthy, and happy.

In *Gathering the Sun,* Alma Flor Ada focuses her lens directly on farmworkers, thereby honoring the lives of Hispanic laborers. *Gathering the Sun: An Alphabet Book in Spanish and English* is a wonderful tribute to the work migrant farm workers tirelessly do for the good of society. In single poems written for each letter of the alphabet, Ada gives praise to the farmers' dignity, their virtue, and their remarkable contribution to our survival and well-being. The poems validate elements that are integral to the lives of the workers, but also speak to each one of the three social themes of preserving humanness, caring for one another, and working for the greater good.

In several of Ada's books, a deep sense of community and caring for others plays a central role in keeping the community strong and intact. This happens in all three of the Hidden Forest books where celebrations are sure signs of the care and concern that the inhabitants of Happy Valley have for one another. Among the inhabitants, though, there is no match for Goldilocks's commitment to keep the community in a good place when it comes to protection, support, and the simple gift of keeping in contact with friends and family. In *Jordi's Star,* another sensitive and touching story, the environment is enriched at the hands of one caring soul. Jordi, an otherwise lonely man, eventually comes into contact with his neighbors through his work on the land. By giving the gift of beauty to society, Jordi comes into a better awareness of himself and the happiness of knowing that he matters to others.

Persistence that leads to putting the world back in balance is an important theme in *The Lizard and the Sun,* a bilingual (English/Spanish) retelling of a Mexican folktale. After the sun disappears for several days in what is pictured as the richly colored world of the Aztec empire, various animals fail to find the sun when they look for it in such places as rivers, lakes, the jungle, and the high volcano. When the animals give up the search, only Lizard, out of her concern for the health of the community, continues until she finds the sun encased in a mysteriously glowing rock. With the sun back in the sky, light and warmth are restored, crops are able to grow, and life can return to normal for all the worried folks and animals. Lizard's perseverance saves the day.

In contrast to many of Ada's stories that highlight the good deeds of responsible, caring characters, *The Three Golden Oranges,* another folktale known throughout the Hispanic world, stands out because of the competitive nature of the two older brothers. When the three of them are encouraged by their mother to find wives, Santiago, Tomás, and the youngest brother, Matías, are directed by the local wisewoman to retrieve three golden oranges from a faraway castle with the promise that by doing so they will find the wives they seek. At the same time, she warns  them that they must work together if they expect to find their hearts' desire. However, when they are motivated by self-gratification, the two older brothers abandon Matías in order to reach the orange grove ahead of him. Since they neglect to follow the wisewoman's advice, they fail in their attempts to break an enchantment and thus miss the opportunity to meet their brides. In this cautionary tale, the brothers' dismissal of their responsibility to each other further emphasizes the profound value of those virtues that thrive in the good- natured communities that Ada builds in so many of her books.

Alma Flor Ada also interprets responsibility as a commitment of the individual to reach out to the world and also to take charge of one's life. This pledge to personal responsibility is manifested in her books by making each day a little more generous and each life more courageous and authentic, by developing love and respect for humanity and all forms of life, and by accepting responsibility to personal growth and development.

All three themes of personal responsibility emerge in *The Malachite Palace.* The princess makes a better life for herself by finding the courage that she needs to break loose from the smothering attention of her elders. The actions of the princess create a contrast to this lack of generosity. Once she realizes that her condition is no better than that of the caged bird, the princess can no longer abide by her elders' scorn and takes responsibility for her own freedom. Only when she commits the generous act of setting the bird free does she finally break the ties that bind her to her insulated life. Defying her elders' bigotry, she joins the very children who have been oppressed through the elders' cold disregard.

Taking personal responsibility is also at work in *With Love, Little Red Hen.* Goldilocks's love and respect for humanity is evident when she organizes her friends to help Red Hen by encouraging them to secretly work in her garden. Goldi's generosity pays off through the personal rewards gained from those who helped. For instance, Peter Rabbit comes to a personal realization that it is much more rewarding to be kind to people than sneaking into gardens to steal their vegetables. For Little Red Riding Hood, painful blisters and a backache from working in the cornfields help her gain a deeper appreciation for the hard life of a farmer and the possibility that a good crop might fail. This insight gives her the opportunity to embrace the *other,* expanding her own respect for all of those who make up her community. Although Red Hen realizes that the Happy Valley contains some nasty folks, through the kindness of others she also realizes that she is surrounded by many good friends who are willing to help her out.

A strong need for companionship motivates Field Mouse in *Friend Frog* as he refuses to give up their potential friendship just because he cannot do all of the things that frog can do. Even though he cannot jump, hop, and croak, Field Mouse acts on his responsibility to himself to not give up on their friendship. Field Mouse takes a risk, reaches out to someone different, and gains a sense of his own worth, while also making a friend.

In *The Gold Coin,* Doña Josefa's acts of kindness and her spiritual beauty profoundly affect Juan. Her entire journey is taken up with using her sacred gift of healing powers to help others. As it turns out, her selflessness is contagious. Juan, the thief, catches it as he moves from farm to farm and listens to tales about Doña Josefa's generosity. In the beginning, Juan would do anything to get his hands on the healer's gold coin, but he eventually comes to realize that the value of wealth is not so much in having the coin, but in living an honest life that is fulfilled by helping others. The turning point in his moral outlook occurs when he generously offers to help Doña Josefa by repairing her hut. At the end of the story, he not only refuses the coin, but he also comes into his own sense of responsibility.

If there is one memorable ideal that Ada conveys to her readers, it is the belief that ordinary people can and must be agents for change. She told us, "I grew up knowing that one could give one's life to good causes." These causes take shape in Ada's stories when her characters pursue the liberatory transformation of spirit and mind, celebrate the possibilities of a community united around the common good, and work for basic human rights and freedoms. Ultimately, what drives Alma Flor Ada in her work is what sustains her in her daily life, which is a genuine love for the world and its people and a profound social commitment.

Notes

1. Paulo Freire, *Pedagogy of the Oppressed.* New York: Continuum, 1970, p. 76.

2. Paulo Freire and Donaldo Macedo. *Literacy: Reading the Word & the World.* South Hadley, MA: Bergin & Garvey, 1987, p. 29.
3. Alma Flor Ada, Telephone interview by authors, tape recording. Kent, Ohio, 18 January 2004.
4. Donaldo Macedo, *Literacies of Power: What Americans are Not Allowed to Know.* Boulder, CO: Westview, 1994.
5. Paulo Freire, *Pedagogy of the Oppressed.* New York: Continuum, 1970/2000, p. 85.
6. Donaldo Macedo, *Literacies of Power: What Americans are Not Allowed to Know.* Boulder, CO: Westview, 1994.
7. *Children's Literature Review* 62 (2000). Detroit: Gale Research, p. 90.
8. Alma Flor Ada. *Yours Truly, Goldilocks.* Illus. Leslie Tryon. New York: Atheneum, 1998, unpaged.
9. For more information about Virginia Hamilton's notion of parallel cultures, see Nina Mikkelsen, "A Conversation with Virginia Hamilton," *Journal of Youth Services in Libraries* 7 (1994): 382-405.
10. Anthony M. Manna, Janet Hill, and Kathy Kellogg, "Alma Flor Ada and the Quest for Change," *Language Arts* 82, no. 1 (2004): 77.

Bibliography

Ada, A. F. Presentation at the 19th Annual Virginia Hamilton Conference on Multicultural Literature for Youth, Kent, Ohio, April 2003.

Ada, Alma Flor. Telephone interview by authors, tape recording. Kent, Ohio, 18 January 2004.

Children's Literature Review 62 (2000). Detroit: Gale Research.

Freire, Paulo. *Pedagogy of the Oppressed.* New York: Continuum, 1970/2000.

Macedo, Donaldo. *Literacies of Power: What Americans are Not Allowed to Know.* Boulder, CO: Westview, 1994.

Manna, Anthony M., Janet Hill, and Kathy Kellogg. "Alma Flor Ada and the Quest for Change," *Language Arts* 82, no. 1 (2004): 76-79.

PEDAGOGY OF THE OPPRESSED

Para Alma,
alma de muita
gente, frater-
nalmente,

Paulo Freire

1983

Introduction

As I share my books with children, parents, librarians, and teachers, I find that behind each one there is another story. These "stories behind the books" can be just as rich as the ones in the text, and their veracity adds to their appeal.

But there is more to a book than even a story: there is also the worldview that is embodied in the choice of theme, of conflicts, and of solutions. The values that are present may speak in a more subtle voice or in a bolder one, yet in either case they sustain and shape the nature of the book.

No matter how different from the author's own life and experiences a story may be or whether it occurs in an imaginary setting or in another time and place, its essence is likely to reflect who the author is, along with her or his deeply held beliefs and feelings. This is why, in attempting to reveal the "stories behind the stories," the genesis of each book I have written, and their possible "hidden meanings," I have been finding in my stories not only the echoes of my own childhood experiences, as well as those of my children, but also the traces of long-held dreams, of my steadfast faith in life and human beings, and of my wish for a world of understanding, solidarity, justice, and peace. One writes who one is, or so it seems to me now more than ever, but one also writes one's hopes and dreams.

Here, then, are the experiences that inform the stories: the experiences of a long life lived in many different settings and rich in adventures, a life lived with careful attention to many small details—colors, sounds, fragrances, as well as the nuances of places, people, and speech. Here are the longings and the dreams, the awareness of loss and the joy of discovery, the sustaining forces of family and friendship, the pride of belonging to a rich culture. And here is the gratitude I feel toward all those who have gone before on the many roads I have traveled, as well as the irrepressible delight of setting forth on uncharted paths.

My gratitude goes out especially to all those who have nourished my work. My grandmother, Dolores Salvador Méndez, whom I have written about in many of my books and will mention more about in this one, has been a lifelong source of inspiration. Although she died before I was seven, her presence has informed my entire life. My parents, Alma Lafuente Salvador and Modesto Ada Rey, worked very hard and made many sacrifices for my education, and no amount of gratitude could ever repay their generosity. The instances of their love are too many to mention, but 1 will always bless my mother's foresight in giving me a portable electric typewriter for my eighteenth birthday. It became an invaluable tool for my

studies, as well as the means for earning a living for many years afterward while I was an impoverished immigrant student in Perú.

Many years later, her gift of a *Selectric* typewriter—a big sacrifice at the time, as she was supporting herself and my youngest sister on a teacher's salary—allowed me to continue my writing in the United States. Those gifts of love made a world of difference in my life. Although my father died much too young, when I was just becoming an adult, his conscious way of living—always paying attention to details and offering his thoughtful reflections on everything he read or saw, experienced or pondered—has been an incomparable legacy. No day goes by without the gift of his memory enriching my awareness.

Every one of my books, and this one is no exception, is indebted to my own children, Rosalma, Alfonso, Miguel, and Gabriel Zubizarreta Ada, for their constant and generous support. They have been a continuous source of inspiration, and it is because of their encouragement and love that I have been able to create the books mentioned here. People are frequently surprised that I was able to produce such an extensive body of work while having  been, for much of that time, the single mother of four children. My response has always been that it is because of my children that I have been able to produce so much.

From a very young age, my children have believed in my work and offered their help. My daughter Rosalma began translating my writing into English when she was twelve, and her gift for language and her insights have earned recognition from my editors. My three sons took over many of the family responsibilities early on, not only by helping with household chores but also by working while still in school. Their integrity, sense of responsibility, and dedication to their work and families, continue to inspire me today. My son Alfonso has nourished my work in a special way by creating Del Sol Books, a distributing house and small press, to promote my work and that of Isabel Campoy. Now, owned by his cousin Ray Vance it continues to promote our books and CDs, as well as those of other Latino authors.

My sons Miguel and Gabriel are always close at hand, ready to help with any of my needs, as well as to offer their loving support. Gabriel surprised and delighted me by becoming my co-author of two recent middle grades novels, *Dancing Home* and *Love, Amalia.* My children's faith in me has been my greatest strength, helping me to prevail over the challenges of being an immigrant and a nonnative English speaker. And now, in addition to the many  joys of being a grandmother, I am enjoying the further blessing of seeing my grandchildren begin to show an interest in my work.

I want to make a special mention here of my gratitude to the late Bernice Randall, an extraordinary editor with whom I had the privilege of working closely for many years. I learned enormously from Bernice about the care that goes into creating a final text and into the many subsequent steps before a book is finally printed. I continue to draw on her lessons with each new book.

This book is particularly indebted to Sherrill Brooks, excellent editor and supportive friend, who carefully edited the original manuscript, and to my daughter Rosalma Zubizarreta, for her valuable comments to the final text.

My gratitude also goes out to all of the friends, too many to mention, who have shown an interest in my work, and in particular to the numerous librarians, teachers, and parents who have helped to make my books available to children.

For after all it is truly the children for whom so much of my work is intended. It is their smiles, their joy in the language, their delight in the stories, their heartfelt comments and reflections that continue to make the labor of writing so extraordinarily worthwhile.

Words of Hope: Living to Write, Writing to Love

My fascination with books, which has been an integral part of my whole life, began at a very early age. Yet even before I ever experienced the wonder of a book, I had already developed a love for words. Surrounded by a family who loved and created poetry and songs, who read and memorized stories or created their own, words were a constant presence.

Words from the old ballads that my mother sang as lullabies sparkled in my imagination:

Las mañanas de San Juan	*On the Feast Day of St. John*
se levanta el Conde Niño	*the Child Count arises early*
a dar agua a su caballo	*to bring water to his fine horse*
a la orillita del mar.	*by the edge of the bright sea.*

Living on an island, I knew well the joys of being by the sea. I could easily imagine a fresh seaweed-scented breeze and the taste of salt on my lips. Yet the words of the ballad called forth images unlike anything I had ever known. What would it feel like, to be out by the seashore, giving water to my horse in the early morning hours? And how could a child be a count? My anticipation of the romance that would develop between the count and the young princess who watched him walking his horse on the sand only added to the pleasure of hearing the ballad one more time.

Words shone in José Marti's verses, sung in my grandmother's voice to a tune that she herself had composed:

Quiero a la sombra de un ala	*Beneath the shade of a bird's wing*
contarte este cuento en flor	*I'll tell you a story in bloom*
la niña de Guatemala	*of the Guatemalan girl,*
la que se murió de amor.	*she who lived and died for love.*
Ella dio al desmemoriado	*She gave to her careles swain*
una almohadilla de olor.	*a tiny pillow filled with fine herbs*
El volvió, volvió casado.	*He came back, a married man.*
Ella se murió de amor.	*Broken-hearted she died of love.*

What magical images those words evoked! In the tropical island of my childhood, shade is always welcome. Yet to imagine sitting beneath the subtle shade of a bird's wing, listening to a story in full bloom, provoked an indescribable joy in me. What kind of illness was love, that it could cause the death of a girl in Guatemala? How could the poet have forgotten her, she who loved him so dearly?

Words sparkled in my grandfather's poem, which my grandmother had me memorize and recite:

Almita de cristal
espíritu soñado en mis quimeras
espíritu divino
más sutil que el ensueño del poeta...

> *Young crystal soul*
> *spirit I have glimpsed in my dreams*
> *divine spirit*
> *gentler than a poet's vision ...*

These surprising images took on new dimensions each time I repeated the words. I knew well that *"Almita de cristal,"* "crystal soul," was a reference to my own grandmother. Yet knowing that I was called *"Almitaflor"* gave those words a special meaning to me. Maybe I, too, shared in the love between the poet and his beloved, and somehow existed already in their dreams.

By the time I was three years old, my grandmother had already taught me to read. Combining her love for learning with her love for the earth, she traced for me on the dirt the names for the animals and plants that we saw on our daily walks through the old farmstead. For each new letter, she created a story inspired by its shape: the **v** of *vaca,* cow, was shaped like the horns of the cow that a farm helper was milking to offer us a glass of fresh milk. The **b** of *burro,* donkey, resembled a donkey's long ears. I don't remember all of the stories, but I can feel even now the warmth of the sun on our faces as she traced the word *rosa,* and told me how the **r**, in her old-fashioned handwriting, resembled the wall of a garden, and how the little loop on top was a rose that had climbed up that wall in order to gaze at the marvels of the world that lay beyond. Looking up at our own garden's walls and hearing the wonder in my grandmother's voice, I felt that this letter held both the fragrance that enveloped us as well as the promise of adventures to come. Many years later, in the rose garden of Santa Rosa de Lima, as I chose the name *Rosalma* for my daughter, I felt the blooming of that seed of wonder that was planted when I first learned the letter **r**.

The joy of learning to read was followed by the magic of the first book my mother gave me, which was her own long-treasured copy of *Heidi*. Over the years, the magic of that book was followed by the magic of many others. I discovered the perfect place for reading among the branches of an old tree that, downed by a storm, had refused to die. With new branches sprouting up toward the sky from the side of the wide, fallen trunk, the tree resembled a green harp. I could hide there and enjoy the company of my dearest friends: a tree and a book. Perched on that tree trunk I sailed the straits of Malaysia with Salgari's *Sandokan,* and saw the brave prince fight the invading British forces. I trembled with fear and hope on Stevenson's *Treasure Island* and laughed at the mischief and misadventures of Richmal Compton's *William.*

While I enjoyed the new worlds that books opened for me, what I savored most was the feeling that they had been written just for me. How special they made me feel, how well understood! While it's hard to imagine two more dissimilar landscapes than our Cuban farm and the Swiss Alps, I identified so completely with Heidi that these differences did not matter. The wind whispering through our bamboo grove by the river was the same wind she heard whistling through the pine trees, and I knew just how she felt when she visited Peter's blind grandmother because I had my own blind great-grandmother whom I would rush to visit whenever I returned from my outings. Above all, I understood as no one else could possibly understand her love for her surroundings: It was my own love for mine.

Likewise, the more I read and reread Louisa May Alcott's books, the more it seemed to me that she could not have been writing for anyone but me. And how could Sarah's misfortunes and her resilience, which I encountered as I read and reread *A Little Princess,* be anything other than a call to my own soul? Of course I knew that other people had read these books and continued to do so; still, I felt that somehow they had been written uniquely for me.

Today I have arrived at the extraordinary realization that I was right—that what could be construed as a preposterous, childish idea can also be seen as an extraordinary insight. Because indeed, contrary to what the proponents of standardized testing would have us believe, each text is written to come alive in the interaction with each individual reader and is rewritten with each individual reading.

This is so because in order to be meaningful, reading has to be a dialogue. It is only when readers engage with a text—bringing their own full range of feelings, emotions, and experiences; comparing and contrasting their own lived knowledge with what is being proposed by the author—that true reading begins. It is only when readers recognize the ideas in the text, or are surprised by them, that reading
becomes enriching; and it is only when readers ask themselves meaningful questions that reading achieves its real purpose. Why did the people around her have such conflicting opinions about Heidi? What did each of them want from her, and for her? What could Jo have done to curb her temper? Why was it important that she continue to nurture her dreams? These kinds of questions can lead us to observe more closely the people around us, and to a deeper understanding of their motivations. They can inspire us to become kinder, more caring, and more supportive of others, and strengthen our determination to never forfeit our dreams.

For this kind of dialogue to take place, the reader needs to be moved to ask true questions, relevant questions: What if *something* had been different? What other possibilities might there be? Who is missing here? Who has been left out? Who will reap the benefits of this? What will the consequences be? Who will be affected, and how? What can I learn from this that will help me become kinder and more courageous, that will help me grow into the person I want to become? What have I gleaned here about how we might make the world a better place for all?

When we become inspired to ask these kinds of questions as we read, what would otherwise be a bundle of sheets with some ink marks on them can become a true friend, a companion, a guide—not just because of the author's talent, or will, or effort, but because the reader has accepted the invitation to join in the individual adventure of discovery that each act of reading entails.

Yes, those extraordinary books had been written especially for me, just as they had been written especially for all those other readers who saw in them a path into their own hearts and minds and souls. An author cannot create alone a gift of knowledge, of experience, of ideas, of feelings, of discoveries; the gift is created together by the author and the reader. This is what makes the reading process so valuable and unique.

It is from this profound intuition of the avid child reader I was, and from the profound respect and love for dialogue that I have developed as a teacher, mother, friend, aunt, grandmother, woman, Latina, and human being—that I began to write and that I continue writing, always aware that my writing is only an invitation for you to use my words to discover the inner cadence of your own, as a mirror for you to find the radiance of your own soul.

And so it is with profound gratefulness to you, as reader, that I offer this book of reflections on my own life as a reader and author. I also dedicate this book, with much appreciation,

- to the *juglares,* the anonymous minstrels who created the ancient ballads, and to the mothers who have sung them for centuries to their children;
- to the creators of the traditional tales, and to those who have kept them alive in the retelling;
- to parents who invent stories to explain life's mysteries to their children, and who tell the stories of their own lives and struggles;
- to teachers and librarians who understand that it is necessary to "read the world" in order to read words, and that reading words becomes more meaningful when it allows us to continue reading the world;
- to teachers and librarians who know that children's souls are thirsty for words—rich, sonorous, musical words—and who find ways to offer students of all ages a new poem, a new song, a new story each day;
- to teachers and librarians who understand that they have the opportunity to either honor or devalue a family's home language and culture, and who find multiple ways to

show their respect for that culture with its wealth of knowledge, experience, caring, and strength;

- to teachers and librarians who encourage meaningful conversation at home between students of any age and their parents, knowing that such conversations will have a strong positive impact on students' well-being as well as on their academic growth;

- to teachers and librarians who embrace technology in all its forms as a way to project, highlight, preserve, and disseminate the voices of their students, to magnify and share students' drawings and words with the whole class,

- to record their speeches on audio and videotapes and to produce multiple copies of student-authored books;

- to teachers and librarians who teach by example, who risk being creative themselves so that children and youth can also become creative; who risk questioning and doubting and searching for new answers, so that their students can see that questioning and doubting and searching for new answers are all essential to finding new solutions; to teachers who are willing to learn from their students and see each class as an opportunity for reflection; to teachers who engage in their practice as an opportunity for ongoing growth and learning.

I am also deeply grateful to all of you, the readers of this book, who know that while our achievement reflect our efforts, our imperfect societies also reflect our own imperfections. You are willing to continue believing and teaching that, just as our species has expanded beyond our own physical limitations in order to explore the depths of the ocean and the furthest reaches of the universe, to explore the mysteries of DNA and to perform surgeries that border on the miraculous, we also can and will find ways to end poverty and injustice, discrimination and violence, environmental pollution and oppression. Yes, we will continue to hope and to turn our hope into words and our words into action.

Over the years, readers have posed questions in their letters, at presentations, and during school visits that have provided opportunities for me to reflect on the stories behind some of my books. Yet writing the two volumes of *Alma Flor Ada and You*, [Libraries Unlimited], and fusing and upgrading them to produce this book allowed me to deepen those reflections while undertaking a journey into my own childhood and youth that has revealed long-forgotten treasures.

The highly creative activities designed by dedicated teachers and librarians have delighted me, providing additional insights. I am pleased to share some of them, as well as various websites maintained by Isabel Campoy and myself:

On the totality of my work:

www.almaflorada.com

For ample use of specific books:

www.yeswearelatinos.com

www.sisomoslatinos.com

www.islandtreasuresbook.com

On the process of authorship:

www.authorsintheclassroom,com

On the literary award Premio Campoy-Ada:

www.premiocampoy-ada

On books published by Mariposa Transformative Education

www.mariposatransformativeeducation.com

On Isabel Campoy's work:

www.isabelcampoy.com

On her book **Maybe Something Beautiful** [Tomás Rivera Award] www.maybesomethingbeautiful.com

A **Themes and Values Index** at the end of this book identifies specific topics.

The **Transformative Calendar / Calendario enriquecedor** suggests books, poems, songs appropriate for specific days each month. It can be accessed in www.almaflorada.com

It will always be a pleasure to hear from you and I will be very grateful for your comments and activities. You can write me at: almaflor@almaforada.com.

Suggestions for using this book

These pages offer librarians, teachers, children's literature specialists, and any reader interested in children's books, or my work in general, a window into the process of authoring a book, as well as some accounts of the varied and surprising effects that children's books can have on their readers.

Adults who wish to encourage children to read will find here the "stories behind the stories": the elements of personal life and the peculiar moments of inspiration that can spark the creative act. Nowhere else have I explored as fully the intimate connections between my life and my work—connections that can be used to introduce a particular book or to add depth to an author's study.

It was a great challenge for me to organize the many and diverse picture books I have written into a set of categories to present to the reader. Once these categories began to take shape, they served as a reminder that I have always written eagerly but never in the same place, or at the same time of day, or under the same conditions. Instead, I have written anywhere and everywhere: on the beach, under a tree, during boring faculty meetings, or in airports while waiting at the gate. I have written on all kinds of materials: white or yellow tablets, the recycled backs of old manuscripts and envelopes, the end pages of paperbacks, even assorted receipts found in my purse when no other paper was handy. I have written what I felt like writing, whenever I found a minute to do so. Yet, while I have written fiction and nonfiction books, prose and poetry, plays and song lyrics, fantasies and realistic chapter books, there are also some recurring themes that underlie this diversity. Writing this book has helped me to discover those constant threads and may help others to do so as well.

Some of the picture books have been organized by genre, as in the section on folklore and legends. Other books have been grouped together because they share a similar format, such as the books that consist of a series of letters between various characters. In most cases, however, I have organized the books by topic or theme.

The initial description of each book, or group of books, is followed by a section called *Sharing with Readers*, with suggested follow-up activities for the classroom or library. Readers who would like further suggestions along these lines may be interested in *A Magical Encounter: Latino Literature in the Classroom. Third Edition* (2016). In this book I explore in greater depth the process of sharing literature including: ways to introduce and read a book; suggestions for fostering a truly transformative dialogue; encouraging oral and written responses to the reading; research and discovery activities to delve more deeply into the topic or setting; inviting dramatic and artistic responses; "culminating" activities that expand beyond the confines of the classroom; and last but by no means least, the significant connections between the classroom or the library and the home that can be woven as part of sharing a story together. While the examples focus on Latino authors, many of the ideas can be adapted for use with other books and authors.

Although some degree of overlap is inevitable, I have chosen as much as possible to not duplicate here the content of *A Magical Encounter*. In fact, most of the activities I include are authentic examples of ways in which teachers, librarians, and children have responded to the books I have written. In the very few cases where I suggest an activity that I have not yet seen enacted, I say so.

I hope you will enjoy the fact that these suggestions and activities are drawn from real experiences. At the same time,

please understand that they are only a small sample of many more possibilities. Also, many of these activities could easily be adapted for use with other books, different than the ones in the original example, and I am sure that many people have already done so children you work with might respond to the stories.

Two books, co-authored with F. Isabel Campoy offer suggestions for exploring poetry and songs. The structure of Spanish poetry and suggestions for its best implementation in the classroom are the focus of *Está linda la mar.*

The possibilities of language enrichment and creative reading through songs are presented in *Música amiga: Aprender cantando,* which offers suggestions on the use of more than 300 songs in Spanish. The enthusiasm of teachers who attended presentations given by Suni Paz and myself on this topic, led me to record professionally the talk on the role of music in the classroom

enlivened by examples of songs presented by Suni. This recording is now available in the CD *Aprender cantando.*

The suggestions and examples offered in these books and CDs are not meant to limit your own creativity in any way, nor constrain how you present the books, poetry or songs, rather they are an invitation for you to discover what best works in your classroom or library.

What happens between a child and a book can indeed be an encounter full of magic and wonder. Sometimes, it is an encounter to be savored in privacy or in silence, one that may take a long time to be fully understood. At other times, your invitation can help create a bridge, encouraging a reluctant reader to become absorbed in a book, to realize that what is on the page is only the beginning of an extraordinary journey of reflection and discovery. As we read, we awaken to the shining truth that a good book can illuminate for us many things about ourselves, about the depths hidden in other human beings, and about the wonders of life itself.

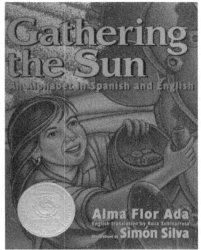

By encouraging children to engage in a dialogue with the text and inviting them to see the relevance of their own feelings and experiences for understanding the story more deeply, something else even more wonderful can take place. Children can begin to discover that they, too, are central characters, that they have the responsibility and creative possibility of being the protagonists of a set of extraordinary stories: the stories of their own lives.

May you enjoy great satisfaction as you invite your students to encounter the magic and wonder of books, of life, and of their own radiant and loving selves!

Part I: Becoming an Author

An Author's Journey

I was born on January 3, 1938, in the outskirts of Camagüey, a colonial city in Cuba at la Quinta Simoni, an old house that our neighbors believed was haunted. Many years before, that house had been the home of Amalia Simoni, a patriotic woman married to Ignacio Agramonte, an important leader in the Cuban struggle to win independence from Spain. Amalia was taken prisoner and forced to go into exile. Ignacio was killed in battle and the family never returned to live in the Quinta Simoni. With the years, all kinds of legends were spun around the large house. People often claimed to see the ghost of Agramonte riding his white horse into battle, although more likely that they were catching a glimpse of the high masonry arch next to the river, behind the flame trees.

While I did not believe the gossip people spread about the house, every evening as we watched the sunset I listened with rapture to my grandmother's stories about the struggles for freedom, equality, and justice led by Agramonte and his fellow patriots. Her stories made the house even more special to me.

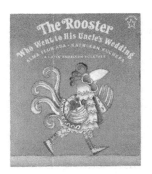

She spoke with tenderness of Ignacio and Amalia's love story and with admiration of the patriots who wanted to end slavery and make Cuba a place of justice for all.

My grandmother, Dolores Salvador Méndez, was called Lola. Her ability to make history come to life planted in me the seed of knowing that children can listen to very significant topics if they are presented as good stories. Many of my picture books and chapter books explore issues such as identity [**The Unicorn of the West** and **El unicornio del oeste, My Name is María Isabel** and **Me llamo María Isabel**]], finding one's own values, **The Malachite Palace**, discovering ways to better the world around us, **Jordi's Star**, and ending discrimination, **Friends** and **Amigos**. I've found that children can easily enjoy these books as engaging stories and do not find it hard to understand the issues that these stories illustrate.

At times, my grandmother told me playful stories about animals, such as the story of a rooster who, in a hurry to get to his uncle's wedding, forgot to eat breakfast. When he stopped to eat along the way, he got into quite a fix— he got his beak all muddy and one cannot go to a wedding with a muddy beak! In my grandmother's stories, the animals were mostly kind and clever, and the smaller animals often outsmarted the larger ones.

It has been a joy to share with children the folktales my grandmother told me. Many of my stories are based on hers [**The Rooster Who Went to His Uncle's Wedding** and **El** *gallo que fue a la boda de su tío, Medio-pollito-Half-chicken*] and those that involve the dear characters *Cucarachita Martina* and *Ratoncito Pérez*. And so, many years after her death, her gift to me continues to be renewed and passed on to others. But my grandmother gave me more than just stories.

She also gave me permission to change the traditional tales, to adjust them and modify them, just as she did whenever she told a story. She had a gift for adding new characters or details that had to do with the present moment, in order to help the stories she told come to life and become more exciting to the listener.

In addition to her wealth of folktales, my grandmother liked to recite poems that she often set to music and to turn history unto fascinating tales. She delighted in introducing me to the Greek gods and goddesses from Mount Olympus. Every morning she would say, "Here comes Apollo on his golden chariot!" When there was a tropical thunderstorm, she would say, "Zeus must be in a bad temper today."

When my grandmother mentioned that the gods and goddesses ate only nectar and ambrosia, I asked her what these delicacies tasted like. She told me that nectar and ambrosia tasted like *nísperos* and *caimitos,* two of my favorite tropical fruits. In this way, she made the food of the gods seem so real that I was always expecting to find Athena or Aphrodite savoring one of the fruits of the *níspero* tree in our garden. Even as a grown-up, I still consider fruit to be the food of the gods.

Yet my grandmother was not the only storyteller in my childhood. Everyone in my family loved a story well told. My uncle Manolo, recounted old family stories very vividly,

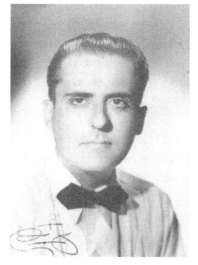

including himself in the action. He did this even if the story had actually taken place long before he had joined our family by marrying my Aunt Lolita. Sometimes the story he was telling had occurred even before he was born, and still, there he was, one of the characters in the story! No one was ever able to set the record straight, as his storytelling was so convincing that everyone, including himself, ended up believing that he had actually been there.

Where the Flame Trees Bloom, in Spanish ***Allá donde florecen los framboyanes***, and ***Under the Royal Palms***, in Spanish ***Bajo las palmas reales***, real-life stories about my childhood are part of this legacy of family stories. They are published in their

individual versions, and also compiled, with some additional stories in ***Island Treasures: Growing up in Cuba***, in Spanish ***Tesoros de mi isla. Una infancia cubana***.

My father was also a storyteller, but his stories were of a different kind. Each night, he created a new chapter in the unending story of human beings on this planet. He was not concerned with the history of kings or well-known figures, but rather with how ordinary people's ingenuity had developed civilizations, one step at a time.

He would start with a few questions: "Who do you think was the first person to ever cook food?" "How did it happen?" "Do you think it might have been an accident, a hunter dropping a piece of meat into a campfire and later realizing that it tasted better than raw meat?" Then he would create an entire story, rich in details and well-developed characters, to bring the incident to life. He told me stories about the first person who used a hook for fishing and the first person who thought to hollow out a tree trunk for a canoe. He invented stories about the people who discovered how to create shoes, clothing, needles, clay pots, and knives of sharpened stone. He admired the people who had figured out how to cultivate different kinds of plants and created a compelling story that told of how the ancient people of the Americas had selected the best seeds year after year. By persevering generation after generation, they finally transformed a scraggly weed into the rich corn plant.

This combination of reality and fantasy delighted me. And the fact that he created these stories just for me formed a very strong bond between us. It inspired me to become more observant about the small details in my environment, so that I might notice more clearly how life unfolded each day. I have recounted many of these observations in the collection *Cuentos con Alma* (Stories with Alma) which includes **Barriletes** (Kites), **Días de circo** (Circus days), **Pregones** (Vendors' calls), **Pin pin sarabín** (Childhood games), and **Barquitos de papel** (Paper boats). New versions of these experiences are now included, under the collective title "Days at La Quinta Simoni" in the already mentioned **Island Treasures: Growing Up in Cuba**.

My father's example instilled in me a sense of respect and appreciation for the people who, through their daily labor, bring forth nourishment for us all. I sing their praises in **Gathering the Sun**, an homage to farmworkers. This tribute was highly enriched by the art of Simón Silva and the beautify music composed and sang by Suni Paz in a CD of the same title.

My father also gave me the gift of fantasy, which allowed me to invent my own worlds. Some examples of this are **The Unicorn of the West** in Spanish **El unicornio del oeste,** and the world of Hidden Forest developed in **Dear Peter Rabbit**, in Spanish **Querido Pedrín; Yours Truly, Goldilocks**, in Spanish **Atentamente, Ricitos de oro; With Love, Little Red Hen;** and **Extra! Extra! Fairy-tale news** *from Hidden* Forest, in Spanish *¡Extra! ¡Extra! Noticias del Bosque Escondido*.

As a rather quiet and observant child, I felt very lucky to be allowed to spend long hours in nature by myself. A bird, a flower, or a leaf could fascinate me for a timeless spell. I lived next to a river, a source of constant wonders: leaping frogs, funny tadpoles, skittish turtles that disappeared into the water at the slightest noise, dragonflies, egrets, and cranes. All so alive in my memory that they have found their way into my writing in books such as *¿Quién nacerá aquí?* in English *Who's Hatching Here*, *La canción del mosquito* in English *The Song of the Teeny-Tiny Mosquito*, *Friend Frog* and *Daniel's Mystery Egg/El huevo misterioso de Daniel*.

Books, too, were wonderful companions, and their characters felt completely real to me. This may be why I have delighted in creating exchanges between familiar storybook characters. At times I have played with having them write letters to one another, as in *Dear Peter Rabbit, Yours Truly, Goldilocks*, and *With Love, Little Red Hen*. I have envisioned storybook characters reporting their latest news in *Extra! Extra! Fairy-tale News from Hidden Forest* and savored being an invisible witness to their everyday happenings as they celebrate a birthday in *Feliz cumpleaños, Caperucita Roja*, in English *Happy Birthday, Little Red Riding Hood* or furnish a new house in *El nuevo hogar de los siete cabritos*, in English *The New Home of the Seven Little Kids*, the last two co-authored with F. Isabel Campoy.

When I was eight years old, we moved to the center of town, Calle República #465. There, I discovered a world full of people. Every human feeling and thought seemed to exist around me if I just listened carefully and reflected on what I saw. Over the years, many of these people have also found their way into my books, sometimes as real-life characters in ***Under the Royal Palms, Where the Flame Trees Bloom***, and ***Pregones*** [Vendors' calls], other times as fictional characters in made-up stories and in my novels for adults.

As a young child, I greatly admired Louisa May Alcott's character Jo March and the creative learning environment of *Jo's Boys.* During the tedious years of fourth and fifth grade at school, I dreamed to create schoolbooks that would be delightful and exciting to read. I even thought to open t someday a boarding school in our old Quinta Simoni. In my imaginary school, the most exciting thing was that every year all of the students would study a culture from a different part of the world during a certain historical period. We would all, students and teachers alike, dress, eat, and behave according to the norms of that culture, engaging in its typical activities. Later in life, when I have encountered Renaissance Fairs in the United States and Medieval Fairs in Spain, I have remembered my own childhood dreams. I marvel at the imagination of the child I once was, who while growing up was so thirsty to experience other times and other places.

Still, I never really believed that I would be a writer. As a teenager, I thought I would be a journalist and became a teacher instead. However, my love for words, for books, and for creativity led me to eventually become an author, and the rewards have been many. Authoring books has allowed me to preserve memories and revisit life experiences in order to share them. It has also allowed me to work collaboratively— with my daughter, Rosalma Zubizarreta, who has translated or edited much of my writing, with my son Gabriel Zubizarreta co-author of two books, and with Isabel Campoy, with whom I have co-authored extensively. Being a writer has given me the gift of seeing my texts beautifully illustrated by extraordinary artists and put to music by Suni Paz. Above all, it has allowed me to meet many children, teachers, and librarians throughout the world, perhaps including you. What a joy that has been!

Childhood Years

My parents, who were great believers in the value of education, wanted to provide me with the best educational opportunities. Many of the families in our old colonial city took pride in knowing that their ancestors had lived in Camagüey two or three hundred years. In those days, most families who could afford to pay tuition sent their children to private schools. The public schools were only for the most economically disadvantaged. As a result, there was a great variety of private schools with different orientations. Since we were not Catholic, and my family viewed Catholic education as too old-fashioned and restrictive, they ruled out all Catholic schools for me. Still, this left a number of different possibilities. As my parents did not hesitate to have me change schools frequently in their ongoing search for good schooling, I experienced quite a number of different educational settings.

My first school experience was a neighborhood kindergarten, which I found terrifying. I hated having to be indoors, for I was used to being outdoors, or at least on the tall, open porches of the old Quinta Simoni, the house of my childhood, which was almost like being outside. Although the simple kindergarten I attended must have been held in a regular-sized building, I could not escape the claustrophobic feeling that the ceilings were caving in on me, and from that time on many classrooms have brought back this sense of imprisonment.

Being firm believers in having children learn additional languages at an early age, when they are most suited to acquiring them in a natural, effortless way, my parents next chose for me the *Colegio Pinson*, an American school run by Methodists. There, half of the school day was taught in English, while the other half was taught in Spanish. The school was a long way from our home, and the only reason I was able to attend first and second grade there was that my aunt Virginia, my mother's recently divorced oldest sister, had returned to live in the Quinta Simoni with her two children, my older cousins Jorge and Virginita.

Tía Virginia was a professor at the Normal School for Teachers, which was in La Zambrana, the same area of town as the *Colegio Pinson*. Thus, every morning we took a long, brisk walk together along General Gómez Street to the streetcar stop, followed by an even longer streetcar ride. At the school we were half-boarders; that is, while most of the day students went home for lunch, as was the norm, we stayed at school and ate lunch with the boarding students.

When I was going to start third grade my parents and my aunt Virginia decided to move my cousins and I to another American school, the *Colegio Episcopal de San Pablo*, this one run by Episcopalians. Again, my cousin Virginita and I were half-boarders, since this school was also far from the Quinta Simoni. Unfortunately, shortly after the beginning of the school year, Tía Virginia and my cousins moved to La Habana. I would then travel alone by public bus. Although there were bus stops right in front of the Quinta Simoni and the school, it was rather daring of my parents to send such a small child alone on the crowded public bus. Their intention was to teach me resilience and survival skills. At the same time, it was very frustrating since in those times Cuban buses were notoriously unreliable. No matter how early I arrived at the bus stop, the bus was frequently so late that I could not make it to school on time.

The school day began with a service in the chapel. On the lucky days when I arrived while the students were still in chapel, I learned to hide in the bushes outside the chapel and sneak into my classmates' line as they returned to the classroom. On the unlucky days when I was too late for even this subterfuge, I would stand in fear and shame outside the closed classroom door, dreading the scolding I would receive for something beyond my control. I did not want to upset my parents with the problem and never brought it to their attention. This made for an unhappy experience throughout the rest of second grade and all of third.

Other issues contributed to making this experience difficult for me. Since we were not Episcopalian, on the days that I arrived early enough to attend chapel I had the strange feeling of not belonging, of being in a place where I had no right to be. This sense of alienation was heightened by two other experiences at school, one having to do with math and the other with meals.

My father, a high school mathematics teacher, had made learning math fun and interesting for me. As a result, I was ahead of my classmates in this subject during my elementary school years. When they began teaching us division, I already knew how to divide. The problem was that my father had

taught me using Hispanic notation, while the school taught

the American way. Although the basic concepts and the results were identical, the fact that the process looked so different visually was very hard for me. Whenever I was called on in class, I could give the right answer; but when I was asked to go to the blackboard and show my work, I was always scolded and forced to redo my calculations the American way. Since no one thought to explain that both ways were perfectly acceptable, each time I was forced to redo my calculations using the American method, I felt it as a direct criticism of my father. Since my admiration for him was profound, this pained me immensely.

As a half-boarder, I had lunch at the home of the De Jongh family, who ran the students' boarding house. They were very strict about table manners following the American way. This meant one had to keep one's left hand under the table on one's lap; but, of course, there is nothing more improper than this if one is following the Hispanic way! So I was constantly being scolded at school for keeping my left hand on the table, and at home for putting it on my lap. How tiresome and confusing it was to have the adults I was supposed to mind behave in such contradictory ways!

I must confess that there was one saving grace to this dueling set of table manners: My fees as a half-boarder included an afternoon snack, and once in a while this snack was a kind of sweet bun, unknown in Cuban bakeries, and filled inside with a generous portion of apple or mint jelly. These exotic flavors were foreign to the Cuban palate, and I ate those delicious treats slowly while waiting for the long bus ride home, knowing that a second afternoon snack of Cuban crackers with guava paste and cheese would be waiting for me there. This was the only compensation for my confusing double life.

Nevertheless, I looked forward to fourth grade. Ms. Gladys Carnero had the reputation of being one of the best and kindest teachers at school, and I could not wait to be in her class. The first months of school were a haven for me that year. My parents had moved to town, and while I sorely missed the Quinta Simoni, it was a relief to be able to walk to school, to always be on time, to come home from lunch and to spend the day with such a wonderful teacher. Everything she

taught us was clear, exciting, and fun, and I was enjoying every minute of class, delighted to discover that school could truly be the wonderful place I had always been promised. And then Ms. Carnero got married and moved to La Habana. Our new teacher was stern Ms. De Jongh, and I was not able to cope with an enormous change. Can children get sick from grief? I did.

There had been too many losses in my short life. Both my beloved grandparents had passed away suddenly, yet as long as we lived in the Quinta Simoni their memory and their spirit felt so present that I still felt nourished by them. But then an accident happened that took the life of my young uncle Medardo, a tragedy I much later described in "Broken Wings" in **Under the Royal Palms**, or **Bajo las palmas reales**, now included in **Island Treasures** or **Tesoros de mi isla**. This sad event led the family to disperse. The two sisters who were still living in the Quinta Simoni at the time, my mother and my aunt Lolita, moved with their respective families out of the old ancestral home, which was too large for two young couples to keep up. My Tía Virginia's move to La Habana had deprived me of the company of my beloved cousin Virginita, whom I looked up to as a big sister. And now the teacher who had offered refuge and inspiration was also gone.

Every childhood illness imaginable: a string of colds, the mumps, some form of measles (although I had already been diagnosed with measles at a much younger age), bronchitis, plagued me that year. After I had been sick at home for several weeks, and seeing how unhappy I was at the thought of returning to *Colegio Episcopal,* my parents decided to try a new school. Thus, in the middle of fourth grade I began attending *Colegio El Porvenir.*

As educational experiences go, this was not a very joyful one. This old-fashioned school was located in a large house in the center of town. To maximize the use of the building, students attended either a morning or afternoon session. Fourth grade was held in the afternoon, so I had all morning at home, and after a rather early lunch I would walk to school. *Colegio El Porvenir* did not have a large campus like *Colegio Pinson*, or even the green gardens and yard of the *Colegio Episcopal*; it had only a small cement patio where the girls could hardly find a free corner to jump rope, and even so were not safe from all the balls the boys  were kicking or throwing around. But what was most devastating for me was that we were assigned seats based on our performance: the best students sat closest to the front, while the worst students sat in back. Since I had arrived at midyear and had no performance record at that school, I was given the last seat in the class. I was younger than most of my classmates by a year or two, and I was also the shortest one in the class. Sitting in the very last row behind the taller and rather unruly boys did not help me to understand the teacher's explanations, and since no one had discovered yet that I needed glasses, the blackboard, where all the work took place, was for me an indecipherable blur.

At this school Math was done the Cuban way, but since by now I had become accustomed to the American way, this became just one more aggravation. What was truly unbearable was the long portion of the day devoted to something called morphologic and syntactic sentence analysis. "Conjunction" and "preposition" felt like such ugly words to me, and I could never tell them apart, while "pluperfect subjunctive" seemed utterly disgusting! Since I had never been exposed to this kind of grammar before, there was no way to imagine how fascinating it might be under different circumstances. Certainly, the way it was drilled into us at *Colegio El Porvenir* was a nightmare, although I confess it taught me something very valuable: how *not* to teach!

As a Language Arts teacher, I tried to ensure that each precious hour that students spend in class and each precious page of a textbook were neither wasted nor used to bore, disgust, or frighten students as they were in my own fourth- and fifth-grade grammar classes. I have delighted in inventing stories about a galactic journey undertaken by a being from a planet where the only form of communication is with signs. This character travels in search of oral language, and visits the Planet of Sustantives, where inhabitants speak only in one-word utterances made of nouns; then travels on to the satellite of Adjectives, where inhabitants use two-word phrases—a noun and a modifier; then sojourns at the asteroids Singular and Plural, and the Planet of Verbs; and eventually discovers the rich communication made possible when all of these parts of speech are combined.

I have also chosen to teach syntax by having students reflect on how they feel when others speak about them, to better understand in a personal way such concepts as "subject" and "predicate" and explore the consequences of using language to support, inspire, hurt, destroy, uplift, or heal.

The other terrifying experience during those two miserable school years at *Colegio El Porvenir* consisted of being made to memorize lists of the unending geographical accidents of the extensive Cuban coast: keys, bays, harbors, points, peninsulas, swamps—about 2,400 kilometers worth of shoreline! I was a passionate lover of the sea, and fortunate to have parents who loved adventure; thus, we experienced many summers of joy exploring the coast. I was also an avid reader, and my imagination had been stirred by *Treasure Island* and by the knowledge that I lived on an island that had once harbored buccaneers and been frequently visited by pirates. Yet not once was any connection made in class between the names we had to memorize on those long lists and their present-day reality or historical relevance. Instead, they remained only names with no rhyme nor reason.

I loved memorizing Rubén Dario's long poems in 14-syllable verse, as their splendid words and sounds awoke all kinds of sensations in me. I also memorized with pleasure my grandfather's poems, which, while somewhat abstract, still had a suggestion of spirit within them; and the long, traditional ballads whose unfinished stories kept me guessing what might have happened afterward. But those lists of names with neither color nor fragrance were a total impossibility to remember! Oh, if I could only have seen a connection between the names on the list and the white powdery sands or the musty mangrove swamps, the calm waters of secluded bays or the waves breaking upon the cliffs! With what joy those names would have turned from a senseless nightmare into a pleasant dream!

Mercifully, I made it to sixth grade, and my wise parents, knowing that there was an exceptionally good sixth-grade teacher at another school, transferred me once more. This would be my fourth school, and in contrast to the previous three, it was a public school. In class-conscious Cuba, many of my parents' friends were horrified that they were choosing to send me to a public school; but my parents were not constrained by such prejudices and valued what this exceptional teacher had to offer. This school was the practice site for the teacher's college, la Escuela Normal, where my aunt Virginia had been a professor.

The school's goal was to serve as a model, and no one could have exemplified good teaching better than Dra. Rosa María Peyrellade, the cultured, stern, and outstanding woman who was my sixth-grade teacher.

We lived close to Dr. Peyrellade, and since the school was far away and my parents did not own a car, she offered to have me ride with her and three other teachers in the large old automobile belonging to her foster mother. She rode up front alongside the elderly driver, while the teachers rode on the back seat. I sat, facing them, on a small folding seat that extended  out from the back of the front seat. I felt as though I was under constant scrutiny. Yet it was the happiest, or more aptly, the only happy year of elementary school, and it certainly made up for all the rest!

This picture with the beloved teacher and my daughter Rosalma was taken several years ago in Los Angeles during a ceremony where I was being recognized as an outstanding educator. I had the great joy of dedicating that award to her. She was then in her late eighties; and she lived far into her nineties. After moving to this country, she taught for about twenty years. As she proudly told me, she only missed school twice, in both cases to attend the funerals of dear friends. When I asked her for the secret of her outstanding health and energy, she attributed it to three factors: being a lifelong vegetarian, eating very slowly and chewing each mouthful multiple times . . . and never holding on to a negative thought towards anyone or anything!

Adolescence

When I was growing up, the Cuban educational system was very centralized and prescriptive. After six years of elementary school, came two years of middle school. Once students had obtained an eighth-grade diploma, those who wished to continue their education could attend one of the following institutions: the Instituto de Segunda Enseñanza, a very rigorous school where students could obtain a *bachillerato,* a five-year degree that prepared one to enter the university; the Normal School for Teachers; the Normal School for Kindergarten Teachers; the School for Teachers of Home Economics; the School of Commerce, where one studied bookkeeping and accounting; the Technical-Industrial Institutes; and the School of Arts and Manual Professions. Students could begin working toward the *bachillerato* at the age of twelve, and the entrance requirement was either an eighth-grade diploma or else a passing grade on a challenging entrance exam. All of the other institutions, with the exception of the School of Arts and Manual Professions, were administered by the state and offered free tuition, although they accepted a limited number of students. They also had a minimum entrance age of fifteen and required an entrance examination.

A large number of students after finishing the eighth grade enrolled in the *Instituto* to bide their time until they reached the required age for taking the entrance exam for the school of their choice. A positive outcome of this was that many students obtained some valuable general education in the meantime. A detriment was that those students who were not committed to completing the *bachillerato* were often inattentive in class, not to mention that they contributed to an extremely large class size. As a result, there was very little interaction between students and faculty.

Although I did not yet know what field I wanted to study, I was determined to pursue a university education. Thus I entered the *bachillerato* program when I was twelve. I had not yet completed the eighth grade, but chose instead to take the entrance exam. As a result, I was one of the youngest in the class.

I was in awe of the majestic building where my grandfather had taught and where my father was still teaching. My father and my mother had met at this building, when she went to take her entrance examination and my father was a young professor monitoring the exam.

The *Instituto* had several hundred freshmen, all of whom were following the same curriculum. The students were divided into two groups: those who attended the morning session (8 a.m. to 12 noon) and the ones who attended the afternoon session (1 p.m. to 5 p.m.). I was delighted to be assigned to the morning session, yet it was only many years later that I realized why most of my close friends from that time have last names that begin with letters from the first half of the alphabet! The few who don't had asked to be transferred to the morning session, since it had the reputation of being attended by the most eager students.

The classes were held in large lecture halls, and each class consisted of a one-hour lecture. In most instances the professors lectured for an hour and then left. Some allowed a few minutes for questions and answers, yet most did not. No homework was assigned, although we were supposed to take notes during the lectures, read the textbooks, and prepare on our own for the end-of- the-semester exams.

I vividly remember the first class, a lecture on the intricacies of the Spanish language. I was dismayed at my inability to write down all that the professor was saying, especially as this course did not follow one specific textbook; instead, the professor recommended various readings as he went along. I looked around to see how others were faring. A girl who sat a couple of chairs to my right took this as a silent plea, and then and there, without even knowing each other's names, we made a commitment through nods and gestures to alternate taking notes, a paragraph's length at a time.

When the lecture was over, the other girl and I rushed to compare notes. Yes, we had found a perfect way of handling the problem of taking down most of what the professor said; we could compile our notes afterward to create a cohesive narrative. My new friend's name was Marta Carbonell. From then on we sat next to each other in every class, and a friendship was forged that has lasted a lifetime.

Martha Carbonell

During the first three years of the *bachillerato,* the number of students progressively diminished. Once we reached the fourth year, our class size stabilized: Those who began the fourth year usually continued on until graduation. When we entered the fifth and last year, we were also divided differently: those who intended to pursue a liberal arts education attended the afternoon session while those interested in a scientific career attended the morning session.

Each subject was one year long. In December, we were given a midyear exam. The passing grade was 60 out of a total of 100. Anything between 60 and 70 was considered the equivalent of a C—; a score between 70 and 80 corresponded to a range from a C to C+; between 80 and 90 was a B— to a B+; and from 90 to 100 was an A— to A+.

A grade of 45 to 60 was a provisional passing grade. Anything above a 45 allowed a student to take in June an exam covering only the second half of the course. To pass the course required an average of at least 60 points from both exams. Students obtaining less than 45 points in the first half of the course, or less than an average of 60 between the two exams, were required to take an exam covering the whole year's content in June or September.

If a student failed one or more courses, below a certain maximum, he or she was allowed to continue on with the following year's curriculum, with the added obligation of studying to pass the exams for the courses that he or she had failed that year. However, students who exceeded the maximum number of failures would have to repeat the entire year.

By the end of the first semester, it began to be obvious that there was a core of us who would be able to pass enough courses to continue on with next year's curriculum, yet there was also a large number who would be repeating the year. Even then, at the age of twelve, I was beginning to feel that something was not right in a system that set so many students up for failure.

As for myself, that first semester I passed all of my courses except for math, where I obtained a provisional passing grade of 50. I was therefore faced with the tremendous task of obtaining 70 points in the second semester exam, in order to achieve an average of 60, the minimum grade for passing the course. I felt an enormous sense of shame knowing that this must be an embarrassment for my father, who taught math at the Institute.

The exams were rigorously anonymous and conducted with great solemnity: we had to show our photo IDs issued by the Institute in order to be allowed inside the examination room. Then we each wrote our name on a piece of paper that was sealed in a small envelope. The envelope was stapled to the blank examination paper, and a seal was stamped on both. The envelopes would not be opened until after the exams had been graded.

We were not allowed to bring in anything but pencils (and in certain courses a logarithm table that was closely inspected, a ruler, a protractor, and a compass, all to be carried in by hand, as no book bags or other containers were allowed). We were asked to sit far apart from one another, and several teachers walked around monitoring the room. A tribunal of three or four teachers presided over the room, looking down at us sternly from the high platform in front of the class.

Never again have I been subjected to such rigor, neither in the two colleges I attended in the United States nor in the two universities I attended abroad. Yet I enjoyed the challenge and loved what I was learning. I felt that my teachers were highly qualified, and that I was extremely privileged to be able to learn from them. I have had proof of this later, as most of my teachers from that time went on to become university professors in the United States. At the same time, I also felt that something was deeply wrong with a system where most of the students did not get to experience the joy of learning as I did. They were not reached by the process and were letting the opportunity slip by, either just marking time or else preoccupied with trying to find a boyfriend or a girlfriend.

All of these high school experiences have had significant implications throughout my life. In the first place, my professors' extensive knowledge base, and the love and appreciation they had for their respective disciplines, inspired in me my own thirst and appreciation for knowledge.

Second, I developed the strong conviction that, when it comes to teaching, other factors can be as important as knowledge. It is also important to make what we know accessible to others, presenting the material in an inviting and interesting way in order to engage our students' motivation to learn.

Third, my own personal commitment to work for justice and equality were strengthened. Seeing how so many of my classmates gained very little from the years they spent at the Instituto, and observing that those who succeeded were primarily the ones who came from situations of privilege, I became convinced that the social systems that perpetuate inequality need to be changed. Placing all of the responsibility for success or failure on those who the system is supposed to serve is not a valid answer. Later on in this book, in the section on theatre, I explore further some of the feelings that my classmates and I shared about these issues.

Finally, all of my high school experiences continued to have a lasting impact on my own teaching when I became a high school teacher and later, a university professor.

After starting my college education in the United States and Spain, I went to Perú. In Lima, while working on my doctorate, I became a high school teacher, and my first books were high school textbooks based on the classroom materials I created for my own students. This led to my books for children and to the various kinds of writing that I do today.

To celebrate my 80th birthday Isabel Campoy organized a family reunion in Camagüey of family members living in the United States and in Cuba.

One of the photos on the next page shows our Senior class, the other, the family members that traveled from various parts of the United States in 2018 to celebrate my 80th birthday, both at the front steps of the Instituto where my grandfather and my father had taught, where my parents met when my mother was a student and my father a professor. met.

**On the front steps of the Instituto de Segunda
Enseñanza de Camagüey, Cuba**

Class of 1955
I'm on the front line, sitting, extreme left

Lafuente-Salvador family visit to Camaguey on 2018
to celebrate Alma Flor Ada Lafuente's 80th birthday.

Becoming an Educator

Among the many questions I encounter during visits to libraries and schools, as well as presentations at conferences, the most frequent ones include, "When did you decide to become an author?" "How did you begin to write?" and "Where do you get your ideas?" I have therefore often found myself in the somewhat awkward position of trying to explain that I never decided to become an author and that I had published several dozen books before I ever began to think of myself as one. I often tell children that, for me, becoming an author was like becoming a grandmother and discovering my hair had turned white; it was something I never really planned for, but that happened in the process of living.

The first books I published were not children's books. They were not literature, either, but scholarly and pedagogical works instead. Very early in my college career, I fell in love with the poetry of Pedro Salinas, one of the Spanish poets of the generation of 1927, which included Federico Garcia Lorca, Jorge Guillén, and Rafael Alberti, among others. Salinas's poetry spoke deeply to my soul, as if it had been written especially for me. I was fascinated by his love poems, perhaps the best love poems written in Spain in the twentieth century. I was also deeply touched by his book *El contemplado* (The contemplated one), which he wrote in Puerto Rico as a paean to the Caribbean Sea, the sea of my childhood and youth, my own beloved sea. While his are probably the best poems to the ocean ever written in the Spanish language, they are also

Pedro Salinas
El diálogo creador
PRÓLOGO DE JORGE GUILLÉN

Alma Flor Ada

much more, conveying the poet's deep reflections on that which is infinite and that which is immanent.

All through my college years I studied the works of Salinas. This eventually led to my writing a dissertation on his complete work as a poet. In turn, the dissertation earned me an unexpected appointment as a scholar at the Radcliffe Institute at Harvard and a Fulbright Scholar Exchange grant. At Harvard I had the privilege to revise and expand my work under the guidance of an extraordinary mentor, Raimundo Lida. Thus, the depth of feeling that Salinas's poetry awoke in me, along with my admiration for the poet himself, led to the publication (under my married name, Alma de Zubizarreta) of a scholarly four-hundred-page book, ***Pedro Salinas: El diálogo creador*** [Pedro Salinas: The creative dialogue, 1969]. The book included a preface by Salinas's best friend, the equally great poet Jorge Guillén, and was published by the prestigious Biblioteca Románica Hispánica of Editorial Gredos, Madrid. At the time I was the first Latin American woman whose work they had published. This book opened the doors for me to begin my teaching career in the United States as an Associate Professor of Romance Languages at Emory University. Something I had done simply out of admiration and love, without any professional ambitions, surprised me by leading to a career as a university professor.

The book has been reprinted under my own name, as ***Pedro Salinas: El diálogo creador.*** [2da. Edición. Mariposa. 2017].

My initial experience teaching college courses was rather unusual. After graduating from high school I received a scholarship to Loretto Heights College in Denver, Colorado, thanks to a wonderful woman, Yolanda Faggioni, a librarian for the United States Information Service, the only public library in my hometown. As an alumna of Loretto Heights, she had suggested to the college administrators that I could be useful assisting with the Spanish courses.

This was in 1955, before language laboratories were readily available, so my task would be to serve as a language and pronunciation model. At the time, it was common for professors who were teaching a foreign language to be well versed in the history of the language, its linguistic elements, and its literature and culture, yet not be able to speak the language fluently. This was the case with one of the professors at Loretto, so I was offered a working scholarship in return for the assignment of demonstrating the language in the classroom.

Concerned about leaving their daughter in the care of strangers, my parents decided to drive me all the way from Cuba to Colorado. It was a marvelous trip, beginning with a ferry-boat crossing and my mother's subsequent impulse to buy a very small used trailer that was being offered for sale along the roadside in one of the Florida Keys. It took us a full two months of travel, including one detour to drop off my young cousin Nancy at a boarding school in St. Louis and other detours to visit Yosemite and the Grand Canyon. Finally we arrived in Colorado. My parents, my aunt, and my sister entrusted me to the Sisters of Loretto, with just one week left before school was to begin, for me to adapt to a very new and unfamiliar reality.

The day before classes were to start, the elderly professor I was supposed to assist had a stroke. I was asked to take over her classes until a new professor could be hired. A few weeks later, it was decided that the "Cuban girl" was doing such a good job that there was no need to hire anyone else. Thus, at the age of seventeen, I found myself teaching two full classes of Spanish 101 and 201, in addition to the courses I was taking as a student. During spring semester, the arrangement continued while I taught Spanish 102 and 202.

Having come from a family of educators probably helped me to live through this experience! When I was younger my three student teachers boarded in our house, and my mother would coach them on their demonstration lessons. And now, the admirable Sister Concilia, the other Spanish teacher at Loretto Heights, was willing to hear my lesson plans. I must confess, though, that what helped me get through a very difficult first class had a very different source.

During that first class, the students laughed at me mercilessly throughout the entire period. I was ignorant of the difference in the pronunciation between **v** and **b** in English, since in Spanish, both of those letters have exactly the same /b/ sound. Therefore, I repeatedly insisted that Spanish would be very easy for them to learn, since it only had five "bowels." I am afraid what kept me going, in spite of the laughter, was not good-heartedness but a serious case of ethnocentrism. You see, I had known people from the United States mainly as tourists. They were unable to speak any Spanish, even though it was such a simple language. They were unaware of the strength of the Caribbean sun and were willing to roast themselves in it. They wore unbecoming shorts and shirts with loud, flowered prints in the middle of the city, and appeared to be continuously surprised by the most ordinary things. We saw them as "aging children" always ready to have a laugh at anything. Therefore, my students' laughter in response to my simple statement about the five Spanish "bowels" only confirmed the attitude that prevailed in my hometown about Americans. I was convinced that I would need to draw on all of my reserves of patience and kindness in order to teach these joyful but oh-so-naive girls.

After a year of study in Denver, where I turned 18, I returned to Cuba during the summer. When I told my parents that I had decided to become a nun and join the Sisters of Loretto, whose unique combination of profound spirituality and concern for social justice had deeply inspired me, they refused to allow me to go back to the United States. Instead, I was to attend the University of La Habana. Unfortunately, during those harsh years of the Batista dictatorship, the university was shut down for an entire year in order to prevent student protests and demonstrations. So, after spending a year in Cuba without being able to go to school, my parents decided to send me back to the United States, this time to Miami.

There, I was able to overcome the initial disbelief of the Dominican sisters at Barry College (now Barry University) that I had taught college courses. Only after taking directly to Loretto Heights College President and hearing her praise for my work was Barry's President willing to offer me a scholarship similar to the one I had held at Loretto Heights. Again I was given full responsibility for teaching college courses, which on paper had been officially assigned to a sister who knew almost no Spanish. But of course, this was not a new experience for me by now. What was new, and much more difficult, was being the person in charge of two teenagers, my sister Flor and my cousin Nancy. They were great girls, but I was much too young for such a big responsibility. I felt inadequate to the task of giving them the guidance and the supervision they needed to manage a difficult adjustment to a new culture. I ended up getting sick from exhaustion at the end of the academic year and that brought my mother to Miami to oversee the situation.

To continue my education in a Spanish speaking country was my hope. My first choice was Mexico. I admired the achievements of the Mexican Revolution and the extraordinary cultural renaissance brought about by painters like Diego Rivera, David Alfaro Siqueiros, and José Orozco (I must confess that at that time I knew nothing about Frida Kahlo who I have grown to love and admire so much), by the Ballet Folklórico de México, and by writers like Juan Rulfo and Agustín Yáñez. But sending me alone to Mexico was beyond what my parents were willing to consider at the time. Instead, I was offered the option of studying in Madrid where I could stay with my mother's uncle and his family.

When I arrived in Madrid I held the false assumption that I could simply continue the liberal arts education I had begun in the United States. It is surprising to me now that neither my parents nor my relatives in Spain had discussed a real plan of study. I can only attribute it to the strained situation in Cuba at the time under the Batista dictatorship. With the Cuban National University at La Habana closed and the widespread fear that young people who spoke their mind would be prosecuted, jailed, or even assassinated, many parents were sending their college-age children abroad to study. The general assumption seemed to be that if they sent their children to a Spanish-speaking country, all we would need to do was walk in to the university and register.

Looking back, I realize how much the situation I encountered in Spain differed from the rather structured and protected life I had known earlier. I arrived with no idea of what the university requirements would be or what I really wanted to study. I soon found out that the Spanish system did not allow for undergraduate general education; I would have to choose a career from the start. There was no system of reciprocity that would serve to recognize my two years of undergraduate courses in the United States. Even obtaining verification of my *bachillerato,* or Cuban high school diploma, would require a lot of bureaucratic maneuvering. Therefore, I registered in the *Curso de Estudios Hispánicos* offered at the Universidad Complutense in Madrid. This was a one-year program  designed mainly for European teachers and professor of Spanish and Spanish literature.

This choice turned out to be the best possible one for me. The program had been started by the great philologist and poet Dámaso Alonso, and all the professors involved were of the highest caliber. Dr. José Cepeda taught the history of Spain. Dr. Pita Andrade, who later became the director of the Prado Museum, taught the history of Spanish art. Carlos Bousoño, the great literary critic, taught a course on Stylistics focused on the poets Federico García Lorca and Vicente Aleixandre. Dr. Elena Catena, who later became a mentor and a dear friend to me, taught both History of the Spanish language as well as Spanish literature.

The last course was geography of Spain. Geography had always seemed a very dry subject to me before. While I have forgotten the name of the professor who taught the course, I have not forgotten that for the first time ever, geography came alive for me, since the professor structured his lessons around passages drawn from works of literature.

This exceptional program was designed for European professors of Spanish language and culture, but a few Latin Americans with interest in the Spanish language and culture were attending the same year.

Fascinated by the richness and depth of the information I took avid notes and participated enthusiastically. After I had spent a few weeks in the Curso de Estudios Hispánicos, Dr. Catena convinced me that I should apply for admission to the Facultad de Letras for the regular undergraduate program leading to a *licenciatura* and   following Dr. Catena's advice, I did all the paperwork to get my Cuban *bachillerato* validated.

So, while attending the Curso de Estudios Hispánicos as a regular student I was registered as an independent first-year student working toward a *licenciatura.* This meant that I had the right to attend classes at the Facultad de Letras, if I wished, but the professors would not acknowledge my presence. I was to take final examinations in June or September. My classmates had all taken seven years of Latin and two of Greek, so the classical language courses were completely beyond my reach. I had to hire private tutors to help me bridge the gap. I did not even attempt to take the exams for those two subjects in June, but instead studied nonstop during the summer.

In September, I was able to pass the Latin exam, but decided I was still not ready for the Greek. I also passed the Philosophy examination, which I had flunked in June something that initially filled me with anguish. Philosophy had been one of my favorite subjects both at Loretto Heights and Barry College. Based on the topics of the syllabus, I thought I was well prepared. Yet I had become used to the open-minded professors in the Curso de Estudios Hispánicos who encouraged ideas and dialogue. What I had not realized was that even the works of St. Thomas and St. Augustine that I was using as references were far too liberal for the fascist professor who taught the philosophy course at the Facultad de Letras.

By September, I had learned that the only way to pass the exam was to memorize and regurgitate certain paragraphs of his textbook. With the encouragement of don Alonso Zamora Vicente, who first congratulated me on having flunked the exam in June and then assured me that sometimes the only way to win in situations like the one I was struggling with was to pretend to play the game, I was able to pass the philosophy exam. After having experienced the situation in Cuba under Batista, this was now my second experience with totalitarian dictatorships and the restrictions they can impose upon freedom of thought.

My time in Spain proved to be one of the richest experiences in my life. The country was so severely repressed by the Franco regime that the few real intellectuals that remained were forced, out of necessity, to host small gatherings where true dialogue could flourish. I was extraordinarily fortunate to be embraced by people of the caliber of don Alonso Zamora Vicente, who later became Director of the Dictionary of the Spanish Language Royal Academy, his extraordinary wife, the dialectologist

doña María Josefa Canellada, and their disciple Berta Pallares Garzón in Salamanca. Dr. Elena Catena, who later became the first woman ever to be a Vice-Decana at the Complutense University, was my mentor in Madrid.

All of these fine scholars offered exemplary models with regard to knowledge, art, scholarship, rigorous thinking, moral courage, and human warmth. The opportunity to be a part of that world was a miracle that fills me with gratitude to this day.

That particular year, several Latin American students who would later become well-known for their literary and academic accomplishments also attended the Curso de Estudios Hispánicos. Mario Vargas Llosa and Jorge Cornejo Polar from Perú and Ambrosio Fornet and Silvia Gil from Cuba were my classmates and friends. In recognition of the high caliber of the students that year, the professors decided to create a Premio Extraordinario, which had never been awarded before. As the recipient of this honor, which was presented by Dámaso Alonso, I was asked to speak on the graduation ceremony. A brief notice appeared in Madrid's newspaper ABC, filling me with pride. It was the second time my name appeared on a newspaper not for a social purpose, but connected with an award, but it was the first time in Spain.

On transcribing the note I have retained the word *beca* which, in this case represents the ceremonial sash which is conferred to students upon graduation. Mine, representing the special recognition, was made of silk, rather than felt, and has the shield of the University embroidered in gold thread.

GRADUATION CEREMONY CURSO DE ESTUDIOS HISPÁNICOS

The culmination of the IX Curso de Estudios Hispánicos, has taken place in the amphitheater of the Faculty of Philosophy and Letters, presided by the Dean, Señor Camón Aznar; the Ambassador of Honduras in Spain, and the director of the program , don Dámaso Alonso. After parting words from Professor Camón Aznar and Professor Alonso, the Beca de Honor was presented to Srta. Ada Lafuente, Cuban, who in the name of all her classmates pronounced words to thank the Faculty and professors who during nine months have taught them about the Spanish language and culture. After her words, the rest of the students received the Diploma of Estudios Hispánicos and corresponding becas.

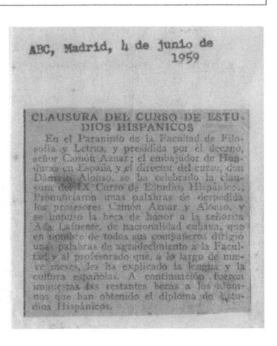

ABC, Madrid, 4 de junio de 1959

CLAUSURA DEL CURSO DE ESTUDIOS HISPÁNICOS

My life in Spain was further enriched by the loving friendship of Felisa de Unamuno, daughter of the great humanist don Miguel de Unamuno. During my stay in Salamanca, summer and fall of 1959, Felisa opened her home and heart to me, allowing me to know other dimensions of the Spanish society. It was particularly enjoyable to visit different areas of Castile with her in my old used Citroen. In her humility and kindness, gave me another example to follow through life.

With Felisa de Unamuno, on the Castilian plains.

With the walled city of Ávila in the background

At the Picos de Europa, with Felisa's sister, María de
Unamuno, who was visiting from the United States, where she was
a college professor, with a colleague.

Leaving Spain, and leaving this intellectual world behind, would have been unthinkable if not for the fact that my mother was expecting a child.

The new sibling, Lolita, would be fourteen years younger than my younger sister Flor, and twenty- one years younger than me.

My mother had decided to leave Cuba and move to Miami, where her own younger sister Lolita had been living, and my father wanted me at my mother's side. So, on a cold December morning, I boarded a Portuguese ship at A Coruña, the city where my paternal grandfather had been born, for a long and turbulent voyage to Ft. Lauderdale, Florida.

My father had chosen that ship because after Curazao it would make a stopover in La Habana. He wanted to join me onboard, be the first one to welcome me back, and travel with me to Florida. I realized later that he also wanted to give me his assessment of what had been taking place in Cuba during the time I had been absent, the first year of the Cuban Revolution. He also wanted to share with me his own personal anguish at being torn between my mother's determination to be in the United States and the decision made by his own father and brothers to stay in Cuba.

The shock of the disparity between the rich cultural life I had been living in Spain and my new circumstances was nearly unbearable to me. In Spain, my life had been marked by material scarcity but was full of constant intellectual and artistic stimulation. Now in Miami, I was working as a switchboard operator. While I was grateful to be able to make some money to contribute to my family, I felt totally devastated. My father, who could not bear to see my sadness, decided to find the means to send me to Perú to continue my studies at the Pontificia Universidad Católica del Perú.

Although travel out of Cuba was very restricted at the time, I was able to return to La Habana and depart again with a student permit since I already had the status of a "student pursuing studies abroad." Our financial resources in the United States were very limited, and my stop-over in Cuba allowed my father to purchase a one-way plane ticket from La Habana to Perú with some of the money that he was not able to take out of Cuba. It also gave my aunt, Mireya Lafuente Salvador, who was still living in La Habana, the chance to pack a suitcase for me with clothes she had carefully chosen for their classic look so they would not become outdated too soon. I was to live for many years out of that suitcase of black, grey, and white dresses with matching shoes!

During my first year in Perú, I worked at a wide variety of jobs, none of which paid very much, as full-time work was not easy to find. However, being bilingual did open doors for me. I began working as a compiler of what later become the *Simon and Schuster English-Spanish Bilingual Dictionary*—there is quite a story there to be told someday! Later, I was hired as a teacher at the Peruvian-American Abraham Lincoln School. Since I was probably not the most experienced candidate among the many applicants for the position of high school teacher of Spanish language and literature, I think I was given the job in part because I was the only candidate for that

position who could converse fluently in English with the recently appointed American principal. One of the many times in which being bilingual was almost significant asset.

At the bilingual Abraham Lincoln School and later at the trilingual Colegio Alexander von Humboldt, I was not very happy with the textbooks I was given to use with my students. I was worried that these textbooks would instill in my students the same abhorrence I had once felt toward grammar, instead of helping them understand the wonders of language that I had eventually discovered. Out of this concern, I began to develop my own loose-leaf teaching materials and to mimeograph them for my students.

Page after page I told the history of the Spanish language, introducing a variety of literary and grammatical concepts and creating exercises that would inspire my students to want to write. Yet I never thought of these materials as the beginning of a book, much less a series of books. It was the philosopher Augusto Salazar Bondy, a great educator and caring friend, who, upon seeing my teaching materials, had the generosity and vision to suggest that they should become books. It was through his kindness that I was introduced to Boris Romero from Editorial Arica (later Editorial Brasa), who would become the first publisher of my educational books and later my children's books.

Mr. Romero's response to my materials was initially lukewarm at best. I am certain that it was only out of deference to Dr. Salazar Bondy, one of Perú's most respected intellectuals, that

Mr. Romero finally agreed to publish a small portion of my work. He was interested in the materials that were least meaningful to me: the spelling exercises I had developed when I finally realized that I needed to do something about my students' disastrous spelling . . . as well as my own! It was a humble book, but it did quite well, and that prompted Mr. Romero to want to publish others.

The second book was a collection of the creative writing exercises I had designed. I called the book ***Ver y describir*** [Observing and describing], and to everyone's surprise it became a best-seller, something unheard of for a textbook.

Ver y describir, and its companion ***Oír y narrar*** became adopted textbook for many high school and college courses, more surprisingly, they were also purchased quite widely by individuals, which convinced me that there are many people who hold the secret wish of wanting to write.

The interest received by these books prompted the publication of a book on the elements of literature ***Iniciación literaria*** which was equally well received by educators and the public at large. For the cover of this book I chose an image that has always fascinated me. Most of the funerary statues found in Spanish churches depict noble men in either of two positions: laying down holding their long sword over their body, or, kneeling down in prayer. Yet this young man, known as *"el doncel de Siguenza"* is doing what no other man was depicted doing: he is reading.

The idea of an afterlife of reading really appeals to me!

In 2017, while attending the 50th anniversary of the High School graduation of my Alexander von Humboldt students in Lima, Perú, during the lovely party that my children's cousin, Max San Román and his wife, had organized for me in their residence I was given a great surprise.

One of my former students brought with her an old gentleman from the Sierra, who, after speaking to us in quechua, showed us copies of both ***Ver y describir*** and **Oír y narrar**. Although the books looked like new, showing the care they have received, they were close to 50 years old, and had been used by the gentleman's mother in her classes, just as he was still using them today.

What surprises authors can receive when they find out how far and for how long their books have been read and studied!

Another extraordinary quality of books is that they can be resurrected even long after their initial printings cease to be, either as a reproduction of the initial version, enriched or modified. Recently, more than 40 years after that first ***Ortografía práctica*** a new book on Spanish spelling and vocabulary ***Palabra amiga*** was created in collaboration with Isabel Campoy. This book is enriched by magnificent photographs of places and people of the Spanish-speaking World by Gerardo Piña-Rosales, President of the Academia Norteamericana de la Lengua Española [ANLE]

And, getting a first book published with a publishing house, can lead to furthering a relationship leading to more publications. Isabel and I are delighted that after this first publication with Velázquez Press, its President Mr. Arthur Chou decided to publish a book we had been working on for a long time ***La fascinante historia de la lengua española***.

The publication of this book gave Isabel the opportunity to complement the photographs of Dr. Gerardo Piña Rosales with reproductions of many of the pieces from our collection of popular art found during our travels, and other art pieces from our walls.

Since we had worked on this manuscript for years, in different settings to incorporate in it now pieces that are part of our everyday experience seemed just a perfect complement in celebrating the richness of a language created by millions of speakers in vast areas of the World all contributing to make it a vehicle of union for all of us.

The book ***A Lifelong Journey: Becoming a Teacher***, is a retelling of my life as an educator. I am very grateful to my son Miguel Zubizarreta for asking me to write it.

There I write at length about my life both as a high school teacher in Perú and as a Professor at the International Multicultural Program at the University of San Francisco. I describe different projects in which I was involved as well as the *Reading the World Conference.*

The title refers to the fact that I value education immensely and believe that, while one may be born with the passion and ability to teach, it takes a long process to become a true educator.

As it always happens to me on writing memoirs, I make valuable discoveries in the process of revisiting the past, an experience I encourage everyone to go through, since I believe everyone would find equally valuable.

Beginning to Write for Children

Based on the ongoing success of the early books, on Creative Writing and Literature Mr. Romero, the owner of Editorial Brasa in Perú, was willing to publish my complete language arts materials. By then, I was at Harvard as a Radcliffe Institute scholar and was living in Winchester, Massachusetts. One day, while I was working on the high school language arts textbooks, my five-year-old daughter Rosalma challenged me. She had been diligently working with paper and crayons on the carpet next to my desk, then she turned to me and said, "Why don't you ask me what I'm doing?" When I obliged her, she responded very sternly, "I'm making a book."

Not suspecting anything, I said, "How wonderful!" She then replied, "Why do you say it's wonderful when you have not asked me, 'Why are you writing a book?'" Realizing by now that there was more going on than I had surmised, I asked her why she was writing a book. "Because the ones you make are so ugly!" she replied.

These words, of course, went deep into my heart. I knew that she was not just passing judgment on my books for high school students, which could certainly seem ugly to a five-year-old, but was also letting me know loud and clear that I was dedicating time to my students rather than to her.

As a fourth-generation educator—my maternal great-grandparents owned a school in Madrid, my maternal grandparents owned a school in Cuba, my father was a professor, and my mother and her sisters were all teachers—I was familiar with the complaint of how parents can dedicate time to their students to the dismay of their own children. While I felt compelled to respond to Rosalma's request for a book that was written for her, it seemed to be a tall order.

Growing up in a family of clever, witty people, I had always felt that I was the serious one, the one who lacked the playful, creative attitude required to write for children. I truly did not know where to start, nor did I believe myself to be well suited to the task. The only things I had to rely on were my love of stories and of words. Finally, I had the idea of returning to the stories of my childhood, and I began to rewrite *The Rooster Who Went to His Uncle's Wedding, Half-Chicken, Cucarachita Martina,* and the other beloved tales.

This process of collecting and retelling the well-loved rhymes and poetry from my own childhood led to the publication of my

first book for children, in collaboration with a friend who had written a few original stories of her own. My children and our friends' children were enjoying the stories we were writing, so 1 decided to take the collection to Mr. Romero to be considered for publication. Since the only books he was publishing at the time were textbooks, we presented our collection of stories as a reader. It was one of the first readers in Latin America, if not the first, that was comprised exclusively of enjoyable literature free from the moralizing tone that was common at the time.

The initial run was small, a timid edition that alternated black and white pages with full-color ones in order to limit the cost. Still, the was a great success. It was titled *Sonrisas* [Smiles]. Since the book has been out of print now for many years, the title was used for a completely different book, a book of biographies co-authored with F. Isabel Campoy.

Teachers loved the idea of teaching reading through good literature, and soon *Sonrisas* was followed by *Alegrías* [Joy], *Maravillas* [Wonders], and *Triunfos* [Triumphs]. With the addition of a primer, *Cascabel* [Jingle bell], these books became

a popular reading series called *Edad de Oro* [The Golden Age]. The series was named in honor of José Martí, the famous Cuban poet and patriot whose literary magazine for children, *La Edad de Oro*, was a major contribution to the beginning of Spanish-language true children's literature in the Americas.

The positive reception received by these books and the increasing number of copies in each new print run helped me

to convince Mr. Romero to start a trade branch in his educational publishing house. Thus, collections of poetry, folktales, biographies, plays, and riddles were added to the *Edad de Oro* series. My involvement with these books was total, from creating the dummies with the layout of text and art, to helping mount the four-color negatives on the glass tables, to supervising the quality of the printing while the books were in press.

My children spent many hours with me in the huge print shop observing the different aspects of producing a book, having their names set in lead strips by the kind men who worked the linotypes, or simply diving into the big bins filled with shredded paper. It was a great experience for all of us to witness the many steps involved in printing one book.

In our current era of advanced technology, most of these processes are now obsolete. And from a purely physical perspective, the books in *Edad de Oro* are a far cry from the beautifully illustrated and printed books that we take for granted today. Yet, there was so much joy and love invested in the laborious production process, and their inexpensive format served to bring wonderful literature to thousands of children. Gazing out the windows of the buses I rode daily in Lima, I would see children throughout the city sitting on their doorsteps reading avidly from the *Edad de Oro* readers. The feelings this awoke in me have been unsurpassed, bringing with them the knowledge that I would always want to write for children.

Becoming a published author in the United States was a very long process. When I moved to this country in 1970, I was a professor of Spanish literature, first at Emory University in Atlanta and later at Mercy College in Detroit. Still, my love for children and for children's books continued. At one of the early conferences on Spanish reading in Austin, Texas, I heard Anne Pellowski for the first time, and I marveled at her gifts as a multilingual storyteller and a scholar. When I went to congratulate her, she recognized my name; she had recently been in Perú and had read my work. It was an extraordinary gift for me that someone of her stature would think highly of my writing. Not long after, E. P. Dutton contacted me with a request to translate books by Evelyn Ness and Lucille Clifton. It was Anne Pellowski who had recommended me, and I am still very grateful to her for this introduction.

From that time on, translating wonderful children's books has been a cherished activity. I consider it an art, as it involves more than knowing a language well. It also requires being a good writer in the language into which one is translating, as well as having a special sensibility and respect for the author's style and intent. By this I do not mean sticking too closely to the original text, which is often not possible anyway. Instead, a translator needs to recreate something in the new language that conveys the spirit of what the author created in the first language.

Translating has offered me many opportunities to explore both the Spanish language, as well as the craft of writing, and has opened the doors for some rich conversations on language with many people. These include other translators whose work I admire: Bernice Randall, one of the most gifted editors I have ever known; and my daughter Rosalma Zubizarreta, with whom I have collaborated on many translations and who has translated much of my work. I still enjoy doing translations, these days usually in collaboration with Isabel Campoy. I often use a musical metaphor to describe my work: If I were a composer, I am sure that I would enjoy playing other musician's compositions as well as my own. Translating a book is creating an interpretation of another author's work and is a very valuable process.

Nevertheless, for many years it was very frustrating for me to be seen only as a translator. Often, I found myself offering a number of suggestions about content, especially in the case of books about Latin America or about Latino culture written by authors from outside the culture. I am always glad to help make a book more authentic. Still, it did not feel fair to be enhancing the work of others who were being published, yet to continually be turned down when I approached publishers with my own writing.

It took me twenty years—until 1991—to have my first book accepted by a major American publisher, and I will always be grateful to Ana Cerro and Atheneum for welcoming *The Gold Coin,* published later in Spain as *La moneda de oro.* Before that breakthrough, I had continued to publish children's books in Perú and Spain. I had also been publishing textbooks for children in Mexico, Colombia, and Panamá.

A significant moment occurred when my juvenile novel *Encaje de piedra* [Stone lace], a mystery story that takes place during the building of the Burgos Cathedral in the Middle Ages, won the Marta Salotti Gold Medal in Argentina. It was lovely to receive this award surrounded by good Argentinian friends, among them Marta Dujovne and Victor de Zavalía, Kuki Miller, Esther Jacob, and Delia Seoane.

Marta, Esther, Kuki and I had become friends through our work on the *Asociación Internacional de Literatura Infantil y Juvenil en Español y Portugués* [International Association of

Children and Young Adult Literature in Spanish and Portuguese]. We shared a common interest in promoting children's books that represent our Latin American reality, uncovering both its richness and its inequality, and specially books that promoted ideas of social justice.

Delia Seoane had been my very dear friend during the time at the Complutense University in Madrid. Together we had taken many cultural trips through Spain and France.

The ceremony became even more meaningful with the presence of Suni Paz. Suni has created music for many of my poems. Her musical talent, her creativity and her unique voice have been an extraordinary gift.

For this ceremony she created music for my poems *Dónde termina el nacer* and *Iguazú*, now included in the CD **Como una flor**.

**Receiving the Marta Salotti gold medal
for *Encaje de piedra*.**

In 1990, Santillana begun to publish my books in the United States. I am very grateful to Sam Laredo, president at that time of SantillanaUSA, for his encouragement and support. He published separate English and Spanish editions of *Stories the Year 'Round / Cuentos para todo el año,* a twelve-book collection, as well as *Stories for the Telling / Cuentos para contar,* a collection of five books for young readers and *El manto de pluma,* a series of realistic fiction stories based in Latin America. Over the years, Santillana has continued to publish my work under their Alfaguara imprint, later under Loqueleo. They have recently been bought by Vista Higher Learning and I have been pleased to see my books on this new publisher's catalogue.

Through the long association with Santillana, I have worked with some extraordinary editors whom I am proud to count as good friends: Emiliano Martínez, Antonio Ramos, and Amaya Elezcano Tolosa in Spain, and Silvia Matute and Isabel Mendoza in Miami.

Sam Laredo moved on to create his own publishing house Laredo Publishing where he published the series *Cuentos con Alma* which included five moments of my childhood: *Pregones, Barriletes, Barquitos de papel, Pin-pin-sarabín* and *Días de circo,* as well as the realistic stories *El pañuelo de seda* and *El vuelo de los colibríes* and *El reino de la geometría,*
a story that presents the difficult topic of segregation and discrimination to young children with geometrical figures as characters

Many of the books that became very successful when they were eventually published by major trade publishers, such as *The Rooster Who Went to His Uncle's Wedding, Mediopollito-Half-Chicken,* and *The Lizard and the Sun/La lagartija y el sol,* were stories I had written many years before. I had been unsuccessfully attempting to get these stories published in the United States during the twenty years before *The Gold Coin* was published. If it had not been for my daughter Rosalma's insistence, this book would have been printed in Argentina or Spain where I knew publishers who were eager to have it. But Rosalma held to the dream that this story should be read by every child in this country, and she discouraged me from publishing it abroad, encouraging me to persist in spite of a long list of rejections. At the time, it seemed presumptuous to imagine her dream coming true, but somehow I did persist.

Many years after it was first published by Atheneum in 1991, *The Gold Coin* has been included in its entirety in several reading series, including ones by Harcourt, Scott, Macmillan-McGraw Hill, Scholastic, and Houghton Mifflin. As a result, quite a few children in this country have indeed been able to read it! *The Gold Coin* was also awarded the Christopher Award Medal, an honor that opened doors and made it possible for me to have other children's books published in the United States.

I only tell this story to encourage others who also want to write for children. It is my firm belief that, if you want to write, you should do so. And when you have a finished manuscript, you should seek publication, without becoming discouraged by the long road ahead. Of course, the ideal situation is to be working with the active encouragement and support of an editor who believes in your work. Yet those ideal circumstances are not always present. Believing in one's own work and continuing to write is the only guarantee that one's words will become a text—and once the text is created, it will require steadfast effort to nurture it through the process of becoming a book.

The book *Authors in the Classroom: A Transformative Process* (2004) co-authored with Isabel Campoy chronicles the work we have done with classroom teachers, encouraging them to initiate a classroom publishing process that involves teachers, students, and families as authors. In it, we also discuss extensively the process of authorship and what that can mean in a person's life. I don't want to repeat what I have already described elsewhere. However, I do want to share my strong belief that we are all the authors of our own journey through life, and as such, we empower ourselves when we find the words to communicate and record our thoughts, feelings, experiences, and dreams.

The website www.authorsintheclassroom.com describes the process and offers guidelines and numerous examples of books created by teachers, students and their families.

The original of the numerous books and poems written by teachers, students and parents, both those included in the website and many more, are now been preserved by Kent State University, Ohio, at the Reinberger Children's Library as part of the Alma Flor Ada and F. Isabel Campoy Collection that contains a great deal of our work.

For me, writing for children has been a process of authenticity. While I have striven throughout my life to be authentic in all that I do, this becomes even more important when I am writing for children.

Imagination is unlimited, and I want all children to be given the time and space, the support and freedom to use their imaginations to the fullest. At the same time, imaginary worlds need to be authentic; that is, they need to be approached with responsibility, commitment, devotion, and truth. These are the guiding lights I strive to follow in my writing.

Children deserve to be treated with care and respect. The world of children's literature offers us as authors the opportunity to create books that reflect that care and respect. The degree to which we are able to do so is reflected in the quality of the final product.

All my writing has been about the things that matter to me. I write because I breathe, I write because I am alive, and I hope I will write as long as I breathe and as long as I am alive. I write when I have stories to tell, but also when I need to explain life to myself. I write to celebrate and to mourn, to remember moments that I would like to preserve, and to preserve moments I have invented.

The values that inform my life inform my writing. I was taught to treat everyone with respect, to wage peace and struggle for justice, to have the courage to speak the truth and to live by it, to make a continuous effort to be kind and generous, understanding and forgiving. But when I write, I am not consciously seeking to teach values; instead, I am seeking to share life.

As a Spanish-speaking Latina, I face some significant challenges in writing and publishing in the United States. Some of my most creative work has been the poetry I have written in Spanish, and many of my children's books have been written in rhyme. In Spanish, my prose has a distinctive rhythm that children recognize quite easily. I have been told several times by teachers that they have read a book aloud to their class, pretending it was a book I had written, and that the children immediately recognized the ruse. Conversely, many teachers have read one of my stories aloud without revealing the name of the author and discovered that the children could easily guess who had written the book. However, much of this word play is lost in translation from the Spanish, and I have yet to find a true poetic voice in English.

Thus, when writing for an English-speaking audience, I need to rely more on other literary resources, such as the strength of the story, the depth of the characters, or the richness of the descriptions. The resources I have when writing in Spanish—the musicality of the language, the potential puns, the vivid images—are not as available to me.

Still, I do live in the United States. During the many years I have lived here, I have dedicated myself to protecting the right of all people to maintain their home language and to advocating for the value of bilingualism and multilingualism for all children. I want Spanish-speaking families to be able to enjoy wonderful books that are written originally in Spanish. And, at the same time, I also want to write for **all** of the children of this country. This includes some of the children in my own family who only speak English, as their parents are still searching for a way to give them the gift and the power of speaking two languages.

All of my efforts are amply rewarded by the happiness I feel whenever I read the letters that children write to me or hear their comments as I visit their schools. 1 am deeply gratified each time I learn that a child has been touched by one of my books, has felt a connection with someone who cares, has been inspired to see his or her own life in a new light. In the following letter, a young reader communicates this message very eloquently:

> *Dear Alma:*
>
> *Thank you so much for the copy of your book, Under the Royal Palms, I have greatly enjoyed reading it. I love hearing about the bats that lived between the ceiling and roof, the tinajones, and the porrones. The stories you tell are so well described, I can picture myself there, watching everything happen. Books like yours have always enthralled me, I am glad to have been able to read your book, and I hope to be able to read your second book Where the Flame Trees Bloom. Reading your book has opened my eyes to my own childhood, and made me realize how much I enjoy my life, and even though not everything that happens in life is good, or enjoyable, I love the things I have learned by experiencing the bad times. As you said in my copy of Under*

the Royal Palms, "Feel the love around you and the love of those who think about you." I have learned to realize how many people really do care, and how widespread that love is. All is well with me, and I am back in school. I can almost run again, and as the day I do grows nearer, the smile in my face grows broader. It is nice to know, I am no longer the person I was before, but I am better in the way that I have matured and grown to understand the real meaning in life. It is not the time we are given, but what we do with the time that is given to us. Thank you again for the copy of your book, and I hope one day I can meet the inspirational author of the book Under the Royal Palms.

Always,

Briana Haller

Part II: Sharing the Joy of Creation

Hearts and Minds: Illustrating Children's Books

by Leslie Tryon

When I wake up every morning between 4 and 4:30—yes, I said *every* morning—the first thing I do, after brushing my teeth, is drink a big glass of water. The second thing I do is make myself a cup of strong coffee—just one cup. The third thing I do is read newspapers. For the next two hours I read all of my favorite parts of five different newspapers. (These days 1 do most of my reading online.) Newspapers have always played an important role in my life. I did freelance work for the *Los Angeles Times* for many, many years. I even wrote and published my own little eight-page newspaper I called the *Pleasant Valley Enterprise.* You would think that creating a newspaper for the characters that live in Hidden Forest would have been the first thing that popped into my mind. It should have been, but it wasn't.

It was the first thing that occurred to Alma Flor Ada. That's just one instance that demonstrates that two minds are better than one. No author or illustrator can think of everything all the time. Of course, when you are doing children's books, if you are working with someone—an author, an illustrator, a songwriter—it is equally true that two hearts are better than one. The product of collaboration must be a creation of the heart and the mind.

Alma Flor Ada and I began our collaboration before we knew it would become collaboration. Our wonderful editor, Jonathan Lanman at Simon & Schuster, brought us together. (We didn't actually meet in person until the book *Dear Peter Rabbit* had been published. Jon took us to lunch in Miami.)

As often happens, an editor will have in his hands a manuscript he is anxious to publish, a story that moves him or her. It is important to mention an editor's emotional reaction to a story because that reaction is what guides the editor to send the story to one illustrator rather than another. Something about Alma Flor Ada's manuscript made Jon think about me. He sent the story to me; I read it and I reacted to it immediately, in my mind and in my heart.

I had written and illustrated many adventures for my character, Albert. These stories, all picture books, take place in a fictional place I call Pleasant Valley, a place I had created. Jon wondered, even though I had my own series of books, if I would  like to illustrate a book about traditional fairy-tale characters, all living in a fictional place Alma Flor called Hidden Forest, a place she had created. The chance to illustrate beloved characters like Peter Rabbit, Goldilocks, Little Red Riding Hood, the Three Bears, the Three Pigs, two Big Bad Wolves, and Mr. McGregor was a remarkable and delicious offer. But that wasn't the best part. These characters were writing letters to each other. This was as much a book about letter writing as it was about inviting friends over to celebrate a birthday party.

I love letters. I had a rare opportunity as a child to live in East Providence, Rhode Island, in the house my mother was born in. My mother was the last of eight Sullivan children, all born in that house. I slept in the same bedroom she slept in as a child, only I shared it with my great-aunt instead of three older sisters like my mother had. Under that bed there were boxes of letters written by three generations of Sullivans. My great-grandfather wrote letters to that house when he was away, serving in the Civil War. My great-uncle wrote when he was serving in the Spanish American War. My mother's brothers were sent to France in World War I, and they wrote home to that same house at 68 Mercer Street.

There were other letters, too, written by those who traveled to New York or Boston. Letters that were written "home" had always been stored in those boxes. Being a curious child, I quickly discovered the treasure under my bed. Those letters became some of my favorite reading material. I would prop up my pillows and take out a letter written by my great-grandfather. I would hold the paper and trace my fingers over the lines and think, *He touched this paper,* I was touching something he had touched. Here is something he wrote in one of his letters, "Although the hour is late, I don't want to close because I so enjoy talking to you." I felt he was talking directly to me.

Alma Flor cares about letter writing and I care about letter writing; it's another heart-mind connection. These are subtle connections but they are what create a solid foundation for a fictional world.

Dear Peter Rabbit was received very well. Because the book was a success, our publisher wondered if there were other stories about the residents of Hidden Forest. At the same time the publisher was wondering about these things. Alma Flor was wondering how the plans for a house-warming party were going for the Three Little Pigs. Rumor had it that Pig Number One may have been planning just such an affair. Jon, our editor, was enchanted at the thought and so was I.

Alma Flor had written about the social structure of the community of Hidden Forest, and I had created the look of the place. I had illustrated *Dear Peter Rabbit,* never thinking there might be another book to follow in its footsteps. The locations shown in those illustrations were confined to their borders. You couldn't fly an airplane over Hidden Forest in that first book. Before I began work on the second book, *Yours Truly, Goldilocks,* I needed to create a bird's-eye view. Just exactly where did all these characters live? I needed a map.

All the clues I needed to create the map were there, in the letters Alma Flor had written; I simply had to go back and play detective cartographer. The two Wolves, Wolfy and his cousin, Fer O'Cious, needed a central vantage point, from which they  could keep a clandestine eye on everyone else. Mr. McGregor needed plenty of room for his garden. The addresses in the letters indicated places like Hollow Oak, Hidden Meadows, Woodsy Woods, Vegetable Lane (which became Veggie Lane), Dark Forest, Cottage in the Woods, and Riding Lane. At last, I began to actually see the community of Hidden Forest. I created the map, and I placed the names of the characters around the border. I added a compass rose made out of binoculars and had two little characters—a cardinal and a mouse—hold the pencil and the pen, symbols for writing. (In *Extra! Extra!* these same two characters appear on the masthead of the *Hidden Forest News.)*

HIDDEN SECRETS IN HIDDEN FOREST

It's fun adding details to an illustration that a reader might discover on a third or fourth reading. For example, in the book *Yours Truly, Goldilocks,* when we see Red Riding Hood in her room, writing a letter, you might notice that, in the background, the closet door is open and there are other Riding Hoods hanging there. We can suppose that the only reason we have the story of Little Red Riding Hood is because the event happened on the same day that she had decided to wear the red hood instead of the green or the turquoise.

Or, in *Dear Peter Rabbit,* you might take another look at all those tails hanging from the ceiling in Speedy Raccoon's shop. There are some bats hanging there among all those tails. Look very closely at the bowl of bunny tails; the back of one reads, "Peel and stick." It isn't written anywhere but I've always thought of that illustration as "Tails of the Vienna Woods." That's because Speedy Raccoon studied tail and tooth replacement in Vienna; one clue to his time spent in Vienna is his little goatee.

In *Dear Peter Rabbit* we see poor Peter, in bed, with the covers pulled up over his nose while his mother and brothers try to comfort him with a nice warm mug of chamomile tea. This composition is homage to one of my favorite artists, the Dutch painter, Jan Vermeer. If you look at his painting, *Maid Pouring Milk,* you will see the subtle influence in my illustration of Peter, lying in his sick bed.

There is just one place where a tiny bit of my character Albert appears in Alma Flor's world; it's in *Yours Truly, Goldilocks,* in the illustration of Goldilocks sitting in her window seat composing a letter to Baby Bear. If you look on the bottom shelf, directly in front of her, you will see the title, *Albert's*

Alphabet, written on the spine of one of the books. As I explained earlier, placing little secrets into illustrations is fun.

Writing and illustrating children's books is fun. It is also work. Hard work. Whether I have written the book that is about to be illustrated or the book was written by Alma Flor Ada, one fact applies—words come first. People think of me as an illustrator but illustrations come only after the words have made a strong case for a fictional world that can pictured.

When I talk to children, I tell them that there is an invisible—but most important—part of every book; you can't see it, touch it, hear it, feel it, or smell it, but without it you will not have a book. That invisible part is the IDEA. The children and I agree that we all get ideas all day long; some ideas are quiet and little, some ideas are medium-sized, and some ideas make you want to jump up out of your chair. I tell them that I look for the ones that make me so excited I want to jump up and run around the room.

Once I have my idea, if I am the author, I will write it down in the form of a story. As an illustrator, the next thing I will do is make drawings of the characters; then I will make a storyboard. A storyboard is like a roadmap; it has a little box for every page

in the book. Once I sketch something into each of those boxes, I have the equivalent of a picture story all on one piece of paper.

The next step is to create a dummy. I will take every one of those pictures in those little boxes and draw it the same size it will appear in the book. I photocopy all those drawings and put them together to form a dummy. When I am finished with the dummy, I will have a paper version of a whole book, cover and all. The editor will look at the dummy and see if it does a good job helping to tell the word story.

Once the editor and the art director decide the dummy is acceptable, I will begin my work on the final art. In other words, I will start all over again, but this time I will do each and every drawing in color. This part takes the longest, usually about six months to finish a 32-page book.

The medium for the illustrations is the same in all four books in the series: *Dear Peter Rabbit, Yours Truly, Goldilocks', With Love, Little Red Hen,* and *Extra! Extra!* First I do an ink drawing on watercolor paper. Next I paint—using very small brushes—with watercolor, being very careful to stay between the lines. Next I color on top of the watercolor with Prismacolor pencils. I love the look of the old children's books and decided that doing my illustrations in that manner might be appropriate for books that tell the stories of traditional characters.

The golden rule of creating children's books is that you must believe completely in the characters and the places that you create. It must be an airtight world. Once your fictional world has reached the point where you know everyone in town, what they like to eat, what games they like to play, what music they like, you can share little details with the reader that they might not otherwise know.

Alma Flor Ada knew that the characters in Hidden Forest had their own newspaper. Of course, I agreed. I wondered, then, who did what on this newspaper. I couldn't pick up the phone and call anyone in Hidden Forest since they don't have telephones. So I decided to travel there in my mind and visit their print shop. Like all newspaper prep rooms and pressrooms, I found a beehive of activity. Red Riding Hood had just stepped out of the darkroom when I arrived, with a dripping photo in her hand. Grandma, the editor and publisher, was busy finishing up the last-minute sketches for an edition that was about to go to press. Papa Bear was following two breaking news stories, one taking place in Italy and the other in Mexico. Little Red Hen was ready to set the type, Mr. McGregor was analyzing samples of bean plants, and eight little Copy Chicks were scurrying around delivering copy, pictures, and type. I peeked into the pressroom where Pigs One and Two were working at the big Gutenberg-type press, printing the latest  edition, while Baby Bear was folding the papers.

Peter Rabbit was in the next room tying up each issue with a red ribbon and piling them into his purple sack. I was very impressed with everything I saw and tried to remember it all so I could go back to my drawing board and draw a picture of what I had seen.

That's what I mean about believing—100 percent—in the characters and the place that you create. You should feel as

though you're dropping in on them for a visit. If it's *real* to Alma Flor Ada and it's *real* to me, then there is a good chance it will seem *real* to the reader.

The world of Hidden Forest has come to life through a collaboration that might never have been had it not been for our editor, Jon, making the heart- mind connection between Alma Flor Ada and me. Hidden Forest is as real to me now as my own little town of Pleasant Valley.

I am in awe of the talents and intelligence of Alma Flor Ada and I just thank my lucky stars that we were brought together to share the world of Hidden Forest. Alma Flor has given me friendship and, through her countless talents, a feast for my mind and my heart to enjoy.

Coauthoring Books with F. Isabel Campoy

Since writing is such a personal expression of creativity, it is not common for literary books to be coauthored. Questions are frequently posed to me about my joint work with F. Isabel Campoy and, in particular, about how we engage in the process of co-creation.

Isabel and I began collaborating in 1994 as co-authors of *Cielo abierto,* a series of books in Spanish commissioned by Harcourt School Publisher. We have been producing books together ever since. We have continued participating as authors in the creation of series for Harcourt (now Houghton Mifflin Hartcourt) in a variety of subject areas. Reading series: *Signatures and Cielo abierto; Collections and Vamos de fiesta; Trophies* and *Trofeos; Journeys and Senderos; Excursions and Excursiones, and Into Reading and Arriba la lectura.* Language Arts: *Language and Lenguaje.* English as a Second Language: *Moving Into English.*

We have been part of the team of authors of the *Frog Street Pre-K Program.* Frog Street is the publisher of our guide for initial Spanish reading: *Spanish Literacy Strategies for Young Learners.*

Our commitment to facilitate the important collaboration between schools and parents lead of to write *Ayudando a nuestros hijos,* published by Mariposa Transformative Education Services and to create with Colin Baker *Guía para padres y maestros de niños bilingües,* published by. Multilingual Matters.

We have also written several pedagogical books. *Authors in the Classroom: A Transformative Education Process* describes the work on promoting creating authentic books in the classroom by teachers, students and their families. A work we have shared throughout the United States, in Europe (Spain, Italy, Hungary, the Czech Republic, Bulgaria), in Latin America (Mexico, Puerto Rico, the Dominican Republic, Costa Rica, Panama), and Micronesia (Guam, the Mariana Islands). examples of this work are presented in www.authorsintheclassroom.com.

Está linda la mar. Para entender y usar la poesía en la clase (Santillana/Vista Higher Learning) provides ample information about the nature of poetry in Spanish and its effective use in the classroom. *Música amiga: aprender cantando* (Mariposa) gives suggestions on the use of over 300 songs in Spanish for language development and creative reading. *Palabra amiga. Domine su idioma* (Velázquez Press) offers guidance on spelling, punctuation and vocabulary of the Spanish language.

In addition, we have also co-authored over one hundred children's books, including anthologies of poetry and plays and collections of folktales. Our desire to help all children become aware of the richness of Hispanic culture inspired the creation of *Gateways to the Sun / Puertas al sol.* This dual-language collection, published by SantillanaUSA, includes anthologies of plays and poetry, books on art, and biographies, as well as an introduction to the history and culture of the Spanish-speaking world. The sumptuous and historically accurate illustrations were created by a multitude of Latin American artists under the highly skilled guidance of Felipe Dávalos and realize fully the intention to honor our cultural heritage.

With the same publisher, we have created *Cuentos para celebrar/ Stories to celebrate,* a dual language series of twelve books that depict the joy of traditional festivities.

Simon and Schuster has published our collection of folktales from Spanish-speaking countries in *Tales Our Abuelitas Told* and its Spanish version *Cuentos Our Abuelitas Told.*

National Geographic has published in a lavish format our anthology of poetry, *Alegría: poesía cada día* with poems for each day of the year as well as some super-sized books with selections from the anthology and a website that offers all the poems read by either one of us and many in musical versions by Suni Paz.

What has made this rich collaboration possible is that, while we have different backgrounds—Spain and Cuba— and different areas of specialization—English and Romance languages—we already had much in common when we met. We both had an interest in linguistics and applied linguistics, although Isabel had focused more on the teaching of English and foreign languages to high school and college students while my expertise was in the teaching of Spanish and in first and second language acquisition in children. We both had and continue to have a profound love for literature in all its genres, especially poetry and theatre, although Isabel has a much stronger background in modern theatre while my experience has been in classical drama. Similarly, we both share a great interest in art, but my education in this field has been predominantly in the classic Spanish and Latin American tradition while Isabel has an extraordinary familiarity with twentieth-century and contemporary American and European art. While our taste may differ somewhat when it comes to contemporary music, we both love classical music, particularly from the Baroque period. We have developed together a passion for opera.

Beyond all of our similarities and differences with regard to our educational and professional backgrounds, we share the deep conviction that all children deserve to have every possible opportunity for learning and that such opportunities need to support children's developing sense of self and their self-esteem. Together, we have sought to create inspiring materials of high aesthetic quality in order to support children's learning.

Both Isabel and I come from families with strong family and close friendship ties and were fortunate to have wise parents who have instilled in us the values of responsibility and service. As a result, we feel a sense of mission about sharing our knowledge and our privileges in order to support the education of all children. We are also dedicated to promoting the contributions of Hispanic culture in its entirety, including the contributions of people from Latin America, Spain, and Latinos in the United States. We firmly believe that Latino children in this country have a right to their own cultural heritage and that a deeper appreciation for their roots will strengthen their sense of self and increase their appreciation for their parents' efforts on their behalf.

We also believe that sharing our Hispanic cultural heritage with non- Latino children may contribute to bringing about greater intercultural respect and understanding. This shared vision supports and nourishes our efforts as we work together on our many projects.

Creating books together, Isabel and I collaborate in a variety of ways. The first step is always to conceptualize the nature of the book, and we do this through dialogue. The nature of the book then determines the nature of our interaction.

Some of the books we have created are anthologies. In those cases, we make decisions together about what selections to include. For other books, each of us contributes some pieces that are our own original work—whether poems, plays, or stories. In still other cases, we actually do the writing together, usually by having one of us create a first draft and then having the other person offer their feedback and input. If it is a longer book, we will divide the work between us at the beginning, each taking different portions of the book to write our first drafts. Yet by the time we have finished editing and revising the material so many times that the books is finally ready for publication, it has become such a tightly woven tapestry that we can no longer easily distinguish who has contributed what!

Sun festival of the Mexica people

This collaborative effort is demanding at times, as it requires some inner and outer negotiations. It is not always easy to take in another person's perspective and let go of a particular word, sentence, or nuance. Yet in the end, we find that the effort we invest in our collaboration is always rewarding, just as the differences in our backgrounds add up to a richer book.

It feels important to write about our collaboration here for two reasons. The first has to do with my readership. In writing this book, I am attempting to answer many of the questions that my readers frequently ask me. The second reason has to do with my own sense of integrity. It would not be appropriate for me to speak about my writing without acknowledging Isabel's significant contributions to many of my most recent books. Even though the byline always acknowledges when a book is a coauthored work, it is important to me to have the opportunity to describe more fully the depth and value of our collaboration.

In the next section Isabel presents her own view of our collaboration.

You can read more about Isabel Campoy, her life, and her creative work in *Something About the Author*, Vol. 143, pp. 21-26, published in 2004 by Thomson/Gale, Detroit and in *Contemporary Authors* volume 365, Gale/Cengage Learning, 2015 pages 62-85.

You are also invited to visit her personal website at www.isabelcampoy.com and the website for her book *Maybe Something Beautiful* www.maybesomethingbeautiful.com recipient of the Tomás Rivera Award.

Writing in Collaboration: One Plus One is One, or Two

by F. Isabel Campoy

How do two writers write one text? If the most frequent question from our young readers is "Where do you get your ideas?" what our adult audiences most want to know is how Alma Flor Ada and I write in collaboration.

It is true that writing is usually done in isolation, and that it reflects the style, thought, and personality of an individual; however, there is a before and an after to the actual moment of writing.

The car we had rented at the airport in Albuquerque was not your typical rent-a-car-to-get-to-the-conference-and-back; it was a red convertible with little space for luggage and a lot of room for adventure. Our plane had landed with much delay, and that car was practically our only choice, except for a ten-seat van that neither Alma Flor nor I felt confident driving. It was early summer and the days had grown longer, spreading out into orange evenings and turquoise skies. Route 1-25 North offered the enticement of a side road that ran parallel to the main road, yet also headed to Santa Fe.  Since it passed through a town called Madrid, we didn't doubt for a minute that it would be a more enjoyable road. It took us forever to wind along that narrow, twisted, two-lane trail, but the enforced slowness of the journey, the closeness to the beautiful arid landscape, and the time for a long conversation led us to design our first series of books together.

New Mexico is a state in which the roots of the Hispanic culture in the United States are intact, and we both felt that it was important to record this history. An idea was born from our

meandering conversation as we discussed our passion for poetry, music, theatre, history, and truth.

I graduated from Madrid's Universidad Complutense, and although the Madrid we found on the Turquoise Trail on our way to Santa Fe had little in common with the cosmopolitan capital of Spain, there were, indeed, a few small parallels. In a little dress shop on the corner of the one-block "downtown," we found a dress made from *mantones,* the richly embroidered silk shawls that women still wear in Spain to a *corrida*, or bullfighting ring, on a summer afternoon. In a gift shop further down the street we found *santos de palo,* statues representing saints carved out of wooden sticks and painted in bright colors, just like the ones I had seen many times in small churches all over Spain. Our conversation ranged from gifts to art, from art to history, and we ended up in a corner of that same shop searching through an old suitcase filled with antique books we simply had to have, knowing that we would regret all that added weight once we surrendered our convertible at the airport.

The process of writing in collaboration probably takes as many different paths as there are authors attempting to do it. Of course, the personalities of the writers involved matter as much as their interests, knowledge of the subject, points of view, and willingness to find a common ground; but most of all, writing in collaboration calls for a firm commitment to the subject and a sincere mutual respect between the authors.

That trip was essential because it provided a stress-free environment, ample opportunity to explore mutual interests, and the discovery *in situ* of a common professional goal: to share with children the richness of our culture. The product of those discussions was a set of various collections of books titled *Cielo abierto* that (Harcourt School Publishers). Anyone who has traveled through New  Mexico will recognize the "Open Skies" that inspired our series' title.

When the boxes of books we had purchased arrived in San Francisco, they were placed in our extensive library by genre and in alphabetical order by author. Although bringing back books upon books from every corner of the world has meant paying extra in airline fees and needing help hauling heavy volumes to and from airports, we know that these books are a crucial tool for facilitating our research, especially when the research is in Spanish. Not many of the titles we need can be found in nearby libraries.

And so the process begins.

First comes opening up the space in filing cabinets, on shelves, and in our computers' memory for what is newly arriving. We are fortunate that the Arne Nixon Center for Children's Literature at Fresno State University has  chosen to archive our work for future generations of students and scholars. Thus, instead of being forced to destroy our previous materials, correspondence with editors, dummies of past books, penciled illustrations, and galleys, and even the three or four drafts each book goes through, the center staff is kindly willing to receive and catalogue whatever we no longer need to keep with us. Those papers are the true trail of the work of two authors who sometimes question each other's reason for a change and at other times firmly refuse to accept a "better" word or sentence on a page of a common manuscript. To the future students of those pages we want to say now that we took the process seriously, but we always had fun!

Once we have cleared enough physical space, we quickly hurry to fill it up. For the way we work, we need to spread long pieces of paper where we can jot down objectives, age of the audience, suggested pieces and genres, nuggets of an idea, even

suggestions for illustrations. Every idea is annotated—this is the moment to let creativity run free! Being who we are, many times we get carried away designing a subproject of the project. Ideas feed new connections to other parts of our work, and trying to do it all at once is a malady we suffer frequently. Returning to our original focus is not always easy.

ONE BOOK, TWO AUTHORS: TWO VOICES

Once we have decided and agreed upon all the main concepts of a project, we determine who will do what, by what time, and how. From this point on, each collaboration develops along its own unique path.

Tales Our Abuelitas Told, which Simon & Schuster published in English and simultaneously in Spanish as *Cuentos que contaban nuestras abuelas,* is an anthology of twelve folktales, each retold independently by Alma Flor Ada or me.

The table of contents identifies the author of each story; however, the selection of the stories and the extensive introduction to the book where we speak about the stories' itinerant nature as they traveled in the backpack of history were both the result of joint work. Our poetry and theatre anthologies have usually undergone a similar process.

ONE BOOK, TWO AUTHORS: ONE VOICE

When Santillana/Alfaguara asked us to write a series of multicultural books for very young readers on the most frequently celebrated holidays in the United States, combining fiction and nonfiction, we were delighted to accept the challenge. Initially, we thought we would divide the titles between the two of us; however, as we continued to talk about the books, our general vision for the series, and the characteristics we hoped to see in each book, we began to bounce ideas back and forth between us and ended up writing the books jointly.

In this process of joint writing, the original idea for any given story could come from either of us, and then one of us would undertake the authorship of the first draft. The second author read, changed, and improved the text as she saw fit and resubmitted it to the first author. This process sometimes went back and forth several times until both co-authors agreed on the final text, which often was so different from the original idea that it would be difficult for us to unravel who had suggested what.

One of the challenges inherent in this series was the need to keep the reading level very simple, while still creating an interesting and lively story. In spite of the multiple drafts we ended up writing for each book before arriving at the final versions, the creative process for this project presented us with many wonderful moments. For example, it gave us the opportunity to consult with many friends and colleagues belonging to the various cultures related to the different holidays. We found ourselves very grateful that our circle of friends is so diverse!

We were also very fortunate to live at that time in Mill Valley, California, which has a most comfortable and beautiful library we know. The librarians there have always been helpful in our research, providing us with the most up-to-date information available. The Mill Valley library is surrounded by redwoods and its cathedral ceilings and glass walls allow the reader to contemplate and enjoy those majestic trees even while reading or writing indoors. For us, Mill Valley's library is as much of an icon as the Golden Gate Bridge, a much more famous icon that is not very far away.

ONE BOOK, TWO AUTHORS: MANY VOICES

Creating anthologies is a unique experience for which planning and preparation are essential, as defining the parameters precisely will save coauthors valuable time.

We have edited a number of poetry anthologies that also contain some of our original poems. The seven poetry anthologies in Spanish that were published by Harcourt as part of the *Cielo abierto* series were our first joint incursions into this field; the four anthologies included in *Puertas al sol/Gateways to the Sun*, published by Santillana/Alfaguara, are more recent. In the *Cielo abierto* anthologies the poems were organized by themes. In contrast, the *Puertas al sol/Gateways to the Sun* anthologies are divided into sections that each feature a particular Spanish-speaking country and a representative author from that country. Another section in each book features Latinos in the United States.

We have also created several anthologies of traditional rhymes, songs, and Christmas carols. *¡Pío Peep! Spanish Nursery Rhymes; MooMuu: Animal Rhymes, Mamá Goose: A Latino Nursery Treasury; Merry Navidad: Christmas Carols in Spanish and English* and *Diez perritos /Ten Little Puppies* are all bilingual books in which the two languages appear on facing pages. The bilingual nature of these books is reflected in their titles.

My passion for art has permeated our work in many ways, culminating in the creation of four books in *Puertas al sol/Gateways to the Sun* featuring the art of the Hispanic world.

Our shared love for poetry has led to the creation of the extensive anthology *ALEGRÍA: Poesía cada día* with poems from great poets of the Spanish-speaking world selected for each day of the year. This anthology and the accompanying giant size books for classroom use have been lavishly illustrated by National Geographic. And to encourage the presence and best use of poetry in the classroom we have written *Está linda la mar: Para entender la poesía y usarla en el aula*, published by SantillanaUSA.

Our joint passion for travel has taken us to Morocco and Guatemala, Greece and Turkey. Our transformational workshops for educators, where we invite them to discover the power of their own voices and self-publish their work as a way of encouraging their own students to also become authors, have taken us to Panamá and México; to Hungary, the Czech Republic, and Bulgaria; and to Spain and Micronesia. This methodology for awakening the power of authorship is described in our book, *Authors in the Classroom.* From each place we have visited, we have brought back notes to expand and develop further whenever we have the time to do so, and which will most likely unfold into another decade of projects.

I haven't expanded here on the process of collaborating with a composer in the creation of musical anthologies such as *Música amiga,* since Suni Paz, our partner in crime in that creative adventure, has written about that beautifully in her own chapter. Still, I need to affirm that her presence in my life has been a source of never-ending joy and boundless fun. It is an honor to have worked closely over time with such a talented musician and generous human being.

In closing, I also need to express my wholehearted gratitude to Alma Flor Ada for her openness to considering the impossible, attempting the unexpected, and working hard to bring the beauty of dreams into material form, while never forgetting to enjoy the simple pleasures of life.

To her, my admiration and devotion.

When Words Sing: Suni Paz

One of the greatest gifts we receive from our own creative expression is that it stimulates the creativity of others. The immense delight of seeing the illustrations that have been created by artists who have been inspired by my stories has been matched only by the profound joy of hearing my words set to music by the very talented composer Suni Paz.

In addition to writing original music to accompany my poetry, Suni has recorded many of these songs in her extraordinary voice. Our collaboration began in 1984, and we will always be grateful to Louise Zwick and Oralia Garza de Cortés for having brought us together at a celebration of Latino children's literature sponsored by the public library in Houston, Texas.

Suni Paz was born in Argentina into a family that appreciated music and encouraged her own and her brother's musical talents. Yet in contrast to the classical music her family enjoyed, Suni discovered her own love for the traditional musical forms, rhythms, and instruments of the indigenous people of the Andes. During the era in which Atahualpa Yupanqui, Mercedes Sosa, Quilapayún, and Violeta Parra were introducing this music to the world, Suni traveled to Chile to expand her folkloric repertoire. Later, she traveled throughout Latin America, familiarizing herself with its diverse rhythms and traditions, and began composing her own songs.

Her loving memories of the songs that she sang as a child, the songs that accompanied her childhood games, led Suni to record six albums for the Smithsonian Folkways label, including *Bajo el cielo de mi niñez* (Beneath the sky of my childhood). When I first met Suni Paz, she was performing some of these songs. To my delight and amazement, these cherished traditional songs took on a new vibrancy, a new sparkle and shine when sung by Suni.

At the time, I was completing a Spanish reading program with the title *Hagamos caminos* (Let's make our own roads) inspired by the words of the great Spanish poet Antonio Machado: "*Caminante, no hay camino, se hace camino al andar*" (Traveler, there is no path, you create the path as you travel). As part of the reading program, I was planning to record a series of cassettes that would include traditional stories and rhymes, in order to offer children additional opportunities for language development. It was immediately apparent to me that having Suni sing the traditional rhymes included in the books would greatly enhance the program's artistic quality.

When Suni agreed to this project and received the books, she suggested that, instead of just recording the traditional rhymes, we also include as songs many of my own texts, both those that were poems as well as others that were simple stories in rhyme. This was a huge surprise to me. Even though I have been a passionate lover of music all of my life, I have little musical talent. Now, here was an accomplished musician saying that it would be an easy matter to set my poetry and my prose to music, as the cadence of the accented syllables was just right!

By the time we completed this project, the *Hagamos caminos* tapes included almost a hundred songs by Suni. Some of those songs are traditional children's songs, but many of them are my poems and stories for the very young, set to original music written, arranged and sang by Suni Paz.

After that initial collaboration, Suni has continued to record cassettes and CDs for many of my books of poetry: *Gathering the Sun* (A bilingual ABC celebrating farm workers), *Abecedario de los animales* (An animal ABC), *Coral y espuma Abecedario del mar* (Coral and foam, an ABC of the ocean), *Arrullos de la Sirena* (The Mermaid's Lullabies).

Suni has also created the music and sang the poems of the anthology of my poetry *Todo es canción* [Everything is song] and a CD of songs for adults, *Como una flor* [Like a Flower]. The poems in this last CD are included in my recent book of poetry for adults and older students *Minuto eterno*.

Isabel Campoy and I co-authored *Música amiga* [Friendly music], a collection of one hundred and twenty songs recorded by Suni, presented in ten books and ten CDs, with twelve songs each. Again, some of these songs are traditional children's songs, a few are poems by famous poets while many are original lyrics by Isabel Campoy or by myself.

Most of the recordings of our work done by Suni have been in Spanish, but she has recorded a CD in both English and Spanish to accompany *¡Pío Peep! Traditional Spanish Nursery Rhymes.* a collection of nursery rhymes that Isabel and I compiled for HarperCollins.

While the books have been published by different companies, all of the CDs we have created after *Hagamos caminos* have been produced by Del Sol Publishing, now an imprint of Mariposa Transformative Education.

The joy I have felt from my collaboration with Suni and the warm reception we have received at our numerous conference presentations over the years inspired me to retell existing stories in verse form, so that Suni could compose music for them and turn them into songs. Some of these musical stories we have created are based on traditional stories that I

have retold in verse, while others are original stories of mine
that I had earlier written in prose.

Examples of traditional stories written by me
in verse, that Suni has set to music include
the fairy tales *Cenicienta* [Cinderella],
Blancanieves [Snow White], and *La bella
durmiente* [Sleeping Beauty], which appear on
the CD *Tres princesas* [Three princesses].

The stories *Los tres cerditos* [The Three Little
Pigs], *Caperucita roja* [Little Red Riding Hood] and *Las semillas
mágicas* [Jack and the Beanstalk] appear on the CD *Cuéntame
un cuento* [Tell me a story].

Other original stories in music format include the twelve stories
from the Spanish version of *Cuentos para todo el año / Stories
the Year 'Round* (Santillana). I have retold in verse my twelve
original stories and Suni has created musical compositions for
them. She has also recorded the five stories in *Libros para
contar / Stories for the Telling* (Santillana). In this collection,
only *Amigos / Friends* needed much rewriting; the other stories
had a cumulative text format that made it easy to turn them
into songs without much modification.

One of our latest collaborations has been *Arrullos de la sirena*.
Suni, with the support of her talented son, has
created a CD with the most delightful music,
tender and suggestive, for these lullabies.

It would not be possible for me to speak about
my books without including all of the work
that I have done with Suni. The songs that we
have created together have delighted
thousands of children. For many of them, it is
the songs that have left the most lasting
impression. It is hard to find words to
adequately express the joy of meeting children, in schools and
in public libraries, who have learned these songs by heart.

Besides being a remarkable composer and a unique singer, Suni is a gifted writer. Her memoir *Sparkles and Shadows*, in Spanish *Destellos y sombras* is a most delightful retelling of her life.

Suni Paz has been well recognized for her outstanding work. In 2003, she received the Magic Penny Award from the Children's Music Network (CMN) for a lifetime of valuable contributions to children's music. One of the most significant recognitions has been the decision made by the Smithsonian Institute, in the year 2000, to include Suni's songs as part of the special platinum recordings they have created to preserve for posterity the best voices of the twentieth century These recordings will be safeguarded in their vaults with the intention of making sure that future generations will be able to continue enjoying Suni's unique voice.

To learn more about Suni Paz and her work, please visit www.sunipaz.com.

When Poetry Becomes Song

by Suni Paz

Since 1984, I have had the joy and privilege of collaborating with Alma Flor Ada, an internationally known poet-author of many award-winning books for children. She has entrusted me with composing, singing, and recording the musical versions of her poems and stories. We share in common our love for education, poetry, and music. When I first met Alma Flor, she was Professor of Education and director of doctoral studies at the University of San Francisco, and I was a performing artist teaching through my songs and through poems, legends, or fables in song form. We have Louise Zwick and Oralia Garza de Cortés, extraordinary librarians and remarkable women, to thank for that first meeting, at a conference they organized in Houston, Texas.

At the time, Alma Flor was completing the writing of a Spanish reading series, *Hagamos caminos,* to be published by Addison-Wesley, and she asked me if I would be willing to record the many folksongs that she had included in the program. When I received the materials, artistically illustrated by Ulises Wensell, I realized that not only would I like to record those songs, but that I could also compose music for many of Alma Flor's poems and even certain of the stories that, while written in prose, had a rhythm that would allow them to be sung.

This was the beginning of our collaboration. 1 called *Hagamos caminos,* our first project together, "my baptism by fire," since I ended up recording 120 songs! For 84 of them, I composed original music. While most of the texts had been written before we began our collaboration, hearing her poems put to music moved Alma Flor to write some special lyrics in honor of the name of the series. *Hagamos caminos* (the name was inspired by the words of the poet Antonio Machado: "We open roads as we walk"). This song, a proclamation of our faith in life and our determination to open roads of learning and joy, of friendship and solidarity, with each step we take, was emblematic of the spirit in which our collaboration would evolve.

The 120 songs for *Hagamos caminos* put my creativity to the test and demonstrated that we could work together harmoniously; all of our other projects have been much simpler by comparison. During the first years of our collaboration, I was living in New York and Alma Flor in San Francisco. We saw little of each other, but we discussed lyrics over the phone, by fax or letter, or when we met at conferences and presentations.

Our next project together was to set to music the poems about each letter of the alphabet from the book *Abecedario de los animales,* beautifully illustrated by Viví Escrivá. For this collection of songs, I found inspiration in the richness of our Latin American folk music. While the compositions are all original, each song exemplifies a different rhythm. Many teachers have referred to this CD as a musical journey through Latin America.

Children most often ask us to repeat over and over the songs for the letter B, in which I play the *charango,* and the letter C, which they delight in singing. I must confess I have a predilection for the song about the letter H. Referring to the fact that this letter has no sound in Spanish, the song declares, "We name it but don't hear it; we write it, but we don't read it." When asked about her preferences, Alma Flor repeatedly insists that she has no preferences when it comes to her work, just as she has no preferences when it comes to her grandchildren. However, I have noticed that she frequently asks me to sing the songs for letters I and L.

For several summers, I joined Alma Flor in Spain for the summer course on Children's Literature in Spanish that she organized for teachers from the United States. Although we were teaching at the Universidad Complutense de Madrid we shared with the teachers our deep appreciation for the farmworkers families whose lives mostly remain unsung, even though there have been a few significant efforts to document their struggles, their suffering, and their courage.

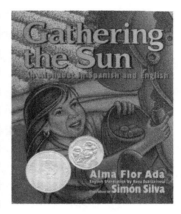

At the height of the farmworkers' struggle in California led by César Chávez, I was a lead singer in national campaigns to raise consciousness about the plight of the farmworkers and the need to join in the grape boycott until the farmworkers' needs for just wages and safe and humane working conditions were met. As Alma Flor had created empowerment-based family literacy workshops with migrant farmworkers families throughout California, particularly in the Salinas Valley and Stockton, it was only natural that our feelings and commitment should find a joint artistic expression.

Alma Flor collected many of the poems she had written after visiting migrant camps and working with farmworkers families into the alphabet book, *Gathering the Sun.* The poems for each letter of the alphabet, written by Alma Flor in Spanish and translated into English by her daughter Rosalma Zubizarreta, express cultural concepts important to Latino communities. The illustrations were exquisitely done by Simón Silva, an artist born into a migrant farmworkers family. In her poetic words, Alma Flor Ada expresses the thankfulness that many of us feel for the gifts we receive from the farmworkers: the fruit of their labor. Her poetry acknowledges, "I will grow stronger and kinder as I eat what you have grown."

The words to the song for the letter O, entitled *Orgullo/Pride,* express the importance of being proud of our origins: of our family, our language, our culture, our people, and who we are. In the song for the letter G, *Gracias/Thanks,* the lyrics express gratitude to the earth and to the elements, such as the sun, wind, and rain, for the delicious fruits we enjoy. The letter C is a tribute to the living memory of César Chávez, while H, *Honor/Honor,* points to the honorable nature of honest work. The arrangements created by Barry Kornhauser for this CD convey the feelings of the songs most beautifully.

Once we had established such a strong working relationship, Alma Flor felt confident about retelling in verse form the twelve stories of her best-selling series *Cuentos para todo el año,* published in English as *Stories the Year 'Round.* Turning entire stories into song was a new kind of challenge for me, but what a joy it is to hear the children follow the songs as they look at the fascinating illustrations by Viví Escrivá! The story *No quiero derretirme,* published in English as *I Don't Want to Melt,* a parable about the cycle of life and death, is for me one of the most compelling pieces I have ever composed. Young children are often mesmerized by *No fui yo,* published in English as *It Wasn't Me,* with its surprise ending. And I particularly enjoy sharing *La piñata vacía (The Empty Piñata)* with its message of generosity and *La jaula dorada* (The Golden Cage) and its praising of freedom, freedom to think, to speak, to love.

Creating music for whole stories in verse form became an even greater challenge when Alma Flor decided to retell six traditional fairy tales in verse. Since the stories were fairly long, the challenge was to compose lyrical melodies that were simple enough for children to learn and sing and that, at the same time, would support yet not interfere with the lyrics. While setting *Cenicienta* [Cinderella] to music, I felt as if I were actually composing an opera!

These delightfully rhymed poems and their musical renditions have waited a long time to be published as they deserve. Espasa-Calpe in Madrid published five of them in two small volumes in a short run with Disney illustrations. We are still hoping they will be produced as beautifully illustrated books. They are available in CDs by Del Sol Publishing: *Tres princesas* [Three Princesses] includes the stories of *Cenicienta* [Cinderella], *La bella durmiente* [Sleeping Beauty], and *Blancanieves* [Snow White]; and *Cuéntame un cuento* [Tell Me a Story] includes the stories of *Las semillas mágicas* [Jack and the Beanstalk], *Caperucita Roja* [Little Red Riding Hood] and *Los tres cerditos* [The Three Little

Pigs]. This latter CD contains two of our signature songs: "Los libros son mis amigos" [Books Are My Friends] and the title song, "Cuéntame un cuento."

In 1998, Del Sol Publishing obtained the rights for the songs from *Hagamos caminos,* which allowed us to create the program *Música amiga,* a set of ten CDs with accompanying small books and a teacher's guide. Thirty new songs were added, created from poems by another gifted writer, Francisca Isabel Campoy. Her lyrics, some humorous, others full of meaning about family relations, our roots, and self-discovery, also inspired lively musical themes with Latin folk rhythms.

By then, all of these experiences had transformed us into a trio of creative, strong, willful women well-versed in collaborating with one another.

Although some people believe that working with others is a hard thing to do, I have to say that, on the contrary, I have experienced few setbacks in my work with Alma Flor Ada and Isabel Campoy. I have learned intensely from both of them and have grown personally and professionally in many ways. I think that our success at working together has been due in large part to the fact the three of us have great respect for one another. For example, whenever I have suggested changes or adjustments to the lyrics, Alma Flor and Isabel have assured me that I am free to make my own decisions, without needing to check in with them first. At the same time, I have never failed to request their opinions and explain the reasons for what I saw as needed changes. Among us, we share great trust, affection, and a mutual desire to bring to life the poems that I set to music, sing, and record, in order to communicate the feelings and values that they hold.

Recently, I composed music to *Coral y espuma: Abecedario del mar* [Coral and Foam: An Ocean ABC], another book of poems  illustrated by Viví Escrivá, this time inspired by Alma Flor's unending love for the sea. The rich and tender imagery Alma Flor uses in these enchanting poems to describe the treasures found in the sea, on its beaches, and in the surrounding landscape stirred my imagination and awakened my inspiration. For example, I was inspired by the poem for the letter U for *Uva caleta* [sea grape] to compose a *guajira,* the popular Cuban style of folk song whose feeling and rhythm is exemplified in the famous *Guantanamera,* in honor of Alma Flor's Caribbean roots. I enjoyed these poems immensely and ended my recording sessions by dancing up and down the studio with tears in my eyes, singing the songs I had just recorded at the top of my lungs. Now I hear from Alma Flor that she is playing these songs continuously as she writes this book.

The book *¡Pío Peep!,* a collection of nursery rhymes compiled by Alma Flor and Isabel, gave me the opportunity to record those beloved songs of our childhood bilingually on a CD of the same title. In a way, it has been a coming full circle, since Alma Flor's initial delight in my work came from hearing the nursery rhymes of my own childhood that I sung in *Alerta Sings* and *Songs for the Playground/Canciones para el recreo.* While I made those recordings some time ago, they have more recently been reissued as a CD by Smithsonian/Folkways in celebration of the opening of the new millennium.

Alma Flor also loved my songs for adults. One of her favorites, "Al ajo" [To Garlic], was included in *From the Sky of*

My Childhood/Del Cielo de mi niñez. Another song, called "Mujer" [Woman] was part of *Entre Hermanas/Between Sisters.* Both issued by Smithsonian/Folkways.

In turn, I have also loved creating songs for the poems that Alma Flor has written for older youths and adults, which we compiled in the CD *Como una flor* [Like a Flower]. One of them, "Iguazú," was conceived during a trip we shared to those breathtaking waterfalls that are on the border between Argentina, Paraguay, and Brazil. By a fortunate coincidence, I happened to be in Argentina at the same time that Alma Flor was there to receive the Marta Salotti gold medal. The ceremony was an unexpected opportunity for me to sing our songs to an Argentinean public in my own hometown of Buenos Aires. The song about growing old, "Donde termina el nacer" [Where Does Being Born End?] moved the audience to tears as they listened to the final words, "*Y no es donde termina/el nacer que no se acaba, /porque me queda la risa/revoloteando en el alma*" [And I don't know when it stops, that unending being born, as I am still left with laughter fluttering in my soul]. I also felt that the audience responded wholeheartedly to our recognition of the uniqueness of every human being conveyed in the title song, "Como una flor."

I believe we are all born with a clear purpose that we must fulfill while on this earth. Mine is to dance, write, compose, play, and sing for audiences comprised of children and adults in all stages of life, here in the United States, in Latin America, and in Europe. I was also meant to find Alma Flor Ada and Isabel Campoy on my path and create beautiful music together. I am grateful to them as well as to the musicians and arrangers, my son among them, who have enlivened my music and challenged me to continue embracing my creativity.

Just as Alma Flor has felt encouraged in her own work by our friendship and collaboration, I too have appreciated her support and encouragement for my own work as an artist. Currently, she has been very enthusiastic about the release of my two most recent creations, *Bandera mía,* a CD on Argentine folk music produced by Smithsonian/Folkways, and my memoir *Destellos y sombras,* published also in English as *Sparkles and Shadows.*

When I was invited to write a chapter for this book, I welcomed with open arms the opportunity to describe these past years of

collaboration with two dear friends—now sisters—Alma Flor Ada and Isabel Campoy, and I look forward with great joy to our future creative work together.

Learning the Art of Translation
by Rosalma Zubizarreta

Just as my mother, Alma Flor Ada, did not set out to become an author, I never intended to become a translator. Instead, it was something that developed out of our shared life circumstances. As a young person growing up in the United States, I was pained by my mother's accent when she spoke English, and even more so by any grammatical errors she made when she wrote in her second language. It felt natural for me to want to help polish her writing, so that it would flow as easily, smoothly, and gracefully as her native Spanish did. For her part, my mother welcomed my help and began to request it frequently, and thus I began to learn how to edit.

At Parque Gaudí, Barcelona. During a trip to
Spain with my mother in 1991.

One thing led to another: At some point I grew tired of teasing out the tangles that can ensue when we are writing in a language that we have learned as adults. "Why don't you just write it in Spanish, especially since you express yourself so eloquently in your mother tongue, and then let me translate it for you?" I begged. And so I began to learn by experience how to translate from Spanish to English.

At the time, my mother was translating into Spanish a large volume of educational materials that had been originally written in English. Translating from English to Spanish was an arena in which I was much less confident, as most of my formal schooling had taken place in the United States in English. Yet my mother gave me a few short pieces and encouraged me to try my hand at translating them into Spanish. With the assurance that she would proofread my Spanish translations carefully and correct any mistakes she found, I began to develop some skills in this area as well.

At the gardens of La Alhambra, Granada.
During a trip to Spain with my mother in 1991.

Later, I began translating children's books from English to Spanish, always relying on Alma Flor's assistance as senior editor. As I started to do more work in this field, I became highly sensitive to the issue of tone in translations. For example, I noticed that many contemporary children's books in English are written in highly accessible language, and in a friendly, conversational tone. I was dismayed to find that some translators were taking contemporary English language children's books and translating them in a manner that sounded quite stuffy and old-fashioned to me. It's not that their Spanish was "incorrect" in any way; if anything, it was too formal. It just didn't feel right to me: I wanted Spanish-speaking children to also be able to enjoy books written in a light-hearted, playful manner.

I had similar concerns about the way that some educational materials for parents were being translated into Spanish. While a particular translation might be perfectly "correct," that did not guarantee that it was accessible, friendly, engaging. When it comes to spoken language, we all know that *how* we say something can greatly influence the message that is conveyed. Yet often people don't realize that the same thing is true about any written translation. The nuances of communication depend upon the words that we choose, their overtones and undertones. There are always many different ways to communicate the same thing, and each of those ways will communicate a subtly different (or not-so-subtle different!) message.

At the gardens of La Alhambra, Granada.
During a trip to Spain with my mother in 1991.

Some of the challenges one encounters in translation are more obvious than others. As you may know, words that sound very similar in two different languages sometimes do not mean the same thing at all. Linguists call this a "false cognate"; for example, the word *librería* in Spanish, while it sounds like "library," actually means "bookstore."

Yet even when two words that sound alike also have a similar meaning, the connotation of each word can be quite different. One example of this more subtle challenge is *discutir* and "to discuss." The denotation, or formal meaning, of both words is fairly similar; if we look the words up in a dictionary, we will find that one of the meanings of *discutir* is "to discuss." However, in Spanish, *discutir* is often used for the kind of discussion that takes place during an argument; in English, the word "discuss" has developed a different, more neutral connotation. Therefore, depending on the context, "discuss" might be better translated as *conversar*.

Of course, in English, we have a word that sounds very similar to *conversar,* in the dictionary we might find the word "to converse." However, "converse" sounds very old- fashioned or even snobbish in English; it is not a contemporary word that we use on a regular basis. In contrast, in Spanish *conversar* is a very popular and everyday word. While the formal meanings of these two words may be very similar, the feeling that they convey is very different. And so we see again that the closest-sounding word may not be the best choice at all, even when it has a similar meaning.

These are just a few examples of how, in order to remain true to the spirit of the original, we often need to choose something that looks quite different. This is true not just of the words and phrases we use, but it also applies to the way we organize our sentences and our paragraphs, and even to the length of a text: some languages tend to use more words to say the same thing than others do! The heart of the art of translation, I feel, is to listen carefully for the shades of meaning in the original text, the feel of the words, the intention of the author, so that we can then re-create that meaning and intention in another language. Next we need to listen carefully to what we have just written: Does it sound natural? Is that how a native speaker would say it? Does it convey adequately enough the richness of the original text?

In all of these explorations into the art of translation and the nuances of language, my mother has been a wonderful guide, support, and companion. She has a great love for the history of words, and has often delighted me with her knowledge of a word's derivations.

She is also an extremely strong advocate for the need to translate in a way that re-creates the spirit and meaning of the original work, rather than remaining fettered to a clunky and overly literal word-for-word process. Indeed, while this book is focused on her work as an author, Alma Flor is also the creator of many exemplary Spanish translations of well-known English children's books. In that arena as in several others, while I have learned a great deal from her, she remains the true master.

In Las Alpujarras. Andalucía.
During a trip to Spain with my mother in 1991.

Within the realm of translation, some of my favorite projects have involved working with poetry and song. Whenever I'm creating an English-language version of a poem or song that was written originally in Spanish, it often feels like I am working on a puzzle. There are so many different elements that need to be attended to! Not just the meaning of the words, but also their sound, their rhythm, their mood. At the same time, I very much enjoy the challenge, and there is a wonderful feeling of satisfaction when I finally come up with something that feels like a good fit.

I have also especially enjoyed working on those books that have to do with family stories, as well as personal experiences that

my mother has had in the course of her life. It's often the case that I've felt that I am getting to know her better as I work on one of her texts—or even hearing about something for the very first time! It just goes to show that, no matter how well we may think we know someone, each person in our life can always offer us an opportunity to learn and discover something new.

Another very meaningful project for me has been working with Alma Flor and Isabel Campoy on their book, *Authors in the Classroom.* Among her many gifts, my mother's delight in encouraging others to find their own voice is one that I particularly admire. After a decade of seeing her be so excited by the results of the workshops with teachers that she and Isabel led, I was overjoyed to see the fruits of that work being compiled to share with others in book form. I was very happy to be able to contribute material on anti-bias education and on facilitating dialogue in the classroom to this book, in addition to my editing skills.

Part of the joy of editing and translating is helping someone's voice to be heard more clearly, and helping a message to be shared more widely, by dissolving any obstacles to communication and understanding. In the process of helping others to be heard, we often learn how to find our own voice as well. I am very grateful for my long home apprenticeship and continuing collaboration with my mother, both for their own sake and also as an opportunity to discover talents and develop skills that I have been able to apply in other contexts.

Perhaps the closest example of how I apply these skills is in my own work as a writer, where I often feel I am "listening" for the words that fit just right. Yet what I have learned as an editor and translator applies to other areas of my life as well, even ones where the connection may not be so obvious at first glance. For instance, in my work as a counselor and social worker, one of my intentions as I listen to my clients is to help them discover their own voice, their own sense of creativity and purpose, and support them in sharing their gifts with the world.

FROM
CONFLICT
TO
CREATIVE
COLLABORATION

A User's Guide to Dynamic Facilitation
with foreword by Peggy Holman

ROSA ZUBIZARRETA

When I work as a mediator with people in conflict, my listening often helps me to "translate" what each person is saying, in a way that the other person is able to hear and understand. And when I am working with a group of people, facilitating a meeting, I am listening to each person with the intention of helping all of the various voices be heard and understood, so that a shared understanding can grow and develop within the larger community or organization.

While my listening work continues to unfold in a variety of ways, I still derive great pleasure from collaborating with others in their writing projects from time to time. And I also continue to enjoy the challenge of translating songs and poems from Spanish to English whenever Alma Flor and Isabel have an idea for a new poetry book!

Some of the many Books with English versions by Rosalma Zubizarreta

The Joy of Co-authorship with a son

Throughout my life my children have been a generous sustaining force. They were interested in my work, my friends, my thoughts and willing to equally share theirs. And whenever they felt they could be helpful they were there without waiting to be asked.

It was this attitude of readiness to be supportive that led to the collaboration with my son Gabriel. I tend to panic when I'm developing a manuscript that all the technological ways of preserving it may fail, and frequently I resource to emailing it to myself. But feeling that if someday I would not be there, none would be able to unravel the multiple unpublished originals in my computer I have sometimes emailed them to one of my children. And this is what happens with the beginning manuscript of *Dancing Home*. I emailed it to my son Gabriel with a subject heading of "Only for safekeeping. No need to read." But, Gabriel, decided to actually read the manuscript, and, always helpful asked me, very respectfully, if I would like to hear his comments.

And because he asked with such kindness, I was very interested in what he had to say. This led to multiple conversations. Fascinated by his good ideas I asked him if he would rather put them in writing, to feel free to make changes and additions on that incipient draft. Then, it became obvious that he was not commenting on my manuscript, that his contributions were far more than merely editorial, he was actually helping me create a new story. And we became co-authors. And **Dancing Home** was born.

The unexpected experience was so positive that I asked Gabriel to help me developed an idea I had for a long time for a picture book but thought that it could be developed further as another middle grade novel, and we engaged in the joint task of creating **Love, Amalia**.

Gabriel's extraordinarily busy professional life has not facilitated further co-authorships, although I do not lose hope that we will still create new worlds together.

His thoughts on collaboration are presented here. Should you want to listen to Gabriel on his experience on co-authoring **Dancing Home** you can watch the video of an interview done by Simon and Schuster included in my webpage. This is the link:

http://almaflorada.com/video-alma-flor-ada-and-gabriel-zubizarreta-discuss-their-inspiration-for-writing-dancing-home/

What is collaboration?
by Gabriel Zubizarreta

Just a quick comment about collaboration... surely you jest.

Collaboration, is everywhere, and every human has been collaborating since inception, literally. The irony is that those things which are everywhere are not so easy to describe in a relevant way.

For example, air, omnipresent, but generally invisible, lest it not be still, but then its name changes to wind. How does one describe air? It has little substance but sustains all. It fills everything and generally represents "absence of anything". It flows to fill areas like water, yet it flows in all directions, seemingly unaffected by gravity.

Ironically, water is also difficult to describe. Known generally as a liquid, it is vapor in the air. As a solid, ice is less dense, so it is literally 'floated up in water' by gravity which keeps our planet from freezing. Our bodies appear solid, yet are over 50% water and all life depends on water in so many other ways.

How does one explain such a simple thing that is so powerful, like gravity?

Oh, gravity, present since birth, acting uniformly on everything, rarely changing. Gravity grounds us and should be easy to explain, but it also presents many challenging ways to describe it.

So, how does one explain collaboration? It's easy...just like rain, the collaboration between water, air(wind) and gravity.

As an author...., ironically, I actually would never have become a creative fiction author without collaboration, because I would never have done so alone.

When two people collaborate to co-create a book, they harness and define several roles to capture a storm onto a written page.

For an author, there is a strong distinction between an author and a writer. Often both, author and writer roles are combined, when only one person in involved, however when collaborating with another person on the same text, these roles can be rapidly switching between the parties.

Something similar could be said about writing and editing, and while the distinction between roles is greater, it can often be blurred when two people are creating one text. Collaboration with external editing is essential to a successful book and gets more complex as the number of relationships double when two people are writing the same text.

The critical reader role, generally an external ally during development is inseparably embedded into a coauthoring relationship.

Nothing written is born without the interactions between the author, writer, editor, and reader; however, when co-creating a book, these roles are constantly collaborating in a tempest of interactions.

Specifically, I will focus on the collaboration between authors which provides a certain magic in various interactions.

Sparks of Inspiration – Creativity is a force outside of our normal state which comes in flashes. When writing creatively those flashes need to be harvested and harnessed into fixed prose. Although solidification seems counter-productive to free-flowing inspiration, it is necessary for writing.

When writing alone, it is difficult to shift between an inspired creative thinking state and the fixation discipline of the written word, which when applied to paper generally loses all inspiration, that is not artfully captured.

Collaboration is like great table-tennis, your best shots are the result of the other players best shots. Without another player's collaboration you cannot be inspired to your best play. Learning to push each other to higher levels is an inspiring challenge that can keep collaboration fresh as long as both participants share a similar vision.

Burst of Momentum – Writing was once described to me as arduous, "bleeding on a page, until there is nothing left inside". The efforts of writing, rewriting, editing, and rewriting more and more, until your never-ending demands are satisfied. It is easy to lose momentum, and a collaborative relationship can be a lifeline to regain momentum and revive a manuscript drowning in the despair of exhaustion.

Reading the additions and changes that someone else has made to your work can infuriate or exhilarate, but regardless, it will revitalize necessary momentum to continue the long migration journey from idea to published work.

Sources of Strength –Writing changes the author and is like plowing a trench through the middle of your life. Many challenges can conspire to derail efforts to dig this transformative trench, and often a collaborator can provide the strength to overcome obstacles, especially ones that are self-created, or appear more powerful than a single person.

Ultimately, collaborative writing is sharing something very personal with someone who can help make some magic together.

Part III: The Readings that Started the Journey

110

[

The Magic of Books

When speaking with teachers and students about the process of writing, I always say that writing begins with reading. I regret never having had the opportunity to take courses in creative writing. It also pains me to confess that, with the notable exception of my sixth grade teacher, none of my teachers ever encouraged me to write.

During my postdoctoral time at Harvard, I once shyly showed some of the stories I had written for adult readers to a professor of Latin American literature. In response, with an attitude no teacher should use with a student, he categorically discouraged me from continuing with something for which, in his opinion, I had absolutely no talent.

The effect of that rejection ran deep: it took me forty years to gather the courage to unveil my first novel for adults, *A pesar del amor,* which was published by Alfaguara in separate editions in the United States (2003) and in Spain (2004). This novel has been very well received by critics and readers alike, and it has been deeply healing to realize that one of the key scenes in the novel is drawn quite closely from one of those stories that was rejected so long ago. There are now new editions published by Mariposa. Transformative Education (2016) and by Editorial Acana in Cuba.

Having a first novel published was a joy I thought would be unsurpassed, but having *A pesar del amor* published in my own home city of Camagüey and with a cover by such an extraordinary artist as Martha Jiménez, has been the fulfillment of a dream I had not dared to dream.

My desire to write, as well as whatever degree of craftsmanship I have developed, has been inspired and nourished principally by means of the familiarity with the written word that I have acquired through reading. Books have been unfailingly kind teachers for me!

Equally amazing has been for me that my novel *En clave de sol* was turned into a radio series. Collaborating with the script writer Aimee Chau Rodríguez in creating the scripts the discovery of a new genre I had not approached before. My gratitude to her and to Radio Cadena Agramonte.

I was given the gift of learning to read very early on by my extraordinary grandmother Lola. She was a teacher, and writing materials abounded at home, including a huge blackboard. Nonetheless, she decided to teach me to read outdoors, while walking around our farmstead. She would point to a well-known animal or plant and write its name with a stick in the dirt, and then invent memorable stories about each letter.

Cows were dear friends to me. We would visit them early every morning and one of the farmhands would squirt some milk directly from the udder into the little jar I carried with me. What a nice breakfast this warm foamy milk was! It made sense that one of the first words I learned to read was *vaca* (cow) followed by *mu* (the sound made by the cow). In Spanish, both *v* and *b* represent the same sound, /b/, and they are usually referred to as *v de vaca* (*v* as in cow) and *b de burro* (*b* as in burro). To help me distinguish between the two, my grandmother taught me to think of *v* as "the horns of the cow" and *b* as "one of the long ears of the burro". To a child not quite three years old, it made a lot of sense! I'm only surprised that, during my many years of talking and reading about Spanish literacy I have never found any one else   describing the difference between the two letters in this way.

One story I remember with utmost detail, right down to the very spot beneath the flame trees where we were standing as my grandmother told it, is the story about the letter *r de rosa* (r as in rose).

My grandmother made up a story about a rose who longed to see the world outside the walled garden where she lived. As she

told me the story, we both looked back at the white wall that enclosed our own courtyard, knowing how happy we were to be on the other side of it, free to explore what appeared to me to be the limitless world of our farm. Then my grandmother told me about how the rosebush grew and grew and climbed and climbed, until the rose was able to look out over the wall and was delighted to discover all the things that she could see in the wide world that lay beyond those walls! In her own handwriting, my grandmother showed me the little head that was peeking out over the top of the letter r, looking to see how far she might be able to gaze.

From that day on, the feeling of continuously striving further to see a bit more of the world became as much a constant feature of my inner landscape as my love for roses. And the story was present in my mind again while, living in Lima, Perú, I frequently visited for a few minutes on my way home from work the rose garden of Santa Rosa de Lima, where one afternoon I came up with the name Rosalma for my yet to be born daughter.

I do not know whether my grandmother was conducting an experiment with me, having fun, or merely planning a surprise for my parents, but I do know that they were truly astonished when she announced to them that I could read. She opened a simple book at random, and when I read a page aloud, my parents accused her of having had me memorize the text. Then she picked up a newspaper and asked me to read the headlines. I can still see the shocked faces of my parents, who seemed to want to laugh and cry at the same time.

My mother then rushed to her room and returned with a big heavy book bound in red cloth, a treasure she had saved from her own childhood. And so it came to be that when I was not yet four years old, I was given my first book, an unabridged Spanish translation of Johanna Spyri's *Heidi.*

When I look at a similar edition today, I marvel at the thought that I could have read every word of that book, but I certainly did, many, many times, until each chapter, each page, each paragraph was engraved in my memory. Each of the three dolls I ever had was named Heidi (which of course I pronounced in Spanish with a silent H), and I dreamed of visiting the Alps.

In retrospect, my own childhood had much in common with Heidi's. Granted, there were significant differences: my parents were alive, we had a large extended family, and the flat tropical plains of Camagüey were very unlike Heidi's alpine mountains. Still, I spent much of my day outdoors in nature, by myself, just as Heidi had spent hers—lost in my own thoughts and sustained by my relationship with the plants and animals around me.

The ideal of the simple life, the desire to scale heights in order to enjoy the vast views from on high, and the dream of having a loft with a window on the roof so that I could sleep beneath the stars, have remained with me throughout my life. And I'm happy to say that there have been times when I have been fortunate enough to be able to realize these fantasies.

My excitement over *Heidi* led my mother to give me the book's sequel, *Otra vez Heidi (Again, Heidi),* as well as other books by Johanna Spyri. I fondly remember *Lorenzo y Margarita (Lawrence and Margaret), Hijos de los Alpes (Children of the Alps)*, and *Sin patria (Without a Country).*

All of these books touched me for the same reason: their praise for the simple life and for the values of caring and friendship. I admired these children who were kind to their elders, who delighted in the pleasures of nature, and who were able to bring about transformations in others through their love and support. They seemed to me to be wonderful examples worth emulating, and while today I might find the religious emphasis in the texts a bit heavy-handed, at the time I did not experience these books as overly moralizing. Instead, I was captivated by the stories and by the depth of the characters, and I felt as if I knew the people in the books as well as or better than the people around me.

The next author I was given to read was Sophie Rostopchine, whom I knew only by her pen name Condesa de Segur (the Countess of Segur). A Russian émigré living in France, she had written *Las desgracias de Sofía (Sophie's Misadventures),* a book that I both liked and disliked. I could not help but feel sorry for the protagonist, a troubled child, even though I found her adventures somewhat too far-fetched for my taste. Yet I was delighted by two other books written by this author. *Memorias de un asno (Memoirs of a Donkey)* awoke in me a greater awareness of the pain that human beings can inflict on animals. After reading it, I was never able to look at a cart horse again, from the horse that pulled the baker's cart to the one that pulled the coal vendor's cart, without wondering about the way they were being treated and about the fate that awaited them in their old age.

Many years later, I would again be deeply moved, this time by Juan Ramón Jiménez exquisite *Platero y yo [Platero and I]*, This story about the author's friendship with his donkey demonstrated that prose could be poetry, while providing one of my first glimpses of the heightened aesthetic experience offered by great literature. Platero remained a beloved figure for my children and I. In the photo Miguel with a statue that reminded us of Platero, and visited wherever we went to the Detroit Fine Arts Museum, while we lived in Michigan.

Miguel. Detroit Art Museum.

The second book by Madame de Segur that excited me was *El General Durakine (General Durakine)*. While I do not remember the plot, I do remember the fascination with the Russian steppes. a fascination that remains to this day.

In my passion for making the stories come alive, I would talk my younger sister Flor Alma, seven years my junior, into joining me in reenacting these adventures.

We would surround ourselves with pillows and pile blankets and towels over us for warmth as we tried to escape in our imaginary sleigh from the hungry wolves that pursued us over the icy steppes. Such was the power of story and imagination that we actually shivered with cold in spite of the tropical heat!

These books, published in Spain by Editorial Juventud, delighted me. The little princess in *Historia de una princesita [The Story of a Little Princes]* by Frances Hodgson Burnett became a source of inspiration. There are other books whose authors and titles I have forgotten, although their plots live on vividly in my memory. I can never watch swallows without thinking of the protagonist of one such book, whose title I vaguely recall as "Little Ray of Sunshine," a young girl who loved swallows and whose kindness influenced her many brothers.

The next author I discovered was Louisa May Alcott, and I could not get enough of her writing. The effect she had on me was that of all good writers: it felt to me as though we were deeply connected and that she was writing for me alone. I was sure that no one else could possibly get as much satisfaction from her books as I did, I thought to myself as I read them over and over again.

Although my parents bought me books frequently, encouraging their children's reading habits more than most of the families in my town, there was no public library in Camagüey at the time. This made it difficult to keep up with my hunger for even more books. Most of the girls I met had fewer books than I did. My older cousins Virginita and Jorge had books I wanted to read, but they lived in La Habana.

During my childhood, I knew only one other girl who owned books I had not already read, and I enjoyed when I could visit her home and read her beautiful collection of fairy tales from throughout the World.

Even though my little library kept growing, there were not enough books for me to read a new one every day, nor even every week, so instead I read and reread old favorites. My pleasure was never dulled by having read a book previously, but heightened instead, as I could take the time to linger over the details without feeling the urge to find out what happened next.

And so I read the three volumes that told the story of the March family many times over: *Mujercitas [Little Women]*, *Hombrecitos [Little Men]*; and *Los muchachos de Jo [Jo's Boys]*.]I also read and reread all the other books by Alcott that I owned: *Una chica a la antigua [An Old-Fashioned Girl]*, *Bajo las lilas [Under the Lilacs]*, *Jack y Jill [Jack and Jill]*, *Ocho primos [Eight Cousins]*, *Juventud de los ocho primos [Rose in Bloom]* and *Cuentos de la rueca* (a title that translates as 'A spinner's tales', which I have not been able to find in English). Although I've never really acknowledged it as such, perhaps the seed for my becoming a writer was planted by Jo March. What I received from Louisa May Alcott and all of the other writers who enriched my childhood was a passion for a well-written book and an awareness of the many forms that stories can take.

While looking up these authors during the process of writing this book, I am struck by how many different books by Johanna Spyri and by the Countess of Segur continue to be in print throughout the Spanish-speaking world. Similarly, all of Louisa May Alcott's books continue to be published extensively in Spanish, in many different editions. While Spanish-speaking book publishers have always been eager to publish translations of children's stories written originally in English, the opposite has unfortunately not been the case.

Traditionally, American publishers of children's books have been very reluctant to publish translations into English of children's books originally written in other languages. Even today, while some of the stories that are published in the United States are set in other countries, the majority of these books have been written here, by authors from the United States. This leaves children without the benefit of being able to obtain authentic glimpses of life in other countries, an experience that I feel very fortunate to have had as a result of my childhood readings.

Nicolás Nickleby and *Oliver Twist,* the first two books I read by Charles Dickens, deepened my empathy for people who live in material poverty while strengthening my conviction that richness of spirit is the wealth to which one should aspire. I was delighted when my son Miguel and his wife Denise chose Nicholas as the name for my eighth grandchild, since the girl I once was had been so taken by the personality of that character.

The thrill offered by Emilio Salgari's writing was a very different kind of experience. *Sandokan* and the rest of his series about Sandokan, the Tiger of Malaysia and the Prince of Momprasen, took me to faraway regions—places that movies had not yet discovered, that I had never seen in a photograph and was not too sure I could find on a map. Yet these destinations felt completely real to me as I read about the brave Sandokan and his pirates fighting against the British colonizers on a remote sea. Straddling the trunk of a fallen elm tree that served as the perfect vessel for sailing across an ocean of green grass, I enacted Sandokan's audacious adventures.

Another Italian author also thrilled me with adventures of a very different sort. Edmundo D'Amicis, who in the late nineteenth century wrote *Corazón, El diario de un niño* (Heart, A boy's diary), brought me to tears again and again over the sad death of many brave children, opening my heart to reflections on human conduct. In his book, D'Amicis promotes the unification of Italy by depicting a diverse group of children in an Italian fourth grade public school classroom. Each month, the teacher tells his students a different story extolling the value of one of the regions of Italy, each one of which is shown as a worthy member of the larger nation. This book became one of the most widely published children's books in the Spanish-speaking Americas. While its popularity may have begun among the numerous Italian immigrants to Argentina, where it was published in multiple editions, it has extended to many other Hispanic American countries, and there are several editions published in Spain as well.

For several generations, the stories and anecdotes of D'Amicis's book have informed the work of other writers, nowhere more remarkably than in the novel *Con las primeras luces* [At early dawn] by the Uruguayan writer Carlos Martínez Moreno. The story takes place during a single night as a young man lies dying in the garden of his childhood home. During those hours he recalls his own childhood and youth, all framed with reference to the stories from *Corazón* that he and his cousins used to reenact.

I have mentioned that, as a child, I acted out scenes from many of the books I read. However, in my case those childhood plays did not include *Corazón*. My response to this book, which always moved me very deeply, was too personal and intimate for me to turn it into a game. I am still amazed by the long-lasting impact of D'Amicis's writing. For a very long time, in my adult life my mother and I referred to these stories in our conversations, just as we referred to real-life episodes from our own family life.

While I appreciated sensitive writing as a child, I also delighted in humor. *Guillermo el travieso [Just William],* by

Richmal Crompton, was one of my favorite books, along with
the rest of the series that I acquired little
by little. How I empathized with the
daring William, whose big heart and wild
imagination got him into so much
trouble!

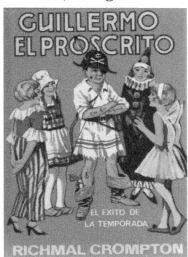

Over the years I have been reminded of
him many times, whenever my good
intentions have not achieved their
intended outcome. Of course, this applies
only to my smaller misadventures; for the
larger ones I have another shining star,
the one who journeyed across La
Mancha. I have mentioned elsewhere in
this book Don Quijote's lasting influence upon my life.

You may have noticed that all of the books I have described so
far, with the exception of *Platero y yo,* have been translations.
The sad truth is that while there were wonderful authors
writing in Spanish for children, such as Elena Fortún in Spain
and Marcela Paz in Chile, at the time their books were not
readily available outside of their home countries. I did not
become aware of these authors until many years later. Most of
the voices from my own culture that I discovered in my
childhood were the poets. Through the work of José Marti,
Juana de Ibarborou, Gabriela Mistral, Alfonsina Storni, Rubén
Dario, Amado Nervo, and Federico Garcia Lorca, poetry became
my friend, offering me the gift of a deeper appreciation for the
richness, musicality, and power of the Spanish language.

While creating poetry anthologies for children, I have felt
gratitude for Germán Berdiales who enriched my childhood
with his anthologies where I found other poets who also wrote
for children, such as Juan Bautista Grosso and José Sebastián
Tallón, creator of the delightful *sapito Glo-glo-glo,* a little toad
that is never-seen although always-heard.

Then there was the Argentinian author, Constancio C. Vigil. Although his work has been disregarded by contemporary critics who find his writing too moralistic, to me his books were a treasure trove. Yes, they were sad; at that time many children died in childhood, and his book *Marta y Jorge* is dedicated to a son and daughter he lost. But what I felt when I read his books was that here was an honest man who was not afraid of sharing his innermost feelings and thoughts with me and trusted that I would understand. I felt that I was being addressed as a human being who did not just wanted to be entertained, but who was also able to think and reflect.

I never received the impression that I was being preached to—and I did know all too well what that felt like, thanks to my experiences with a few teachers and school principals. Instead, I felt I was being invited to ponder and consider matters of significance. After all, one cannot escape a principal's preachy lecture, standing in the schoolyard under the scorching sun. Yet a book can always be put aside, and the fact that I chose to keep reading and revisiting these particular books, even the ones that did not attempt to mask their message with a story, offers a powerful testimony about the way this author reached me.

There were many other books that were important to me: Mark Twain's *Tom Sawyer* and *Huckleberry Finn,* as well as Harriet Beecher Stowe's *Uncle Tom's Cabin* transported me to another time and place. While I understand the contemporary critique of these books, at the time they confirmed my abhorrence of slavery and of any form of oppression or discrimination. Other classics, such as Daniel Defoe's *Robinson Crusoe*, Jonathan Swift's *Gulliver's Travels* and Jules Verne multiple titles, fed my thirst for adventure.

No matter how many books I read, I never lost my passion for listening to stories. In the absence of storytellers, I loved to read traditional folk tales and fairy tales. *Colección Marujita,* a collection of small books published by Editorial Molino, offered a world of gnomes, fairies, and elves who did not hesitate to interact with everyday girls and boys. Although their simple stories were only three or four pages long, I searched avidly for these little books, as I was particularly drawn to the notion that the two worlds of magic and everyday life could intersect.

At the same time, I thirsted for traditional, elaborate fairy tales from around the world. I had seen a beautiful collection of fairy tales in a set of those large and lavish volumes that people often refer to as "coffee-table books." I was enchanted by this treasure trove of stories, but unfortunately, I did not have access to it. I never learned why my parents never gave me at least one of these books, but I suspect that their determination to live simply and to shun the ostentatious displays of luxury that were common among Cubans of their generation led them to stay away from books like those. In addition, my father was not too keen on fairy tales. However, he did not hesitate to become an agent for Jackson Publications and sell their books in our jewelry store in order to obtain a complete set of encyclopedias for me, along with a collection of books about nature and a geography set called something like "Our Marvelous World." He built a special bookcase with glass doors to house these three collections, which were always treated with maximum care and respect. These volumes were a source of fascinating information, enhancing my awareness of the complex marvels of nature and feeding my desire to travel all over the world.

Still, I secretly longed for that beautiful collection of fairy tales. The various editions I did get to read were usually abridged or shortened. *One Thousand and One Nights* was a wonderful book to return to again and again, and I read my abridged version from cover to cover many times. I also loved Hans Christian Andersen's tales, which offered a tiny ray of hope that I might not always remain an ugly duckling in the midst of all the witty, clever, and funny people in my family.

I will always be indebted to the authors I have mentioned above. Along with many other authors whom I have discovered in the course of my lifetime as a reader, they have added immeasurable pleasure and meaning to my life. That I might somehow offer a similar lasting joy to a child has been my dream.

Part IV: Creating Children's Literature

The Special Process of Creating Picture Books

One question frequently asked by both adults and children is, "How do you choose your illustrators?" As you will see, the answer to this question is often surprising, and the results can often be surprising as well!

A picture book is the fruit of the combined labors of an author and an illustrator. Sometimes these are one and the same person, yet many times they are not. In the picture book industry, it is generally held that a story written by an author who is not an illustrator will become a better book if, instead of representing only the writer's vision, it combines the vision of both the author and the artist.

Once the publishing company has contracted with the author for the text, the artist is often selected by the editor of the book and/or by the art director without the knowledge or consent of the writer. Sometimes I have been consulted in this process out of courtesy, but in many instances the final selection was not what I had recommended. While this has often turned out to be for the best, it has not always been easy. For an author like me who visualizes a story as she writes, it can be difficult to subject one's own visual conceptions to the determinations of the editor and art director. At the same time, my collaboration with illustrators has often  been a wonderful experience. I will share various highlights with you as examples of this process.

I did not know Viví Escrivá when Santillana paired us together. Yet from the first, I was delighted by her work. We have since become very good friends and have collaborated for many years, mainly under the Santillana/Alfaguara seal by illustrating the twelve books of the series *Cuentos para todo el año*, published also in English as *Stories the Year 'round*, and four books the collection *Libros para contar*, in English *Stories for the Telling*.

Cinco pollitos

Cinco pollitos
tiene mi tía.
Uno le canta,
otro le pía
y tres le tocan la chirimía.

Vivi's art is engaging for young children. Bright and luminous, it is tender without feeling condescending; light and fun, while deeply sincere. To my great joy, we have finally collaborated on three books published by Putnam for the American mainstream trade book market. Vivi's charming illustrations for *¡Pío Peep!* and *MooMuu,* both bilingual collections of nursery rhymes that Isabel Campoy and I compiled, have received well-deserved recognition as had her endearing illustrations for *Merry Navidad* our compilation of Christmas Carol from all over the Spanish-speaking world organized to tell the Nativity story.

Viví also illustrated three books published by Editorial Espasa-Calpe, Madrid. Two alphabet books: *Abecedario de los animales* [Animal ABC] and *Coral y espuma. Abecedario del mar* [Coral and Foam. An ABC of the Sea] as well as the story *¿Quién cuida al cocodrilo?* [Who   will take care of the crocodile?].

Those wishing to see more about the life and work of a gifted artist and outstanding human being will enjoy watching the documentary, available in YouTube in Spanish and English versions:

   Cuando Viví dibujó el mundo.
https://www.youtube.com/watch?v=M_viHBRhyPI&t=19s
   Viví Escrivá. Illustrator. When Viví Drew the World.
https://www.youtube.com/watch?v=RIXt_4rWrN0&t=22 5s

When Jonathan Lanman, our mutual editor at Atheneum, asked her to illustrate *Dear Peter Rabbit,* I did not know Leslie Tryon. Yet she was more than up to the challenging task of creating just the right images for familiar storybook characters pursuing new adventures. The joy her illustrations brought to so many children, and to me as well, had everything to do with my desire to create more books about the world of the Hidden Forest. Leslie and I have also become good friends and find our collaboration to be most rewarding as she describes in her own chapter in this book.

Nothing could have made me happier than having Susan Pearson, then at Lothrop, convince Simón Silva to create the illustrations for *Gathering the Sun* and having Karen Wojtyla, then at Dell, select Felipe Dávalos to illustrate *The Lizard and the Sun/La lagartija y el sol.* It has been an honor to collaborate on a book with each of these outstanding Latino illustrators. It is my hope to publish more books with Simón Silva, and I already had the pleasure of continuing to work with Felipe Dávalos in his role as art director of the collection *Gateways to the Sun / Puertas al sol* that Isabel Campoy and I co-authored.

Next is an example of how one's beliefs can grow and change as an author and illustrator join to create a new whole.

When I was first given a contract for *The Gold Coin,* I had already pictured in my imagination how the characters and the

setting would look. I had spent some time in Costa Rica shortly before I wrote the story, and my mind was filled with vivid images of its luscious landscapes.

When I first received the book with Neil Waldman's illustrations, I was somewhat disconcerted. Without question, it was beautiful. Yet it did not feel like the book I had imagined. For one thing, it focused very much on Juan, while I had expected to see more of doña Josefa. Also, the landscape was different than the images I had expected to see. The book felt very masculine to me, quite unlike anything I had ever published before. Yet, when *The Gold Coin* reached the readers, I discovered how

mistaken I was, and how wrong it would have been for the book to be more like what I had originally envisioned.

Neil had enriched the book enormously when it had ceased to be mine and instead become ours! I am sure that his art was significant to the book receiving the Christopher Award, since although the award is meant as recognition of the book's message its lovely presentation must indeed have contributed to make it stand out for the selecting committee.

Neil was absolutely right in focusing on Juan, who is indeed the protagonist, the one who undergoes a most significant major transformation. It was a stroke of genius to keep Doña Josefa so minimally present throughout most of the book. On one level, it accurately reflects the fact that she was not physically present in most of the scenes. Yet more importantly, since Juan is seeing Doña Josefa only as someone he intends to rob instead of as the generous, caring person she really is, it makes sense that the reader is not able to see her either until the very end, even when she is mentioned earlier in the story.

And as the landscape is described in detail in the text, it needs not be emphasized in artwork. In truth, the events could happen anywhere. Instead, the story is really about the characters and Juan's evolution as Neil captures so well.

What has been so significant for the life of the book is the readership it has gained by being somewhat more masculine and formal than what I had originally envisioned. I have received more letters from boys about this book than about any other book I have written, with the exception of *Under the Royal Palms* and *Where the Flame Trees Bloom.* Some are from middle school and even high school students, who mention that they first picked up the book because the man on the cover resembled their father or uncle. Older readers have been drawn to the book because it does not appear too childish, and this has made the book acceptable for inclusion in reading programs for fifth

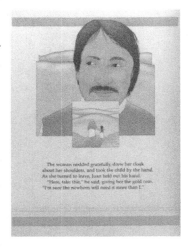

The woman nodded gratefully, drew her cloak about her shoulders, and took the child by the hand. As she turned to leave, Juan held out his hand. "Here, take this," he said, giving her the gold coin. "I'm sure the newborn will need it more than I."

and sixth graders. Most significantly, I once received a very moving letter from a young man who confessed that he had been stealing but, after reading *The Gold Coin,* decided that this was not what he wanted to do with his life.

I can never thank Neil Waldman enough for being the "father" to this book I had "mothered." Our two different sensibilities have helped create a much larger whole. Many art directors hold the theory that if the author and the illustrator work independently, each one contributing their best, the total is not simply one hundred percent, but rather two hundred percent. This may not have always been the case, and I am glad for the many instances in which I have been able to give input during the "pencil stage," before the artwork has been finalized. Yet in the case of *The Gold Coin,* this theory certainly did hold true.

Letters and I

My fascination with letters began very early in life. Every day I watched from the porch as the mailman walked down the street in his heavy shoes, whose many patches told of various repairs. His bulky sack seemed to hold mysterious secrets more fascinating than those carried by Santa Claus, who had begun to appear at Christmastime in shop windows and was beginning to compete with our dear *Reyes Magos* [The Three Wise Kings]. Earlier, they had been the only ones bearing gifts at Christmastime.

The days the mailman stopped at our house were few; mail-order business and advertisements were not part of the Cuban experience at the time. I swelled with pride whenever I was entrusted with letters to hand to my mother, since personal mailboxes were unheard of in Cuba and our old door did not have a mail slot. On the rare occasions when a letter came from Spain in a thin envelope covered with large exciting stamps, I experienced a sense of wonder. I knew that those letters from my grandfather's family would not be opened until after dinner, when they would be read as a family event.

Aware of my enthusiasm for the mail, my sweet, creative mother invented a wonderful game just for me, the only child in a household of adults. In the mornings we would cut small squares of blank paper that she had taught me to fold to make envelopes. I would cut even smaller squares of paper to fit into the envelopes.

We would soak used stamps in the sink to separate them from their original envelopes, and I would sort the stamps carefully, keeping them in small tissue paper packets. My mother would let me sharpen several pencil stubs that she had saved for me from her accounting work and helped me put everything inside an old handbag. She would then write a few "letters" to different people in the household, place them in envelopes, and paste one of the used stamps on each envelope. After that, it was my turn to proudly sort the letters into the cubbyholes of my father's roll-top desk, where I had assigned a slot to each member of the family.

All morning long I would write letters of my own to add to the ones my mother had written; I would cut out pictures from the Sunday paper to make small magazines so that I would have plenty of mail to deliver. In the afternoon, I would take everything out of each cubbyhole, place it in the old handbag that also carried my supplies, and set out for my deliveries. As I delivered the mail to each person, I would also offer materials to write a reply. My father had brought home a bag full of shiny new American pennies after doing some surveying work for the Nicaro-Nickel Company in Oriente. We used the pennies for play money, and when my mother invented the game, she distributed a handful to each member of the family so they could "purchase" my stationery and stamps.

To this day, it is still hard for me to believe that everyone was so willing to indulge me in this game. Even then I had the vague notion that my mother had invented the Mailing Game to keep me busy, particularly on rainy days, while she did her accounting work at home. I also knew that everyone was being kind to me in participating, yet in some way I also felt that they were not being condescending and, instead, rather enjoyed sending their little notes to one another in that long-ago time before e-mail and texting were invented.

As I grew older and my mother noticed my interest in the letters we received from her uncle in Spain, she allowed me to be the one in charge of writing to our relatives with the family news. I swelled with pride at this assignment and very much enjoyed planning the letters, making sure to not leave out any tidbits.

When I was seven, we left the old house on the outskirts of the city and moved into town. Yet we all found that we longed for our beloved Quinta Simoni, where I had been born. After a few years, my father decided to build a small house by the river Tínima, behind the hacienda's large old house. When I was twelve, we moved into this new house that he had built entirely with his own hands. I pestered my parents constantly about my grandparents' books which had been left packed away in the old house. Finally my father built a detached garage with a room behind to serve as my library and they finally opened up the big crates where my grandparents' books had been stored. I will never forget my enthusiasm at

Cartas de
Medardo Lafuente Rubio
a
Dolores Salvador Méndez
Camagüey, Cuba
1910–1917.

being able to get at those books, although most of them were far over my head. Among my grandparents' papers, I found my grandfather's letters to my grandmother. As I read those letters, I fell in love with my grandfather, who had died when I was not yet three years old, and I began to understand the love that my grandmother felt for him. I have published those letters as a book, with one of his greetings as a title: Medardo Lafuente. *Mi cada vez más querida mía* [My each day more beloved] in a private printing. I hope I will be able to publish a Mariposa Transformative Education edition that will be widely available. From the day I read those incomparable love letters written by a young immigrant poet, I knew how important letters could be.

During the summers, my family would travel to the United States. Somehow, I had learned that one could receive letters through General Delivery. Thus, I mapped out our route and gave my friends dates and places to write to me. Since I was the navigator, whenever we arrived at a new town, the first stop would be at the main post office. I would walk out proudly with a bunch of letters in my hand, astonishing my little sister as well as my parents.

In my teen years, I maintained frequent correspondence with two people. One was a young woman from the Dominican

Republic whom I had met briefly while vacationing in Miami. Although she was a woman and I was just a young girl, she was kind enough to write long, meaningful letters about her own life and to respond to my comments about every book I had read and every movie I had seen. It made me feel valued to have someone take my comments seriously enough to expand on them.

The other, was a young Italian man from Napoli, studying to become a naval engineer, whom I never met. During a summer

course in Pennsylvania, when I was fifteen years old, a young Colombian classmate had given me the name of Rudy Veronese, who had been her cousin's fiancé. It intrigued me when she told me how on breaking the engagement her cousin had broken the man's heart and I decided to write to him

Our correspondence was a deep cultural exchange between our two worlds and our very different experiences. He had lived through all the pain of World War II, and his stories awoke in

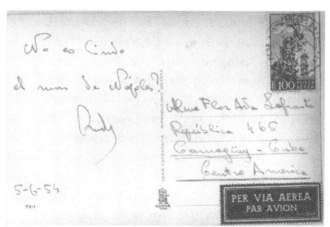

me an absolute abhorrence of war. The world he described was very much like the one I could see in neo-realistic Italian films, such as *Bicycle Thief, Bitter Rice,* and *La Strada.*

It has taken many years for me to find the courage to transcribe Rudy

Veronese's letters, which I have kept for over 65 years, while living in four different countries moving numerous times. I treasured these letters because they represent such a meaningful moment in my life. Since I have none of the ones I wrote, I realize that those long letters must have been the passionate outbursts of a girl who, as my mother aptly put it, "was in love with love." Rudy's are the reflection of a sensitive man, who suffered the conflicts of World War II in a Europe struggling to recuperate from destruction.

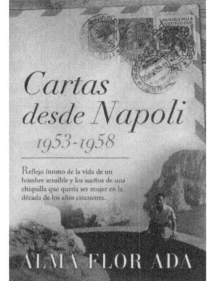

I have now published these letters, wishing we could have maintained a life-long friendship, acknowledging the significance of this relationship carried on thin air mail paper and post cards and through the movies, books, music, we shared, and above all as a tribute to Rodolfo Veronese Cammarata, thankful for the dreams he inspired of a world so far from my Caribbean homeland.

And what a gift Rudy has given me these many years later! My son Alfonso, always such a supporter of my many ventures has been able to find Rudy's children and nieces and now many members of my family and members of the Verenose and Cammarata families are maintaining a thoughtful and loving correspondence by email.

Earlier, I have mentioned Pedro Salinas, whose poetry was the subject of my dissertation. In Salinas magnificent collection of essays called *El defensor* [The defender], he expresses his appreciation for language in its multiplicity of expressions. One of his essays is an impassioned defense of letters as an unsurpassed form of personal communication.

A few summers ago, I received a gift across time upon encountering the recently published collection of letters that

Salinas wrote to his secret lover Katherine Whitmore, an *hispanista,* a scholar of Spanish literature and culture, whom he had met in the famous Instituto de Verano (Summer Institute) in Santander that he directed. Katherine was the inspiration for *La voz a ti debida* and *Razón de amor,* some of the best love poetry written created in Spanish. And what a treasure of intimacy, these letters! More than half a century later, they have retained their poignancy and their power as they offer us a window into the author's inner self. Once again, I found myself falling in love as I read a collection of letters between two people, now long dead, whose feelings were timeless.

The Origins of the Hidden Forest World

How did my love for writing and reading letters transformed itself into a series of children's books? It is a simple but perhaps surprising story.

Several years ago, after teaching at the University of San Francisco, I would drive north to Lake County where I had rented a small house on the top of a mountain. I carried with me a cassette recorder with an extended microphone, which allowed me to use the three hours of driving time to dictate notes to my students. It also served to keep me awake after an exhausting weekend of teaching.

On one of those evenings, tired of dealing with academic matters, yet still needing to keep myself awake, I began talking into the microphone just for fun. And this "fun" came out in the form of various voices: pigs, rabbits, and even wolves that were sending letters to one another!

When I got home, I forgot all about that episode of playfulness. The cassette was put aside and perhaps I would have never remembered any of it, if it had not been that several months later I was looking for a blank tape. Not finding one, I played an old tape to see if I could safely erase it—and out popped a whole story in letters! This became the first of the Hidden Forest manuscripts.

Of course, Hidden Forest as such was truly born when Leslie Tryon began producing her magnificent illustrations. Leslie's whimsical depiction of the characters brought them to life, and her attention to details, most of them of her own creation, substantially enriched the world alluded to in the letters.

Dear Peter Rabbit (in Spanish *Querido Pedrín*), *Yours Truly, Goldilocks* (in Spanish *Atentamente, Ricitos de Oro*), and *With Love, Little Red Hen,* all three illustrated by Leslie Tryon and published by Atheneum, are written in letter format. New stories develop as letters are exchanged between some well-known characters, including Peter Rabbit, the Three Pigs, Goldilocks, the Three Bears, and Little Red Riding Hood, as well as a few new ones, such as the two cousins Mr. Fer O'Cious and Wolfy Lupus. In the third book, we meet Ms. Red Hen and her cousin Hetty Henny. The illustrations add layers of details that contribute to bringing the Hidden Forest to life and engaging children in repeated readings.

In these books, I use situations derived from the original stories to tell new stories, and I also take artistic license as needed. For example, when Little Red Riding Hood is talking to the wolf, it turns out that Goldilocks was a silent witness. Goldilocks also happens to be Mr. McGregor's daughter and thus forms a relationship with the feisty rabbit that has been trespassing in her father's vegetable garden. Instead of one Big Bad Wolf, there are two unsavory characters who also happen to be wolves, Mr. Fer O'Cious and his cousin Wolfy Lupus. They are sometimes joined by the devious Mr. Feline in their pursuit of pigs, rabbits, hens, and girls. To their chagrin, they meet their match in Mrs. Bear, who is always ready to protect Little Bear and his friends.

Another book that does not take place in Hidden Forest, but also revolves around the theme of mail and letters, is *A New Job for Pérez, The Mouse* (in Spanish *Ratoncito Pérez, cartero*) co-authored by F. Isabel Campoy and illustrated by Viví Escrivá. Pérez, The Mouse, or Ratoncito Pérez, is the equivalent of the tooth fairy in the Hispanic tradition. He collects the baby teeth that children place under their pillows and leaves a coin for them in return. One of the most beloved Hispanic folktales tells how Ratoncito Pérez marries Martina, a character who in different versions is a small cockroach, an ant, or a butterfly. In some countries, she is called Cucarachita Mandinga.

These beloved characters appear in *Cuentos que contaban nuestras abuelitas* (published also in English as *Tales Our Abuelitas Told* where I have retold their full story, up to the marriage and beyond. I also brought Cucarachita Martina to present days by transforming the story on that of her granddaughter *La tataranieta de Cucarachita Martina* (published also in English as *The great-granddaughter of Cucarachita Martina*).

In our book, written in letters, Pérez is looking for new work, since most of the children in town have grown and there are not many baby teeth left to collect. He is delighted to be given the job of mailman and enjoys delivering different types of mail to the diverse characters along his route.

Unfortunately, his friend Pig Three does not value the role of postman, since he believes that e-mail has made snail mail obsolete and unnecessary. Seeing Pérez suffer as a result of his friend's disregard for his job, Martina decides to change the little pig's attitude toward postal mail. Her strategy? Mailing him something delicious to eat!

About the Characters

The traditional tales portray Little Red Riding Hood as a disobedient child who does not follow her mother's orders to stay on the path and to not linger or talk to strangers and depict Goldilocks as a nosy child whose curiosity results in encountering the scare of her life. At first glance, the Hidden Forest books may appear to not stray too much from the original stories, but a closer look reveals that the stories provide an opportunity to explore the characters' deeper qualities.

For example, Little Red Riding Hood was indeed a helpful and caring child; otherwise how can we explain her willingness to walk across the forest to carry goodies to her grandmother? In  the Hidden Forest series, Little Red Riding Hood's loving relationship with her grandmother is expanded upon, and the child shows her willingness to help others by organizing celebrations and also by taking on the demanding task of assisting Ms. Red Hen in cultivating her cornfield. That she does this unbeknown to Ms. Red Hen is an even greater demonstration of her generosity.

Goldilocks is adventuresome and curious, as she demonstrated by entering the Bears' house. In the Hidden Forest books, she shows herself to be a good judge of character and ready to befriend others who may not look just like her.

Both Leslie Tryon and I feel a great affinity for the self-reliant Little Red Hen. This beloved character appears traditionally in two different stories. One story tells how she attempts to obtain help as she plants and gathers grain. Unfortunately, the other characters only want to help in eating the fruit of her labors! Another story tells how the resourceful hen is able to escape when she is captured and held captive in a sack, thanks to the scissors, needle, and thread that she carries in her apron pocket. Sometimes both adventures are combined into one story. At other times, they appear separately.

For *With Love, Little Red Hen,* I decided to have each story happen to a different (but related!) character. Ms. Red Hen plants and gathers, while her cousin, Hetty Hen, escapes after having been captured by the mean Wolfy Lupus who is planning to make a meal of her. These two characters have allowed Leslie and me to discover our alter egos. I am the hen with a brood of eight chicks, my eight grandchildren at the time of publication (sorry Collette, you were not born yet!), while Leslie is the elegant and artistic Hetty Hen.

Teachers and Librarians' Ideas

Letter Writing

An obvious role for these books is to encourage children to write letters, and teachers and librarians have often used the stories for this purpose. Sometimes the letters have been addressed to me. At other times, children have written to other authors or to people of significance in their own lives. Some creative teachers have encouraged them to address the letters to storybook characters, either those in Hidden Forest or characters in other stories.

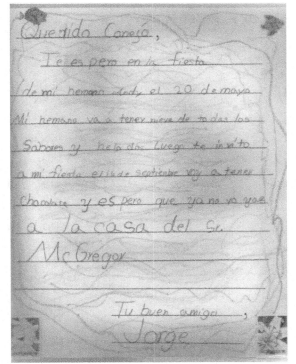

Children have written letters addressed to a character, explaining why they have chosen to write to him or her, and mentioning which aspects of that character's life that intrigue them the most. The two examples here are from a class where all children wrote letters to Peter Rabbit.

Dear Rabbit:

I hope to see you at my brother's birthday party on May 20ᵗʰ. My brother will have ice cream of all flavors, and then I also invite you to my birthday party on September 16ᵗʰ and I hope you will not go again to Mr. McGregor's house.

Your good friend,

Jorge

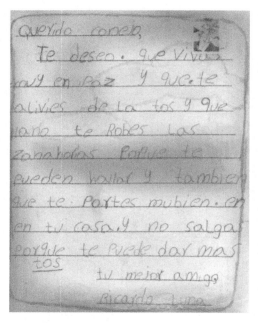

Ricardo Luna

Dear rabbit,

I hope you will live with great peace and that your cough will get better and that you will not steal the carrots because they can find you and I hope also that you behave very well at home and don't go out anymore because your cough can get worse.

your best friend,

Another teacher invited her second grade students to write letters to Mother Bear thanking her for having scared the wolves away.

A boy, writing as Peter, thanked her in his letter for "having saved my furry life." Then, aware of his good use of imagery, he added a P.S. addressed to me, asking: "How did you like that 'furry life'?"
Indeed I thought it was precious!

Maps and Directions

A very creative teacher at Woodlawn Elementary School in Bell, California, decided to use *Ratoncito Pérez, cartero* published also in English as A *New Job for Pérez, The Mouse,* to teach her first graders the points of the compass, how to read and make maps, and how to follow and give directions.

On one full wall of the classroom, the children painted a large watercolor mural as the background for the town, following the map which appears in the book. North, South, East, and West were clearly labeled. Individually or in pairs, the children created different buildings out of paper and pasted them onto the mural with appropriate labels: Library, Supermarket, Little Red Riding Hood's Cottage, The Three Bears, The Seven Goats, The Castle of No Return, and so forth.

Then each child wrote a letter from one of the book's characters to another character. In addition to any personal comments they wanted to include—and they included the most wonderful comments—students were asked to include clear directions on how to get to their character's house, so that the recipient of the letter could come for a visit. The teacher who designed this activity mentioned that this was one of the most exciting projects that she had ever done with her students and that they had never before learned to give directions and follow them as readily.

Creating Books

Some of my favorite activities inspired by these books have come from teachers who have invited students to write their own books, also based on letters between storybook characters.

- *Envelope books.* One teacher devised a very clever way of creating a collective book of letters by spiral-binding a number of white legal-size envelopes, one envelope per student, and placing the students' letters, written on paper of a slightly smaller size, inside the envelopes. Of course, the children can decorate the envelopes before they are spiral bound.

Home-School Interaction

These books have also been used to support the key relationship between home and school. In one fascinating activity, students asked their parents to name their own favorite characters from storybooks or traditional folktales and to explain why they liked those particular characters. The children then wrote letters to the characters explaining why their parents had chosen them.

Newspapers and I

THE ROLE OF NEWSPAPERS IN MY LIFE

Many times I have said in jest that it is not blood but newspaper ink that circulates in my veins, since both of my grandfathers were journalists who owned newspapers.

My grandfather Medardo Lafuente Rubio began his professional life as a freelance writer of literary and political articles. After marrying my grandmother, who was an extraordinary educator, education became one of his themes. His own parents had owned a rather progressive small school in Madrid, Spain, and he eventually became a professor of French at the Instituto de Segunda Enseñanza de Camagüey, our local preparatory high school, which was the highest educational institution in the province. He also wrote poetry throughout his life. None of these other pursuits, however, kept him far from his beloved newspapers. He constantly collaborated with several and eventually had his own, *Camagüey Ilustrado.*

Since my grandfather Medardo died before I was three and the newspaper disappeared after his death, I never had the opportunity to get to know his newspaper office; but I distinctly remember the smell of ink that lingered on his clothes. The hardbound copies of his newspapers always evoked my admiration as I stood in awe in front of the huge, imposing volumes that were stored in our library at the Quinta Simoni. Unfortunately, none of them exist today, or at least I have not been able to locate any.

Through the assistance of some dedicated friends I have been able to access a number of articles my grandfather wrote in several newspapers and journals. They are now collected in the book Medardo Lafuente. *Páginas rescatadas* Third Edition [Rescued pages] published by Mariposa Transformative Education, 2017.

My paternal grandfather Modesto Ada Barral had a fascinating life that I describe in the story "Choices" in *Where the Flame Trees Bloom*, now included in *Island Treasures* or *Tesoros de mi isla.* For several decades in his later years, he owned both a radio station, *La voz del Tinima,* and a newspaper, *El Noticiero.*

Alma Flor and Flor Alma Ada Lafuente, Modesto Ada Barral, my grandfather, Modesto Ada Rey, my father, Alma Lafuente Salvador, my mother, Mario Ada Rey, my uncle.

During my childhood and youth, *El Noticiero* was one of two newspapers published in Camagüey. While it did not have as much circulation as the morning newspaper, *El Camagüeyano,* as an afternoon newspaper *El Noticiero* could focus more on issues than on recent news. Whenever I saw it

I was filled with pride at knowing that it was the product of my grandfather's efforts. After we moved to town, he would take me to visit his offices. He would always ask me to wait
for a few minutes at the door of the print shop to give the men who ran the linotypes a chance to put on their T-shirts, since on account of the tropical heat they mostly worked bare-chested.

These kind men would let me set sentences in type and then would run them for me; these were the first words of mine that I ever saw in print. I collected these treasured pieces of paper and the lead strips in a special box together with a wax seal with the initial A, which had belonged to my grandfather. He had given it to me to seal my letters.

Discovering the inner world of newspapers, which meant understanding the various sections with their different intentions and styles, was one of my first intellectual revelations, and I relished it. I remember distinctly the day that I happened to sit next to a history professor on the public bus, when I was twelve years old and had just begun to attend the Instituto. The professor was engrossed in reading a newspaper, and I silently observed her concentration. She was a rather abrupt woman, and I felt very shy sitting next to her. All of a sudden, as though she had interpreted my silent observation as a criticism, she said, "So you think I'm just reading pages and pages of the same thing? Someday you'll discover that's not true!"

I was chastened and embarrassed but determined to find the secret I felt hidden in her words. For the next few days, I read newspapers from end to end, until it dawned on me that within these lines of print, all so parallel and similar, there was great variety. At last I could sense the difference in style between the terse, crisp international news bulletins, the florid local social chronicles, and the passionate editorials. I realized that certain sections could always be found on the same pages of the newspaper. For all of their family traditions, neither my mother nor my father was very interested in reading the newspaper. My father read journals and magazines, as well as many books, but I do not believe we ever had a subscription to either newspaper. Moreover, at that time and place, the newspaper was not considered part of a school curriculum. The sentences our teachers would write on the board for us to dissect in what felt like unending, useless exercises had very little to do with the content of daily life. No one had ever talked about the sections of a newspaper with me or in front of me; the history teacher's words are the only ones I recall on the subject. Therefore, when I made my discovery about newspapers on my own, I felt that I had conquered an important piece of the adult world, and my admiration for both my grandfathers grew greater. Finding out the names of the different sections of the paper was the next task I set myself, and I felt very grown-up the first time I could talk to my grandfather Modesto about the content of his paper in words that conveyed my growing

understanding.

I have loved newspapers ever since, although many times I do not necessarily enjoy their contents. Therefore, it makes sense that my next book in the Hidden Forest series, while keeping many of the same characters, would be in the newspaper genre rather than in letter format.

The three issues of the weekly *Hidden Forest Times* included in the book allow for the development of one main plot based on the story of Jack and the Beanstalk, along with stories drawn from other cultures for the international news section.

The various other sections—editorials, op-ed articles, announcements, sports, brief news, and classified ads—invite children to remember characters they already know and characters they already know and to enjoy further developments of well-loved stories.

This book will always be very meaningful to me because it is the result of a special collaboration. I tend to have long dry periods during which I don't have many ideas for a new story; but once I do have an idea, I tend to not have much difficulty finishing a book. This time was an exception: I had a clear idea of what I wanted to do, but my first drafts felt incomplete and insufficient. I was working with a new editor for me, Ginee Seo, after the departure of Jonathan Lanman from Atheneum, and she agreed with me that something more was needed.

Then I had the opportunity to visit, as a guest author, the school in Lakewood, Ohio, that four of my grandchildren attended. During an assembly, one of the students asked if I ever had problems finishing a book, and I mentioned that indeed that was the case with my current book. Later that day, my eldest grandson, nine-year-old Timothy Paul, wanted to know all the details. When I explained what the book was about and why it was difficult to complete, he surprised me by coming up with a series of great ideas that not only pleased me but also delighted my editor. She could not believe that such a young reader had come up with such wonderful suggestions!

As I have noted before, my collaborations with various creative partners have been a source of great joy. It was delightful to have the opportunity to collaborate on a creative project with my own grandson!

Teachers and Librarians' Ideas

Creating a Classroom or Library Newspaper

This book can be a good starting point for encouraging children to create their own newspaper. The newspaper could have one or multiple copies; it could be written on paper or

pasted onto poster board to create a mural; but in all cases it should include clearly defined sections: news, editorials, op-ed articles, interviews, announcements.... Students can work on these sections individually or in groups, and they can illustrate the various sections of the paper with drawings or photographs. The overall content can be realistic, including news from the classroom, school, or community. Or, like *Hidden Forest Times,* the "news" can be based on the lives of various storybook characters.

Latino Identity

New realities call for new definitions and nomenclature. The widespread acceptance of these definitions and names depends upon the ever-changing complexities inherent in the reality we are attempting to describe, as well as on who is naming that reality.

It has taken some time for most of us who are called "Latinos" in the United States to agree that this is what we want to be called, for we are far from homogenous. Even those of us who find it important to have a unifying name want to make sure that the label chosen is understood as encompassing a wider diversity.

There are many aspects to our diversity. Some include:

- **Our level of bilingualism or trilingualism**. Some of us can speak both English and Spanish with ease, some of us are monolingual in Spanish or have a limited command of English, and some of us are monolingual in English or have a very limited use of the Spanish language. Some, members of indigenous communities in Latin America may have a third language, an indigenous language (zapoteco, mixteco, maya, quechua, etc.) as their heritage language.

- **Our country of origin and that of our family's ancestors.** Our ancestry may derive from Spain or from any one of the nineteen Spanish-speaking countries in Latin America. This means that we can have both a national as well as a regional identity, depending on whether our family's country of origin is in the Caribbean Sea, in Central America, in South America or, as is the case with Mexico, in North America.

- **Our length of time or number of generations in the United States**. This can vary from less than ten years (if so, we are considered recent immigrants) to many generations back. There are Latinos in New Mexico who trace their roots in this country to the sixteenth century.

- **Our reasons for immigrating to the United States**. These vary from economic hardship in our country of origin or the desire to pursue the "American Dream" to political exile. Among political refugees there may be substantive differences, since there have been refugees both from left-wing and right-wing governments.

- **Our educational and social background, as well as our degree of integration into U.S. society**. As Latinos, some of us live in rural communities as migrant farmworkers, some of us live in enclaves in the inner city, and some of us have integrated into the larger workforce as successful entrepreneurs or professionals.

- **Our mix of heritages**. All Latinos are of mixed ethnicities and cultures, born from the fusion of  people of indigenous, African, Spanish, and Asian origin. The Spanish culture itself is a product of many heritages: Iberian, Basque, Celtic, Jewish, and Arabic. The manifestations of these different heritages vary from group to group and even from person to person. It is not unusual for members of the same family to have different coloring and facial features, which sometimes contribute to different self-identifications. Both Esmeralda Santiago and Piri Thomas have addressed this issue in their writing.

- **Our beliefs and/or religious practices** Contrary to popular misconception, not all Latinos are Catholic, even though the Catholic religion has permeated the culture. Latinos belong to many different faiths and some are decidedly anti-Catholic as a result of the long-term role of the Catholic Church in perpetuating social inequalities. Some are freethinkers, and do not practice any organized religion. Yet even those who are not practicing Catholics may still participate in Catholic celebrations that have become common cultural expressions, such as building a nativity scene at Christmastime, displaying crosses or iconographies of the Virgin Mary and special saints, or having an altar for the Day of the Dead. Some Latinos, particularly those of us from the Caribbean, may have a syncretic set of beliefs that combines Catholicism with ancestral African practices.

Given these many variables, it is not surprising that it would be difficult to define what it means to be a Latino and to find a name that applies to all of us. At the same time, there are various cultural and historical elements that connect us, so that, even with all of the differences among us, we can still recognize ourselves as sharing many things in common.

Every human being can be seen as having multiple identities influenced by many variables. Some of these identities are based on where we were born or where we grew up; others area relational: we are the children of our parents, the grandchildren of our grandparents, as well as sisters or brothers, mothers or fathers, nieces or nephews, uncles or aunts, friends, students, coworkers; others may be related to our profession or area of work: we can be teachers, medical doctors, farm workers. We could see these as concentric circles.

For example, I could say about myself that I am:
- *camagüeyana,* alluding to my city of origin, in order to distinguish myself from other Cubans;
- *cubana,* Cuban, referring to my native country;
- *caribeña,* Caribbean, acknowledging my region of origin and the special connection I feel with Puerto Ricans, Dominicans, Haitians, Jamaicans, and other Caribbean peoples;
- *hispanoamericana,* Latin American, with ties to people from all of the Spanish speaking countries of Latin America, or *iberaoamericana,* to acknowledge a connection that includes the people of Brazil;
- *Latina,* to embrace the cause of a specific community within the United States; and
- *Hispana,* a member of the worldwide Spanish-speaking community, with a particular history and culture that is distinct from that of Canadians, Germans, French, and people from Asia or the Middle East, even though I certainly consider myself a citizen of the world. As José Marti proclaimed, my brothers and sisters are all those who hold kindness in their hearts.

These six different levels of identity do not conflict; on the contrary, they support one another. Depending on the context within which I am operating at a given time, one level may be more pertinent than another, but all of these identities are always with me.

Those of us who choose to be called by the general term "Latina" or "Latino" may also see ourselves as having other identities. We may see ourselves as chicanos, mexicanos, puertorriqueños, dominicanos, cubanos, salvadoreños, venezolanos. . . When children are born to parents from different countries, they may describe themselves as Puerto Rican-Dominican, or Cuban-Peruvian. And, as intermarriage between Latinos from different backgrounds becomes more and more widespread in this country, the process of identifying our diverse heritages will become even more complex.

In Search of a Common Name

When our intention is to identify with others in a joint social action, the need for a common name becomes important. In the 1960s and 1970s, people of Mexican descent in the Southwest and California began a strong movement to affirm their identity. They wanted to emphasize the importance of their dual heritage, indigenous and Spanish, and to celebrate their indigenous roots. In a tactic similar to that of African Americans who wished to vindicate the term *Black* by affirming that "Black is beautiful," these people of Mexican descent validated the term *Chicano* (or Xicano), which had previously been applied in a derogatory way. In a parallel movement on the East Coast, some Puerto Ricans adopted the term *Boricua,* which derives from the indigenous name of their island, "Boriquén" or "Borinquen." Those who wanted to recognize the commonality in the struggle of these two groups adopted the hyphenated term *Chicano-Boricua.*

However, not all people with Spanish-speaking ancestors identified with the ideological stance of these movements. Some preferred to call themselves *Mexicanos,* affirming that regardless of where they lived their identity was based on their country of origin. Others chose *Mexican-American* to signal their dual identity as Mexicans and Americans. A similar thing happened among those with roots in Puerto Rico. Some would call themselves *Puerto Rican* while some from the second and third generations with strong ties to New York chose the name *Newyorican* or *Nuorican.*

A common term that could apply to all of us remained elusive for a long time. Official forms attempted to use *Spanish-speakers,* which was not inclusive since many of us no longer spoke Spanish as a primary language. The term *Spanish-surnamed* was also deceiving, since all of us did not necessarily have Spanish-sounding surnames.

In New Mexico and the Midwest, the favored term was *Hispano.* At some point the term *Hispanic,* seemed to be gaining force. However, for some people this term sounded too much like Spain and carried unwanted echoes of the colonizer. Others saw the term as being imposed by the federal government and therefore lacking in self-definition. Slowly, the term *Latino/Latina* gained wider acceptance.

Personally, it has been a long journey for me to embrace the term Latina. Like many people from the Spanish-speaking countries of the Americas, we grew up calling our part of the world Hispanoamérica and rejected the term Latin America as a name imposed by the United States. We saw it as lumping us together with the French, Italian, and Portuguese, whose languages are also derived from Latin. The use of terms like "Latin lover" made the word feel stereotypical and foreign.

To identify myself as Latina did not initially feel comfortable to me, knowing that historically it had been used by the Emperor Napoleon III of France to justify imposing Emperor Maximilian in Mexico. The only claim to legitimize the French invasion of Mexico has been emphasizing their common Latin roots.

I always felt proud when I was called a Chicana, as I very much identified with the struggle for social justice embodied in the name. However, I did not understand how the term Latino/Latina fit in with a struggle for liberation; the colonizer—Rome, in this case—was simply a little further back in history and the French invasion of Mexico a much closer reminder of colonization. Yet as I continued to live in the United States and to participate in movements to affirm our identity, celebrate our culture, and find unity in our diversity, I felt a growing need to accept the term that felt most representative to most of us, regardless of its etymology or history. In this way, while continuing to recognize our individuality, we could gain strength through solidarity.

As I affirm my identity as a Latina, I do so based on choice and self- determination. Having a set of Spanish words, **Latino / Latina**, into the English language without any modification in spelling or pronunciation is a source of pride!

The desire to make the term inclusive to those not accepting a binary identification the term *Latinex* has been growing acceptance. While I fully believe in the need to modify language to be more inclusive I am saddened and appalled by the choice of a term that goes against the phonetics of the language, since the sound/symbol correlation has been one of the highly positive aspects of written Spanish. For me it would make much better sense to coin LATINES and to adopt the E as substitution of the A/O genre distinction and extend it to words like *Nosotres, Otres,* and *buenes.* The reasons would be:

- it stays in consonance with the nature of the language
- it is easy to pronounce and write, maintaining the sound/symbol correlation
- it already has a basis in the language, in adjectives that do not differentiate in genre: *amable, alegre, noble, inteligente* and in nouns like *estudiante.*

It is good to know that in Argentina and Chile there is a movement to establish this usage.

Yes! We Are Latinos and *¡Sí! Somos latinos* were the product of long years of reflection and study. Isabel Campoy and I wanted to present in a clear and simple way the major issues of our history as Latinos. We decided that to give the thirteen chapters of this book greater appeal for young readers the non-fiction information be preceded by a fiction portrait of an important moment in the life of young Latinos and Latinas from diverse origins and in diverse settings.

We are delighted with the great reception received by this book and have created a website with suggestions for classroom discussions and activities, as well as recommendation of books by multiple authors, for each of the topics. Please visit: www.yeswearelatinos.com. From this website you can also access a Spanish version of the website or you can go directly to www.sisomoslatinos.com.

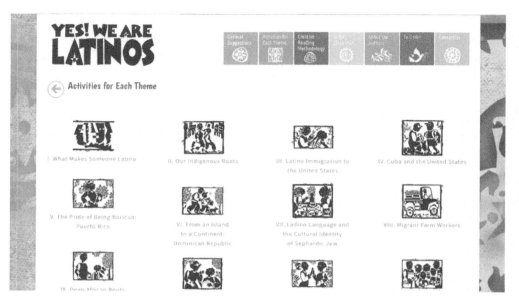

A Dual Heritage

There are growing numbers of children in the United States who have a dual heritage. My own four children have a Cuban mother and a Peruvian father; my nine grandchildren all have Latino fathers and mothers who are not Latinas. But the idea for *I Love Saturdays y domingos*, in Spanish *Me encantan los Saturdays y domingos,* illustrated by Elivia Savadier, was not inspired by my own grandchildren, even though this book has come to represent their circumstances.

In fact, the inspiration came many years ago when I was vacationing in Maui, Hawaii. It was a Sunday morning in Lahaina, and I sat down to observe my surroundings—not so much the ocean as the human landscape. A number of families were walking in the park by the seashore. Some were going to church, others had just returned from there, a few were sharing ice-cream cones, and most were simply strolling about. I was moved by the sense of relaxation and by the richness of their diversity. The families appeared to be Hawaiian, Filipino, Chinese, Japanese, and Portuguese, as well as various combinations of all of these ancestries. I began thinking about how beautiful it was for these children to have so many heritages from which to draw.

That day I wrote the manuscript. As with many books, it took years to have it published. None of my children were married yet when I first wrote the story. By the time the book came off the press, I already had eight grandchildren!

This book has been very well received, and it has been a great joy for me to hear the responses of parents, teachers, and children. Many Latinos have shared their delight at finding a book that reflects their own children's mixed heritage while celebrating the Latino culture and language. Other parents have told me that they have found this book helpful for their children who have a mixed heritage, even though their heritage is not Latino at all but from a variety of other backgrounds instead.

Until the multicultural nature of the United States society is fully recognized, Latino children, born in the United Sates from parents who grew up in other countries, may be puzzled by the contrast between their family heritage and what may be presented to them as the American culture.

This is the situation of Margarita, who prefers to be called Maggie, and reminds everyone that unlike her Mexican parents she was born in Texas, the protagonist of **Dancing**

Home or **Nacer bailando**, a middle grades novel co-authored by my son Gabriel Zubizarreta Ada and myself.

Teachers and Librarians' Ideas

A Family Tree

This book has been a springboard for exploring children's heritage and inspiring them to create their own genealogical tree. However, this activity needs to be approached with sensitivity to the fact that some children may be adopted and that even those who are not adopted may still not have much information about their grandparents. It is important to let children know that not everyone has access to their family history and that whatever information we do have is of value. It is also important to offer adopted children the option of taking on their adoptive parents' lineage, if they so choose, or else to imagine and create the lineage of their choice.

Learning about Grandparents

The children can brainstorm what information they would like to learn about their grandparents and decide who they might ask to learn the answers.

Writing about Grandparents

This topic can be explored from various perspectives:
- describing a grandparent
- talking about the activities they share with their grandparents
- comparing and contrasting one or more grandparents with those in the book
- asking grandparents to offer a favorite story, story character, song, rhyme, game, riddle, or proverb. This information can be compiled into individual books for each child or into a collective book—for example, "Our grandparents' favorite proverbs," or "Our grandparents' favorite songs" (nursery rhymes, riddles, lullabies, etc.), with one page dedicated to each grandparent. Some teachers have asked the children to add the

- grandparents' photos or their pictures as drawn by the students. *A useful tip.* When asking students to draw people, it helps to give them a good-sized circle to use as an outline for the face. If the circle is scaled to the size of the paper they are using, this will help with the proportion of the final picture.

- Suggestions and examples of books written by teachers and students that may be useful in describing a grandparent can be found in the section **A person in my life**, from the website dedicated to promoting and facilitating authorship www.authorsintheclassroom.com

- A loving relationship between a grandmother and her granddaughter relationship showing the transmission of family history and culture is the central topic of the section **My Name is Sultana o Susana I am Sephardic. I live in San Francisco. I am Latina** in the book *Yes! We Are Latinos*. For suggested activities see:

www.yeswearelatinos.com
www.sisomoslatinos.com

The Value of Family

Throughout my life, Family has been my most valuable treasure. As it is natural on life its composition has changed through the years. I was born in my grandparents' home shared by my parents, aunts and uncles. Now my grandparents are no longer with us, and I am in turn a grandmother. From living under one roof we have scattered to live in distant places, our number has grown exponentially: my 2 maternal grandparents had 5 children, in my generation we were 11 cousins, in my 4 children's generation there are 36 cousins, who by now have children and even grandchildren, and yet the common values of responsibility and generosity, the gratitude towards our ancestors and our love for each other have remained strong.

It is natural that this love of family will appear in my writing in multiple ways. The grandparents in my stories are inspired by my own wonderful grandmother Lola and my great-grandmother Mina, as well as my own mother who became mi children's beloved grandmother.

You will find them books like my recent **Abuelita's secret** also

published as **El secreto de abuelita.** The wisdom of the grandmother in the story, who finds an imaginative way to solve the anxiety of her grandchild on a first day of school is very much inspired by my creative mother's attitudes as a grandmother.

A love for a grandmother is central to **La jaula dorada** published also as **The Golden Cage** as is the recognition of the grandmother's values.

This story is one of the twelve of the series **Cuentos para todo el año** or **Stories the Year** 'round which I have retold in verse form. Suni Paz created the most delightful music to the verses, capturing the special feelings between grandmother and grandchild.

Children are the most valuable in the family's treasure, they are as Martí so justly said "the hope of the World, because they are the ones who truly know how to love." My own children have inspired many of my stories, either because the are based on real moments of their childhood, like **No quiero derretirme** or **I don't want to melt**, **Rosa alada** or **A Rose with Wings,** and **El papalote** or **The Kite,** or because they are inspired by their personalities which is the case with **La jaula dorada** and **La sorpresa de Mamá Coneja** or **A Surprise for Mother Rabbit**.

Whether all four children, a daughter and three boys are present in the story, only one of them appears, or the four have turn to eight helpful rabbits, because they truly helped me then, and continue to do now, as if they had been eight instead of four these stories are all an expression of our family life.

Another expression of my love and appreciation of family is present throughout my poetry. On occasions my joy of family has also been turn into song by Suni Paz, as in the joyful **Más que el oro**, an affirmation of the value of family.

My childhood memories, published both in several individual books, and also collected in **Tesoros de mi isla** or **Island Treasures** include many stories based on my family. In **Allá donde florecen los framboyanes** or **Where the Flame Trees Bloom** two stories portray my generous and kind great-grandmother *Muñecas de trapo* or *Rag Dolls* and *Matemáticas* or *Mathematics.* My paternal grandfather's extraordinary story is shared in *Choices* and my father's infinite generosity is seen in the story *Canelo*, about the dog he saved, while his wisdom and kindness show in stories in **Dias en la Quinta**

Simoni or **Days at the Quinta Simoni** *Barquitos de papel* or *Paper Boats, Papalotes* or *Kites* although in subtle ways it permeates all the stories as it permeated all my life.

My maternal grandmother Dolores Salvador, lovingly called Lola, was as I have already mentioned the greatest influence and the most beloved person in my early childhood. Our particular bond is shown in *Murciélagos* or *The Bats* in **Bajo las palmas reale**s or **Under the Royal Palms.**

I have also tried to describe that bond in *My Abuelita, My* **Paradise** in Bonnie Christensen's anthology of many authors recollections of their **grandmothers** *In My Grandmother's House.*

The love of a grandmother and her special bond with her granddaughter is the central theme of **Love, Amalia** or **Con cariño, Amalia** a middle grades novel written in collaboration with my son Gabriel Zubizarreta Ada. This collaboration was of profound significance for me, since it allowed me to share the task I love, with someone I love greatly. At one level it was a process of sharing and learning at another the amazing confirmation of the continuity of family: I was writing inspired by my grandmother, he inspired by his own grandmother, who in turn was my mother.

The second novel we wrote together, whose central topic is identity **Dancing Home** or **Nacer bailando** is a powerful portrait of multiple family relationships, not only parents and children, but also aunt, uncle, cousins, which are very strong in our own family.

While I have mentioned here a few instances where family is portrayed in my books, I should emphasize that love of family is essential to my own being, and whether central topic of a story or poem or not it supports all I write.

Teachers and Librarians' Ideas

Creating their own family poems by substitution

After sharing the poem **Más que el oro** from the anthology **Todo es cancion,** or having the children sing along with Suni Paz in the CD of the same title, have then create their own poem substituting the aspects of their family that are most valuable to them.

Más que el oro	*More tan gold*
El beso de mi mamá	*My mother's kiss*
vale mucho más que el oro.	*is worth much more tan gold.*
La sonrisa de abuelita	*My grandmother's smile*
vale mucho más que el oro.	*is worth much more tan gold.*
El cariño de papa	*Father's caring*
vale mucho más que el oro.	*is worth much more tan gold.*
El cuento de mi abuelito	*My grandfather's story*
vale mucho más que el oro.	*is worth much more tan gold.*
La risa de mi hermanito	*My little brother's smile*
vale mucho más que el oro.	*is worth much more tan gold.*
Mi verdadero tesoro	My true treasure
¡la familia que yo adoro!	*the family I love so much!*

After sharing the poem **Dime una cosa, abuelito** from the anthology **Alegrías. Poesía cada día**, have them create their own poems. They can substitute "abuelito" with any other family member and the third line with anything they like,

The poem:	Example of substitution:
Dime una cosa, abuelito	**Dime una cosa, *mamá,***
Dime una cosa, abuelito,	Dime una cosa, *mamá,*
pero dime la verdad.	pero dime la verdad.
¿Siempre te portabas bien	*¿comías toda la comida*
cuando tenías mi edad?	cuando tenías mi edad?

After sharing the poem *Orgullo / Pride* from **Gathering the Sun**, students can add as many lines as the wish to indicate the things of which they are proud. If the sharing is happening in Spanish, boys can change *orgullosa* to *orgulloso* and they can sing the poem in the musical version by Suni Paz, en el CD **Gathering the Sun**.

El poema: The poem:

Orgullo   **Pride**

Orgullosa de mi familia   Proud of my family
orgullosa de mi lengua   proud of my language
orgullosa de mi cultura   proud of my culture
orgullosa de mi raza   proud of my people
orgullosa de ser quien soy.   proud to be who I am.

Some of the additions students frequently suggest are:

- persons: *mother, father, grandmother, teacher...*
- places: *my home, my school...*
- other more reflective: *my thoughts, my actions...*

A person in my life

For this activity I would like to suggest a visit to:
www.authorsintheclassroom.com
where there are specific suggestions as well as examples of books created by teachers, parents and students on this topic.

The Joy of Traditions

Festive gatherings are very special for Latino people. They offer an opportunity to share meals and music, two very important cultural elements, but above all they are an occasion to get together with family and friends. As a multicultural educator I believe that cultural celebrations must go "beyond heroes and holidays," yet I also acknowledge the importance of celebrations and the memories they create. And since in the Latino tradition festivities are usually intergenerational, shared by members of the extended family of all ages, which includes close friends, this represents an important cultural value, the appreciation of the extended family.

THE YEARLY MIRACLE OF CHRISTMASTIME

Although I grew up in a highly spiritual family that did not practice institutionalized religion and was rather critical of it, the celebration of Christmas was one of the highlights of the year. If asked what they were celebrating, my parents would have responded that they were celebrating the magic of birth and of life, the spirit of peace and goodwill. The Baby Jesus was seen as a reminder of the gift of every child, and as we created elaborate nativity scenes, my sister, cousins, and I were often told about the anticipation and love with which our own births had been awaited.

One of the blessings of an extended family was our family friends. One special friend was a kind gentleman named Rafael Respall, who lived in Havana but always came to Camagüey to spend Christmas with us, his adopted family. On the photo he is with my loving aunt Mireya Lafuente.

Rafael was highly artistic. Using only scissors, glue, and a few flowering branches, his gifted hands could create complete worlds out of empty boxes, butcher and crepe paper. The nativity scenes he created included mountains with brooks and lakes, deserts with dunes made from the sand we collected at the beach every summer for this purpose, and date palms with trunks made from sturdy sticks and fronds of brown and green crepe paper.

Our contribution to the nativity scene was a collection of figurines that grew every year as we added more shepherds and lambs, donkeys and cows, and all sorts of fowl. The process of making these low-cost figures out of plaster, as an alternative for those who could not afford the fancier factory-made ones, is the theme of the story "Christmas for All" in **Under the Royal Palms** now also included in **Island Treasures**, or **Tesoros de mi isla.**

While nativity scenes, called *nacimientos* o *belenes*, are a traditional part of a Hispanic Christmas celebration, Christmas trees imported from the North had already become a popular feature during my childhood, and these two customs, the old and the new, coexisted in harmony. It was the joy of decorating our Christmas tree as a family that inspired **The Christmas Tree—El árbol de Navidad** illustrated by Terry Ybáñez.

This simple cumulative story shows each person in an extended family bringing an ornament for the tree. Each ornament is unique and reflects something about the person who brings it as an offering. Combined, the ornaments decorate the tree, just as the family is fulfilled by the presence of each individual member.

In Hispanic culture, the holiday season begins with the sound of *villancicos,* the traditional Christmas carols that announce the arrival of the holiday season.

Although *villancicos* are extraordinarily diverse, the most traditional center on the story of the Baby Jesus.

In ***Mamá Goose: A Latino Nursery Treasury***, illustrated by Maribel Suárez, there is a section devoted to *villancicos*. In ***Merry Navidad*** illustrated by Viví Escrivá, Isabel Campoy and I offer a collection of some of our most beloved *villancicos,* which we have organized in sections that tell the Nativity story. The sections include the journey to Bethlehem, the anticipation that permeates Christmas Eve, the shepherds' visit to the child, and the Adoration of the Magi or the Three Kings.

In the book we note that many of the *villancicos* are written as lullabies sung by Mary to the Baby Jesus. Many mothers have sung their own babies to sleep with these same melodies. We also remark that Joseph and Mary are often referred to with great familiarity, as if speaking of close, dear friends. There are even some *villancicos* that poke fun at Joseph, in a kind way— for example, pointing out that the mice in the barn have eaten holes in his pants.

Creating this collection has been a special joy, since it has given us an opportunity to remember our happy childhood days. The only difficulty was choosing from among so many carols that we would have loved to include!

Christmas is also an important aspect of the development of ***Love, Amalia*** published in Spanish as ***Con cariño, Amalia***. In this book the annual writing of Christmas cards is one the activities Amalia and her grandmother share and it becomes an important way for her to get to know about the relatives who live outside the United States.

In ***My Name is María Isabel***, published in Spanish as ***Me llamo María Isabel*** both Christmas and Hanukah play an important role as the story gets to its most poignant moment during the rehearsals for the Holidays pageant.

Honoring the rich cultural diversity of the United States, when Isabel and I developed the collection *Let's Celebrate*, in Spanish *Vamos a celebrar*, we included books on Christmas and the feast of the Three Wise Men, Hanukkah and Kwanzaa.

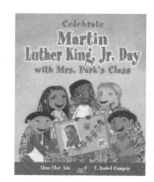

Teachers and Librarians' Ideas
If You Celebrated Christmas, Hanukah or Kwanzaa with Us at Our Home

Following our suggestion to teachers to create their own authentic books to share with their students, a teacher in Texas was inspired to write a book about her own Christmas celebrations as a child with the title "If You Celebrated Christmas with Us at Our Home". Creating a similar book of your own could inspire your students to write about what makes their holiday celebrations unique. What are the distinguishing characteristics of the way their family celebrates Christmas or other religious holidays? What are the sounds, the words, the smells, the activities? This kind of writing project encourages children to pay attention to details and specific nuances, while developing an appreciation for their own family and traditions.

Children's or Family's Own Anthologies
Nothing could be more rewarding than seeing this book become an invitation for children and/or families to create their own collections of *villancicos,* Christmas carols or traditional songs.

If a collective book is created, each child or family can contribute a favorite song and illustrate that page. It would be important to have both the names of the child and the contributing adults on the page, as well as their place of origin. When a family creates its own book, it may contain as many songs as the family remembers and loves.

PIÑATAS: WONDERS AND SURPRISES

Piñatas are frequently associated with Mexico, for their long-established tradition in connection with Christmas and the

Posadas. However, piñatas can be found in many Spanish-speaking countries, albeit with their own distinct styles.

In contrast to the Mexican tradition of breaking the piñata with a stick, in Cuba piñatas are opened by pulling on ribbons attached to a trapdoor. This allows the piñata to be reused several times, and thus they are often very elaborate. Many ribbons are attached to the piñata. While most are designed to simply fall off when the children tug on them, a few actually pull open the trapdoor. Often the ribbons have a little prize attached to the end.

No enterprise was too new or too difficult for my parents to undertake. In the story "Christmas for All" from **Under the Royal Palms**, included in **Island Treasures** or **Tesoros de mi isla**, I tell the story of how they bought a jewelry store. Soon they were not only selling jewelry and repairing watches, but were also offering all kinds of other objects for sale, some of which like the Christmas figurines, they made themselves.

So it was not surprising my mother decided she would make piñatas to sell. She displayed some in the store windows: A duckling, for which we cut huge amounts of bright yellow feathers from crepe paper and a rocking horse. There was no limit to my mother's imagination, it was fascinating to see her create something out of nothing. She would start with a small drawing that she would transfer onto a large poster board, using a grid of squares to guide the enlargement process. Next it was a matter of cutting two identical poster boards for the sides of the piñata and connecting them with more poster board to create the ample body that would be filled with treats. The whole artifact was then covered with endless pieces of crepe paper, which it was my job to cut until I had blisters on my thumb. The charm came from the details my mother added: wings, a beak, and eyes for the duckling, a saddle and reins for the rocking horse. I remember in particular a piñata in the shape of a ship. It was filled with many details, including faces that we had cut out of magazines and pasted to look out from multiple portholes.

When my parents became involved in a project to build low-cost houses, my mother passed the piñata-making project on to a friend who continued to exhibit her samples at the store, where my mother took orders for her. The friend was a seamstress and very imaginative. Once, she dressed her own daughter as a piñata for her birthday—all in pink, with a double-layered tutu skirt that contained all the candy. The girl stood up on a high table while all the guests pulled on the ribbons to create the shower of candy. The Cuban love for costumes, masquerades, and lavish parties led many mothers to order similar "piñata dresses" for their daughters. They were indeed amazing, although I wonder whether the birthday girls had much fun wearing them!

I cherish memories of two very special piñatas. The first was a beautiful rose made for my surprise birthday party when I was in second grade. We were still living in the old Quinta Simoni, and the piñata in the shape of a large rose was hung from the tall archway between the living room and the library.

My mother's aunts and cousins must have worked for hours to string the long decorative chains of palm tree seeds that framed the archway. I had never seen the green palm seeds used for this purpose before, and although it may have been an old tradition, I have not seen it since. The piñata was so high up that even though the ribbons were very long; many parents had to lift their young children upon their shoulders to reach them. All of this added to the glory of the day.

Arch at La Quinta Simoni, characteristic of
Camaguey's colonial architecture

My second cherished piñata was a duckling I made in Perú for Rosalma's birthday. While I was never good at crafting things, I was determined to have my children experience the joy of a piñata, which at the time were not common in Lima. Following cautiously the steps that I remembered seeing my mother take, I came up with a pleasant-looking duckling that not only delighted Rosalma and the children who attended her birthday party but also helped celebrate many other occasions, as I kept passing it on to friends for their own children's parties.

The mother who was so determined to re-create some of her childhood joys for her own children later became the model for the mother in *The Kite,* from the collection *Stories the Year 'Round* or *Cuentos para todo el año.* The object she creates is

not a piñata but a kite, another special memory from my childhood. However, the energy to persist and succeed, in spite of many trials, was actually inspired by my earlier efforts to create piñatas for my children.

When we moved to the United States, I stopped making piñatas since I could now obtain beautiful Mexican ones. I recall various occasions when I traveled a long

distance with a piñata, bringing one back from a border town or from a trip to Mexico. One green parrot piñata lived with us for many years because my son Miguel, for whom it was intended, refused to have it broken open. This green parrot which Miguel kept in his room until he was in his teens brought back many memories of the parrot my great-grandmother had kept on a perch in his kitchen and eventually inspired the bilingual picture book *I Want to Help/Quiero ayudar.*

With all those piñatas in my background, it was natural that a piñata would appear in one of my stories. Young Elena experiences both the gift of generosity and the joy of reciprocity in *The Empty Piñata*, in Spanish *La piñata vacía*, illustrated by Viví Escrivá. Suni Paz has created a beautiful musical rendition of this story re-written by me in verse, for that purpose. It can be found in her voice in the CD *Cuentos para todo el año* (Santillana/Vista Higher Learning).

Recently, Isabel Campoy had the amazing idea of celebrating my 80th birthday at the Quinta Simoni, the house where I was born. My dear cousin Noris Romero Labrada decided we should have a piñata. She and her husband created a very large piñata, made of wood, a faithful copy of the Quinta Simoni. For the children attending the celebration it was, as piñatas are meant to be, a moment of joy... for me this second piñata in my beloved childhood home a magic instance, a coming full circle in the confirmation of the highest of all values, the strength of family.

You can see a moment of the birthday celebration and the breaking of that piñata in YOU TUBE, search for:
Alma Flor Ada Lafuente celebra sus 80 en Camaguey

Teachers and Librarians' Ideas

There are many activities that can be carried out around the theme of piñatas. Some have a more physical dimension, while others emphasize the values illustrated in the story. These various activities can include:

1. Making piñatas
2. Filling and breaking open a piñata
3. Making a mural display in the shape of a piñata with the photos of all the children and their birthdates
4. Using a real piñata or other container as a receptacle for index cards on which each

5. student writes a positive thought or a helpful wish. Then each child can draw an index card from the "piñata" and read it aloud to the class.

OTHER CELEBRATIONS

Living in the United States with my four children, and later my nine grandchildren, new celebrations became important for us. Halloween is always a time of fun and my children enjoyed it to the fullest, including turning our own home into a mystery house which I found as a great surprise when I returned home from work.

But this is too long a story to share here. Since the wonderful

things they came up with as they were growing up deserve to be told I have created a book, *Once There Were Four Children* which I printed in a limited edition as a Christmas gift for my grandchildren, so they would learn much about the lives of their fathers and aunt when they were growing up. I intend to make a more formal edition that will be available through Mariposa Transformative Education.

Halloween as well as other celebrations became an inspiration for some of the titles of *Cuentos para todo el año* published also as *Stories the Year 'round* (Santillana, 1993).

What are Ghosts Afraid Of? or *El susto de los fantasmas,* the title corresponding to October in this series, was born out of one of those questions my children and I enjoyed posing to each other. Once, while getting ready for Halloween one of the children said something like: "I wonder what the ghosts think of all this?"

That interesting question remained unanswered at the time, but one day served as inspiration for this story where two friendly ghosts, to avoid the rain in a stormy Halloween night, take refuge at the home of children who are coming from treat or tricking.

Halloween as well as Day of the Death are featured in the twelve books series described later, *Stories to Celebrate / Cuentos para celebrar* (Alfaguara 2006), which combine stories and non-fiction information about celebrations that take place in the United States.

Respect for Farmworkers

My first introduction to *campesinos migrantes,* the migrant farmworkers who live and work in the United States, was in 1973, when I learned about their ongoing struggle for justice and their dream of providing their children with a good education. My children and I had moved from Georgia to Michigan where I was to teach at Mercy College in Detroit, and my growing awareness led me to organize a number of activities at the college and in the community.

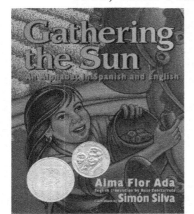

At that time, as I organized at the college some events to support the Farm-Workers efforts to secure just treatment, I had the opportunity to meet several families of *campesinos,* and my admiration and respect for them has continued to grow through the years. Soon after my arrival in California, I became involved in family projects for migrant parents, first in Half-Moon Bay and shortly afterward in Pájaro Valley. I have written extensively about the *Literatura infantil project,* a family literacy program at Pájaro Valley centered on children's literature (1988, 1997). I also included some of this information in my book *A Magical Encounter: Latino Literature in the Classroom* (2004, 2016).
My daughter, Rosalma Zubizarreta has developed a manual to guide anyone interested in developing programs based on the same principles.

Dick Keis, who successfully used the model to create a similar program with farmworkers families in Oregon, has also written about his project and other similar ones (2002a, 2002b). At the University of San Francisco, Karen Kaiser completed a doctoral dissertation analyzing several programs of this nature. Her dissertation is a good source of information on family literacy programs centered on children's literature.

The *Literatura infantil* project at Pájaro Unified School District led to speaking to other groups of migrant parents throughout California and Texas. After the meetings I was frequently motivated to write poetry in Spanish, inspired by their lives. I never thought about publishing them until Kendra Marcus from Bookstop Literary Agency showed them to Susan Pearson at Lothrop. This led to the idea of organizing the poems into an ABC book and having the book illustrated by Simón Silva.

The opportunity to create a book with Simon's powerful art led to considerable modifications. In order to have English and Spanish versions of the poems and to allow sufficient space for Simon's paintings, the texts were substantially shortened. The poems were also simplified to accord with Susan's sense of what was appropriate for a children's book.

This was the birth of *Gathering the Sun* and the CD of the same name, with music and voice by Suni Paz.

While I tell children truthfully that, as an author, I love all of my books equally, it is also true that *Gathering the Sun* is one of the books that has given me the greatest satisfaction. This is in part because of its beauty, but especially so due to the responses I continuously receive from the readers.

People ask me to autograph this book for newborn children, for birthday gifts, for First Communion and Quinceañeras presents, and for graduations and anniversaries. I have dedicated it to unborn children and to grandparents. Over and over, people speak of seeing themselves and their families in the book and of the significance of having their lives and their work be honored and valued.

With this book I have witnessed repeatedly the power that a book has to affirm one's own experience. In our classist society, people are often judged by their income and by the work they do. As a result, students from farmworkers families are often reluctant to acknowledge their parents' work. But when they see *Gathering the Sun* and hear that it was created to honor their families and express gratitude for their work, a major shift in attitude happens. Of course, I do not believe that creating books that celebrate working people is enough to change their living conditions, but I do believe strongly in the power of words, ideas, and images as the seeds of social transformation.

Gathering the Sun received the Once upon a World Award from the Simon Wiesenthal Center at the Museum of Tolerance in Los Angeles. This museum seeks to educate young people about how we can all learn to respect one another as human beings, regardless of the differences we may have among us. It has been extremely meaningful for me to be connected in this way with the valuable work of this outstanding museum.

Teachers and Librarians' ideas

Sharing Other Books and Texts

Reading other books and texts about farmworkers' experiences offers additional opportunities to explore this theme. There are several fine texts on this subject by a variety of authors, and there is still a need for more.

Acknowledging how hard it can be to work the fields and describing how a parent can draw strength from their love for their children is the essence of *My Mother Plants Strawberries* in Spanish *Mi mamá siembra fresas,* illustrated by Larry Ramond.

The warm, realistic illustrations in this book may feel a bit pale in comparison to the muralist brilliance of Simón Silva's art. Yet teachers who introduce this oversized book to young children mention that their students enjoy the story and connect with the joy that mother and daughter feel at being reunited after a long day's work.

In honor of farmworkers' contributions to society, I have co-authored two biographies with Isabel Campoy: "Luis Valdés" in *Voices* (Spanish version *Voces)* and "César Chávez" in *Paths* (Spanish version *Caminos),* both part of the collection *Gateways to the Sun / Puertas al Sol.* In addition, 'Teatro Campesino. ¡Que florezca la luz!" ("Farm Workers' Theatre. May the light bloom!") is included in *Imágenes del pasado* (Images from the past) 1997.

The book *El vuelo de los colibríes* (Laredo, 2016) tells the story of three generations of a Mexican family, the pain of leaving behind what they knew and cherished, the difficulties to come to the United States, and the value of the memories they preserve and share.

Dramatization of *Gathering the Sun*

High school students in San Diego were invited to create a dramatic performance using the songs that Suni Paz has created from the poems in *Gathering the Sun.* Directed by the talented educator Sylvia Dorta Duque de Reyes, the students painted a striking backdrop for the stage, inspired by illustrations from the book. Following the songs played from the CD, students created a magnificent choreography to accompany the words. For the poem "Lettuce," the students, dressed as farmworkers in the fields, had arranged stacks of empty lettuce boxes on the stage as props. Following a beautifully choreographed pattern, they threw heads of lettuce to each other across the stage and packed them in the boxes, all to the rhythm of the music. One of the most moving scenes was of César Chávez walking slowly toward the sunset.

Expanding on the Poem "*Orgullo / Pride*"

"Orgullo/Pride" is one of the best-loved poems/songs from the

book and CD. I have had the pleasure of seeing elementary teachers use this poem as an open-ended structure.

The poem names different things of which we are proud—our family, our mother tongue, our culture, our country of origin—and teachers have encouraged students to add one thing or person (my home, my school, my aunt, my teacher, my friends ...) that they would like to recognize as a source of personal pride.

The students' contributions are then used to create additional lines for the poem or song.

Interviews

Students can interview someone who has worked as a farmworker to learn firsthand about their experiences.

This activity may be easier to carry out in a farm workers community. If students have relatives or neighbors who work in the fields, this is a good opportunity to appreciate the value of their work and to encourage students to honor their families as hard-work heroes.

Biographies of known and unknown figures

Students can write a biography of important figures within the farm working community, based on written information.

They can choose to write about César Chávez, Dolores Huertas, Luis Valdés, Simón Silva, or another well-known person from the farm workers community.

Or, if they know firsthand someone who has labored as a farmworker, they can choose to write the biography of a previously unsung hero.

Examples of writing about "A Person in My Life" can be found in the website: www.authorsintheclassroom.com

Books about the Work in the Fields

Using her camera to document the grape harvesting, Ellen Gillham, a teacher in Exeter, California, created a beautiful self-published book, *A Morning in the Grape Fields,* in collaboration with one of her students, nine-year-old Jeannette Castillo.

The striking photographs show the farmworkers selecting the table grapes, leaving the rest of the fruit on the vines to be picked later for juice, and carefully picking and packaging and loading the boxes of grapes.

Books like this can support children and parents in taking pride in their own work, while helping others learn more about the complexity and dedication that is involved.

Kinder Caminata to Honor César Chávez

It was deeply satisfying to have *Gathering the Sun* be part of a very special project, the Kinder Caminata in Redwood City, California. This was a walk for all kindergarten students in the tradition of the *marchas* or caminatas of César Chávez.

The purpose was twofold: to help children learn about César Chávez and the farmworkers' struggle and to have them walk to a nearby college so that they could begin to see themselves, from a very young age, as future college students. Each child was given a copy of *Gathering the Sun* as an inspiration for their ongoing journey.

Parents as Authors

Inviting parents and family members to become authors is central to the work described in *Authors in the Classroom: A Transformative Education Process.* Listening to the voices of migrant farmworkers and recording their words has been a deeply moving and educational experience for me, and I am grateful that other programs have begun to publish these voices as well. These are a few examples from the book *Corazón: Fuente de aguas puras / Heart: Fountain of Pristine Waters* (1999) developed in the Family Literacy Program Libros y Familias directed by Richard Keis in Independence, Oregon, offers a taste of the wisdom of these voices. María Ramirez writes in Spanish, with the elegance of a haiku:

Agua blanca y cristalina   *Water, white and crystalline*
te veo pasar   *I see you stream by*
sin saber a dónde vas.   *without knowing where you go.*

Aracely Saavedra honors her father's memory as she writes:

Te miré y admiré
cuando levantabas la tierra
como se levanta el sol de la mañana
dando vida a un nuevo día.

> *I watched and admired you*
> *as you turned over the soil*
> *as the morning sun rises*
> *bringing a new day to life.*

For examples of books written by parents, teachers and students in multiple sites, visit:

www.authorsintheclassroom.com

Celebration of Diversity

Nature has always been a great teacher for me. The resilience of a blade of grass growing tenaciously through the cracks in the pavement and the fallen tree trunk that is still sprouting branches have inspired my own endurance and perseverance, just as the colors of the sunrise have spoken to me of subtlety and delicacy. But no lesson has been more important than the assurance that we live on a planet whose essence is diversity.

If we had to choose a single word to describe our planet, it seems to me that the one most appropriate would be "diverse." On our planet, there is not "a" single kind of tree, there are oaks and palm trees, redwoods and sequoias, elms and maples—all of them trees, and yet so different from one another. There is not "a" single type of flower, but instead a world full of jasmine and roses, dahlias and daisies, frangipani and violets. Fruit is not "a" fruit, but rather an apple or a mango, a pear or a coconut. And is it really "a" fish that we see when we visit the aquarium? Or is it a white shark ... or a manta ray ... or...? Just think of the myriad of birds and bugs, each unique, all coexisting! Nature offers us a daily message of harmony in diversity; yet all too frequently, human beings have tried to impose homogeneity as the formula for coexistence.

FRIENDSHIP IN DIVERSITY: THE JOY OF LIFE

Because of my appreciation for this subject, it is not surprising that the theme of celebrating diversity in various ways permeates my writing, as in *Friend Frog,* illustrated by Lori Lohstoeter.

This is one of my favorite books to share with audiences because I like to tell people how much I see myself as the shy Field Mouse who goes out in search of a friend. As Field Mouse, I have had the opportunity to meet many extraordinary people for whom I feel great admiration in much the same way that Field Mouse admired Frog. I often feel that I cannot do the many things that my talented artist and musician friends can do, just as Field Mouse could not leap or hop, croak or swim, as Frog did. Yet, like Field Mouse, I hope to nonetheless be a good friend.

There is a wonderful anecdote related to the illustrations for *Friend Frog* that children always enjoy hearing. After the book was published, the editor told me that when she first proposed the project to illustrator Lori Lohstoeter, Lori was fascinated by the idea of illustrating a story about a frog. But when she heard that the story also involved a field mouse, she did not want to take on the project simply because she did not like mice of any sort.

In the end, Lori decided that she liked the story well enough to do the illustrations, but she felt she needed more experience in order to do justice to the assignment. So she went to a pet shop and bought a mouse, a cage, and all the other necessary equipment and supplies—but only after the shop owner agreed that she would be able to return the mouse once she finished her drawings. Lori did not want to keep the mouse a day longer than was absolutely necessary!

With the mouse as a live model, Lori created wonderful illustrations for the book. When she returned to the pet shop for more supplies, the pet shop owner asked her about her progress. Lori was happy to announce that the artwork was finished, but when the owner asked her when she would be bringing back the mouse, Lori was surprised: how could anyone think she would be willing to give away her beloved pet?

Lori's story is an illustration of how we learn to love that which we truly get to know. This is also the theme of the book *Friends*, a story with an interesting origin. During a one-day workshop for teachers, I asserted that all subjects could be made more appealing by means of a story and that all subjects could be approached from a critical and transformative perspective. A kindergarten teacher challenged me by asking how colors, sizes, and geometrical shapes could be taught in this manner. While I did not have a ready answer, I promised her that I would consider her question.

The lunch break gave me time to open myself to the question. How might the simple concepts of colors, sizes, and geometrical shapes become an opportunity for learning about critical thinking? And that is the story of how *Friends* was born.

Friends (in Spanish *Amigos),* illustrated by Barry Koch, was my

first children's book published in the United States. At the time, Santillana marketed their materials almost exclusively to schools, so the book has not become widely known outside of educational circles, although it has been constantly reprinted and has remained in print for over 25 years. I dream that someday this little book will receive the recognition it deserves, and be published in a new edition with a new design and new illustrations. Unfortunately, the book's success has been its own worst enemy. It is hard to convince someone about the need for a new edition when the old one is selling so well!

For several years before the book was published, I would tell the story in the classrooms I visited about a town where the squares, who lived in square houses with square windows and doors, taught their small square children to not play with rectangles. The squares thought the rectangles were strange because two of their sides were longer than the other two. In turn, the rectangles, who lived in rectangular buildings with rectangular doors and windows, told their little ones to not play with triangles, who only had three sides. The circles, who lived in circular houses on the other side of the railroad tracks, told their young circles to not play with any squares, rectangles, or triangles, as the other shapes would not like them. Until one day, two little circles took a roll into town and helped everyone discover how much more fun they could have together!

One source of enormous gladness is that this book has been translated into Haitian Creole as *Zanmi* for the Haitian population living in the United States.

Since the theme of diversity is so important to me, it can be found as a subtext in many of my books, even in ones that may have a different main theme.

In *A Surprise for Mother Rabbit* (in Spanish *La sorpresa de Mamá Coneja),* illustrated by Viví Escrivá, Mother Rabbit's joy, when her bunnies help with the task of gathering eggs for Easter, is heightened by the fact that each of them returns with an egg from a different bird.

The Malachite Palace, illustrated by Leonid Gore, is essentially a story about friendship and self-determination. Yet at one point in the story, the songbird the princess has freed returns to the palace, to the old cage that has now been changed into a bird feeder. The songbird does not return alone, but is accompanied by many birds of different kinds: blue jays, cardinals, chickadees.... Here again, harmony in diversity is present, even if in this case it demands a degree of poetic license. As a bird lover, I know all too well that blue jays are not very keen on sharing a bird feeder, not even with another jay!

In other books, the joy of diversity is indeed the principal theme. This is the case of the book *In the Cow's Backyard* or *La hamaca de la vaca*, illustrated by Viví Escrivá. One summer afternoon, a series of female animals appears in the cow's backyard. As each one arrives, she is invited by the ant, who was the first to discover the hammock, to join the others as they all lounge in the hammock. When Mother Elephant appears, the last of the animals to arrive, the ant still does not hesitate to say, "Come join us!"

When I tell the story, I enjoy asking children to ponder what will happen if Mother Elephant indeed accepts the invitation. Will the hammock be able to hold such an animal? Will the branches break? And I enjoy even more seeing their delight as I show them the last picture spread: the animals are still on the hammock, which now hangs beneath a canopy on Mother Elephant's back. ("When there's goodwill, there's always a way for one more friend to squeeze in and play! ")

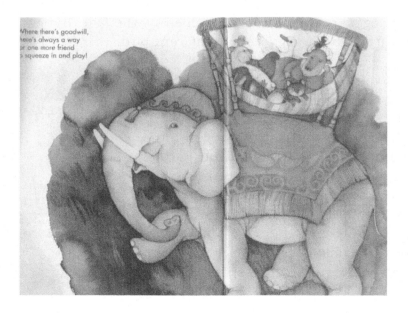

Another cumulative book that illustrates friendship among diverse characters is: *Strange Visitors* (in Spanish *Una extraña visita),* illustrated by Viví Escrivá. The story follows the days of one week. Each day, new animals appear playing different instruments: On Monday, a cricket saws a tune on a fiddle; on Tuesday, two cows are shaking maracas. . . . Finally, on Sunday, the animals are joined by the Seven Dwarves playing fourteen-handed piano. And the *true jarana,* or merrymaking, begins.

Needless to say, when I was playing with rhymes and visual images—*armadillos tocando platillos* and *cigarras tocando guitarras*—I was not making a conscious effort to celebrate diversity, just as this was not my explicit intention in some of my earlier books. Yet my experience has been that when something is held very dearly in one's soul, it will find a way to manifest. And I am very happy to know that teachers are intentionally using these books as a way to encourage a greater appreciation for diversity in their students.

Teachers and Librarians' Ideas

Children's Own ABC Books

Too often there is a tendency for students to always stay with the same group of friends. It can be helpful to create situations that allow students to experience themselves as part of different groupings. One simple way to do so, while at the same time reinforcing literacy skills, is to create a classroom ABC book where children are grouped according to the letters of their names.

The idea is to photograph all of the children whose names begin with the same letter of the alphabet as a group. This photograph is then used to illustrate the page that corresponds to that letter.

Each child will appear once in the book, in a group with others with whom he or she may or may not have been grouped before.

A variation on this theme is to create the groups according to the final letter of each person's name. Most likely the groups that are formed will be very different from the first ones.

Alternatively, one could make a book in which the children appear in several groups, one for each of the different letters in their name. As the children group and regroup themselves in different ways and photographs are taken of the various groups, this provides an opportunity for understanding that in life we end up forming part of many different kinds of groups, and we need to learn to interact with many different people.

Diversity and Freedom

A deeper examination of the value of diversity and the destructive forces that can be unleashed in the name of homogeneity is at the core of *El reino de la geometría* [The kingdom of geometry]. José Ramón Sánchez, who has received multiple national awards in Spain, his native country, accepted Sam Laredo's invitation to illustrate this fantasy. Of course, as with any good fantasy, this story also has implications for the real world.

In the kingdom of geometry, life followed its usual course, some days were better than others. Squares and triangles, rectangles and diamonds, all lived peacefully together... until one day, King Square VII ascended the throne. Very soon after his coronation, his advisors convinced him that a square was unquestionably the perfect figure, with four sides of equal length and four angles of equal value. This led to major changes throughout the kingdom. The palace was rebuilt with only square-shaped rooms, windows, and doors. All of those who were not squares were removed from service in  the palace. Later, they were held captive within the city walls, with only the squares being allowed free entry and exit through the city's gates.

These harsh conditions led Rose, a young square, to attempt to free her friend Violet, a triangle. Rose suggested that Violet and her brother could join together to disguise themselves as a square and thus find a way to escape the city. Yet Violet refuses to flee, as she does not want to leave anyone behind. Then Rose ends up inventing tangrams that will allow all the shapes to group themselves taking the shape of a square and escape to begin life anew in another land where bad days will be followed by better ones.

The degree to which even very young children are able to appreciate this book has strengthened my belief in metaphors and symbols as helpful avenues for exploring harsh realities and for generating creative responses to difficult conditions. The book is in the process of being reissued by Vista Higher Learning.

Teachers and Librarians' Ideas

The Children's Own Kingdom

Some teachers have used this book as an invitation for children to create their own worlds of peace and harmony, elaborating scenes with geometrical figures to represent diverse characters.

Others, have suggested children use various geometrical shapes to create images that represent the qualities that they would like to see prevail in their own kingdoms, such as friendship, love, caring for animals and plants, etc.

Friends Are...

Since it was her friendship with Violet, the little triangle, that inspired Rose to search for a way to free her, teachers have often invited children to create their books about friendship as a follow-up to the reading. In the case of younger children, teachers have invited their students to write a sentence that tells what friends do and don't do. I have seen charming books that include, in addition to more obvious comments such as "Friends play together" and "Friends talk to each other," other telling statements such as "Friends do not pull each other's hair," "Friends do not kick each other," and "Friends share their snacks with each other."

Involving the Families

By encouraging students to talk to their parents about friendship, teachers and librarians can promote meaningful conversation at home, a basic activity for students' growth that strongly supports academic achievement.

Children can ask their parents:
- Who were your friends when you were my age?
- What did you enjoy doing together?
- Did you ever quarrel? How did you make up?
- Did you ever get into trouble?
- What did you enjoy most about your friendship?"

The conversation can also include more contemporary experiences. Children might ask their parents:
- What is friendship?
- What would you do for a friend?
- What would a friend do for you?
- What do you value most in friendship?"

Back in the classroom, teachers can invite students to use what they have learned to write their own books, starring their parents as protagonists.

Relating The Little Blue Square, Friends and El reino de la geometría

These three books all have geometrical characters and each one carries a message. Have children identify the messages:

The bilingual book **The Little Blue Square / El cuadradito azul** celebrates each one's identity. It shows that with interest and practice one can learn and become what one wishes to be.

Friends and **Amigos** shows how prejudice is damaging. The story celebrates friendship and suggests that by interacting with people who may look externally different one can discover they may have much in common with us.

El reino de la geometría denounces the dangers of tyranny created by imposing only one way of being, thinking, and acting.

The World of Nature

GROWING UP IN NATURE

The Quinta Simoni where I was born and raised is acknowledged today in Cuban tourist guides as one of the first and most interesting suburban haciendas or "quintas" on the island. The Simoni family came originally from Italy, and the large house they built, with flat roof and wide porch with open arches on three sides, is a beautiful example of neoclassical architecture not typical to Cuba, where the prevalent Colonial style is the Spanish style of tile roofs

The hacienda was a multifaceted enterprise. The Simonis established a production brickyard next to the Tinima River so that they could use the excellent red clay from the riverbank to make the bricks and tiles for the house. They also created a tannery to tan hides. These provided leather for making the seats and backs of chairs, for making saddles, boots and shoes, and for every other sort of leather artifact.

Like many wealthy nineteenth-century families, the Simonis were fascinated by the botanical diversity that existed in different parts of the world, and they created their own botanical wonderland. Exotic trees, shrubs, and plants from different countries surrounded the house and blossomed in the extensive gardens and in the greenhouse. By the time I was born, only a few remnants of the old grandeur of the hacienda could be seen in the house and farm. But many of the trees still stood on the grounds, and while many of the plants had grown wild, they still offered a world of diversity to my young eyes. It was not until many years later that I learned why there were so many strange plants around my house that did not seem to grow anywhere else.

We were a rather unique family: my bohemian, freethinking grandfather was a sensitive poet and passionate defender of social causes, while my grandmother was a practical feminist who saw to it that the various social justice projects they undertook were carried through to completion. I grew up with a clear sense that we were very different from the tightly bound society around us with its rigid social classes and unquestioning loyalty to the Catholic Church. Our own home did not resemble any other, and its uniqueness was a paradise to me.

In this latter part of my life I have been publishing books about my family, some collecting their own writings, others sharing what I know about them. One of them, *Casa de grandes arcos: dos familias luminosas. 2ds edición* is dedicated to the Quinta Simoni and the two families Simoni-Argilagos and Lafuente-Salvador who contributed to its history.

It was also fortunate for me that my young parents, who cared for me very much, had their own full and rewarding lives. They did not center their lives on me or expect me to live out their unfulfilled dreams. They accepted me and loved me for who I was, and I was left with a great deal of freedom to discover the world around me.

My earliest years were mostly spent outdoors. During the rainy tropical storms, I could stay inside on our open porches and continue to experience the wonders of nature. Even indoors, the high ceilings and vast rooms offered a sense of freedom. Probably as a result of all this freedom, I found it very difficult to go to school and remain indoors. As I shared earlier, I have distinct memories of kindergarten and feeling that the ceiling was caving in on me. While our class must have been held in a regular-sized room, and probably even been large one, I still had a terrible sense of claustrophobia.

Until we moved to the city when I was about eight years old, I spent many hours exploring the open lands of the Quinta Simoni. The river Tínima that crossed it fascinated me. It was easy to watch cranes fishing in the shallow waters, their white feathers a bright contrast to the deep green of the vegetation along the riverbanks. When I moved closer to the water, I could see various fish of all sizes, including some large *biajacas.* Closer to the surface, the tadpoles, or *renacuajos,* moved incessantly. I loved to observe the skittish turtles and learned to be extremely quiet when approaching, since at the slightest noise they would jump into the water from the rocks where they basked under the sun.

While my enthusiasm for nature can be found to a greater or lesser degree in almost any of my books, it is a central theme in some stories, and I will mention a few of those here. Several of the titles in the twelve-book collection *Stones the Year 'Round* or *Cuentos para todo el año*, illustrated by Viví Escrivá, focus on an aspect of nature.

THE WONDERS OF A SEED

The extraordinary process by which a seed grows into a plant,

which amazed me so much as a child, is the main subject of the book *After the Storm*, in Spanish *Después de la tormenta.* Several seeds fall from a sunflower plant to encounter their different destinies. Most of them end up as breakfast and lunch for the chipmunks and the squirrels. But one seed, with the help of wind, rain, earth, and sun, will grow up to become a new plant.

Another book, published by Hampton-Brown, now National Geographic Cengage, **Just One Seed,** in Spanish **Una semilla nada más**, illustrated by Frank Remkiewicz tells the story of a boy who planted a seed:. The young boy is teased by everyone in his family for having planted just one seed, yet he remains confident that it is just a matter of time. The beautiful sunflower that eventually springs up gives him plenty of new seeds to share with others. This young child could be any one of my three sons, who all share a love for growing things as well as the capacity for great generosity.

THE WONDERS IN AN EGG

My extraordinary grandmother Lola, who found time to be a teacher and a principal while still keeping up a farm, was the source of many blessings in my life. One of his gifts was the joy of living alongside a large company of fowl. She kept a large number of hens that roamed among the trees and bushes on a wide area of land enclosed by chicken wire. The hens moved about freely, looking for worms and seeds, sleeping on the lower branches of the bushes. While nesting, they could take shelter in a large chicken coop. We ground corn for their feed, and twice a day, my grandmother and I would walk into the chicken pen with our aprons filled with ground corn. In an instant, we would find ourselves surrounded by a sea of squawking feathered creatures.

One of the scariest moments of my childhood was the time I

tossed all my grain around me in a circle, leaving me no space for retreat. Another scary moment was the time I accidentally attracted the wrath of the flock of geese who roamed in total freedom on our land. The geese were blocking my path, and I decided to try to pass by them anyway. They tore my small dress to tatters, although, fortunately, I escaped unharmed.

The most magnificent of all the birds were the peacocks. My grandmother loved their beauty and was always happy to see them.

My grandmother feeding her chicken

They nested atop the large masonry arch by the river, but but visited the house frequently. At lunchtime they perched on the beam above the French doors that opened from the dining room onto the garden. Later in the day they would walk grandly by the kitchen to receive whatever scraps had been saved for them: vegetables, fruit rinds, rice, or beans. Years later, when I read the poetry of Rubén Darío, I realized how much of my grandmother's taste for blue lamps and a garden filled with peacocks corresponded to the Modernist aesthetic as expressed in his remarkable verses.

One of the members of the feathered menagerie was a lame white duck who surprised us all by becoming my grandfather's pet. My grandfather Medardo was always lost in his books and papers, and I could not imagine him stopping to pet a dog or stroke a cat. However, he had a soft spot in his heart for this duck that hobbled after him around the house and stood by his side during meals. If my grandfather forgot to give him some bread, the duck would pull on the corner of the white starched tablecloth to catch his attention!

While my grandmother collected some of the hens' eggs for our own meals, she also frequently allowed the hens to sit on their eggs. Whenever a hen was nesting, I would wait impatiently for the extraordinary moment when the little chicks, wet and wobbly, would come out of their shells. Usually, I only got to see them after they had already dried out into fluffy balls, all ready to run around. But there were a few times that I had the opportunity to observe my father's efforts to get an egg to hatch  that had been left behind in the nest after most of the other ones had hatched. He would cover the egg with warm ashes from the kitchen stove and monitor it frequently. What a moment of joy it was when the egg started to make slight movements and the chick's beak began to break through the shell!

The wonder of eggs was not limited to chickens and other fowl; there were many other kinds of eggs in my childhood world. One of my fantasies was to see a lizard hatch. I would search through the garden for lizard eggs—small, white ovals whose softness fascinated me. I collected all the ones I could find and placed them beneath the ferns in the old stone fountain that my grandmother had turned into a planter. There I would sit for the longest time, hoping that at least one of the eggs would hatch. Unquestionably they did, because I would eventually find the collapsed shells, with the small opening at one end, that the lizards had left behind; but I never managed to be there at the precise moment when one of the little lizards crawled out.

My fascination with lizards, along with my desire to celebrate the wondrous moment when a chick emerges from an egg, inspired two books whose main character is based on my grandson Daniel Zubizarreta, a very kind and courageous young boy.

The editor agreed to give Daniel's photo to G. Brian Karas, the book's illustrator, so that his illustrations might resemble the real Daniel. I was delighted to see that the illustrator was able to capture the image and character of my wonderful grandson!

Daniel's Pet depicts the joy of having a chick for a pet. In ***Daniel's Mystery Egg,*** a young boy finds an egg, and his friends make all kinds of wild predictions about what kind of creature might emerge from the shell. But instead of the ostrich, the crocodile, or the dragon that his friends had imagined, it is a beautiful green lizard that comes out, much to Daniel's delight.

The desire to share my sense of wonder at what an egg may hide also led me to create another book. First printed in 1990 it has remained in print after numerous reprintings: ***Who's Hatching Here?*** in Spanish ***¿Quién nacerá aquí?***

This story invites children to guess who might hatch from the eggs that are magnificently depicted by Viví Escrivá. Will it be mosquitoes, butterflies, lizards, crocodiles, or snakes? Viví's wonderful art contributes to make this book a favorite. I have visited many classrooms where teachers had used the art from the Big Book edition to decorate their walls.

Years later I came across a similar idea in Ruth Heller's *Chickens Are Not the Only Ones,* which I had the pleasure of translating into Spanish.

baby chicks

mariposas

mosquitos

My own sense of wonder toward the natural world was later enhanced as my children experienced their own awakenings to nature's mysteries. When we lived in Lima, Perú, where my three older children were born, we had a *ñorbo* vine that climbed along the front wall of our house to the window of my small office on the second floor. A particular kind of butterfly is attracted to the *ñorbo* where it deposits its eggs. The larvae will later feed on the leaves of the vine, and finally the chrysalis will hang from the branches with total mimetic resemblance to a dead *ñorbo* leaf.

The children and I spent many hours watching as a butterfly, gently perched upon a leaf, would lift the back part of her body to deposit her tiny yellow eggs, one by one, in perfect rows that covered the entire bottom surface of the leaf. We would wait patiently for the day the eggs released dozens of tiny caterpillars that would spread over the vine, eating incessantly and growing day by day. From our watch at the window, we were able to see all the various stages of the process. A caterpillar hanging upside down from a leaf would secrete a dark, sticky substance that, after it hardened, formed a chrysalis shaped like a dry *ñorbo* leaf. Finally, days later, a butterfly would slowly emerge. At first, her folded wings were wet, and she was not able to reveal the magnificent being she had become until the sun had dried her wings enough for her to spread them wide and fly.

From 1965 to 1967, during my appointment as a scholar at the Radcliffe Institute at Harvard, we lived in Massachusetts. My oldest child, my daughter Rosalma, was four years old at the time, and she wrote about that experience in her first book *How a Caterpillar Becomes a Butterfly*. A kind friend, Rupert Ingram, who was then an editor at Addison-Wesley, was so taken by the realistic pictures that 4 year old Rosalma had drawn from memory, that he made a one-copy mock-up of the book for her. The kindness of a professional adult to a child that young has never be forgotten.

Years later, this firsthand experience with butterflies led to the writing of **A Rose with Wings** [in Spanish **Rosa alada**], illustrated by Viví Escrivá. A child needs to choose an animal to talk about in class. He wants to choose something special, something that is personally meaningful to him. While he is still thinking about what animal to choose, the other children in the class have already selected most of the animals that he would have chosen. Then he finds a small caterpillar and decides to keep it in a terrarium. By observing the caterpillar, he ends up witnessing the process of its metamorphosis into a butterfly!

Gabriel can only say
that his worm eats,
and eats some more.
It looks as if he's healthy—
but who knows if he's bored?

The child who had trouble deciding what to choose for a project was very familiar to me. It seemed to be what always happened to my own children whenever they were confronted with a major class project. They wanted it to be so special that days were spent in the choosing. This generated some anxiety, because at the end the time left to do the project was always shorter than we would have wished. And yet today, as I see the wonderful human beings all four have turned out to be, I wonder if the time taken in choosing may have been well spent. I am glad to have honored the undecided child who needed time to make up his mind and was rewarded with the glory of a butterfly!

No, I Don't Like to Eat Bugs

A very different experience is behind another book, *The Song of the Teeny-Tiny Mosquito* [in Spanish *El canto del mosquito*], illustrated by Viví Escrivá. Living by a river on a tropical island; mosquitoes were a very integral part of our life. They were particularly fierce in the first hours of the evening, and the large family of fruit bats that lived in the ceiling of the old Quinta Simoni was not sufficient to keep them at bay.

While most of the time the mosquitoes attached themselves to your arms and legs, sometimes they would fly blindly into your face. So, if you were speaking, there was the risk that a mosquito could fly right into your mouth. Usually, it was possible to spit out the mosquito, but, every once in a while, there was an unfortunate moment when a mosquito would fly all the way into your throat... a most horrible sensation, I can assure you!

Many years had passed since I had last sat with my family during the evenings on the porch of our small house by the river, built by my father, listening to my parents' stories. Yet one day a vivid memory came back to me of one of those mosquitoes who happened to fly into my throat. I felt a surge of pity for that unfortunate being, along with a sense of my own responsibility for having swallowed a mosquito. There was nothing I could do but turn the incident into a story, a very special story, one that would not only soften the memory but also save the mosquito.

Thus was born this cumulative tale where a mosquito is swallowed by a frog, who is in turn swallowed by a fish, who ends up being swallowed by a duck, who is then swallowed by a crocodile! But in contrast to what happened to the poor mosquito in real life, in the story the crocodile ends up with a tummy ache. He spits out the duck, who in turn spits out the fish, who spits out the frog, who of course spits out the mosquito who is able to happily continue his unending song.

There is a certain risk involved in telling children about the origins of some of my stories. In my video *Writing from the Heart*, in Spanish **_Escribiendo desde el corazón_**, I tell the story I have just shared with you.

Since they had watched the video, I was once greeted with great enthusiasm by a class of kindergartners who exclaimed as I came in, "Here she is, the lady who likes to eat bugs!"

BIRDS AND HELPERS

My son Miguel became an avid bird watcher at a young age and soon had a nice collection of books about birds. Observing the joy he took in identifying the various kinds of birds and their eggs was part of the inspiration behind A ***Surprise for Mother Rabbit*** [in Spanish ***La sorpresa de Mamá Coneja***], illustrated

by Viví Escrivá. In this story, eight bunnies decide to help their mother gather the eggs she will be coloring for Easter. Off they go on their search, and each of the bunnies ends up begging an egg from a different species of bird.

Of course, there are other influences that also shaped this story. I like to tell children that I wrote this book because my own four children have always been so helpful to me. So much so, that instead of having four bunnies in the book, I put in eight to show that each of my children has been twice as kind as one could expect.

The book is also a perfect example of how what we write reflects who we are. A first look at the book ***A Surprise for Mother Rabbit*** would seem to be an Easter book that celebrates both birds and their eggs and suggest it has not much to do with Latinos since the Easter bunny is not a traditional element of the Spanish-speaking world. Yet here in the United States, while we Latinos may continue to celebrate some of our own traditions for Easter, our children have adopted this endearing character. Moreover, this book shows the love found in a caring family where children appreciate their parents and want to help and surprise them, values fostered in Latino families.

Regardless of the outer form a book may take, the story will inevitably be imbued with the author's worldview and values. This book is also a celebration of diversity. When the bunnies show their mother the eggs they have gathered, her delight in their surprise is heightened by the fact that the eggs are all of different sizes and colors, thus reflecting the diversity of life around us.

As with most of my books, I did not set out to give a lesson on multiculturalism. Yet this story of bunnies and birds mirrors the rich diversity I constantly see around me, a diversity that clearly appears to me to be the defining feature of life on this planet. A diversity I have celebrated while teaching the importance of making our education multicultural and free of biases.

My son Miguel's love for birds, his compassion for any wounded animal, and his determination to be of help, are the experiences that inspired ***El pañuelo de seda*** [The silk scarf], illustrated by Viví Escrivá, the story of a young girl who sacrifices her most beloved possession in order to help a wounded bird. I chose to set the story in early California, since this historical period fascinates me and is one I hope to write more about it someday.

Teachers and Librarians' Ideas

After Reading "*The Song of the Teeny-Tiny Mosquito*"

A creative teacher had each of her students write and illustrate a page to create the most charming book: ¡*Oye, insecto!* (*Listen, Bug!*). Each child chose a different insect and addressed it directly.

After Reading "*El Pañuelo de Seda*" (The silk scarf)

I have seen a variety of responses from children to *El pañuelo de seda* [The silk scarf], and some of them have been very moving. In my office I have a pink papier máché plate with a beautifully painted scene from the book. I have seen numerous other paintings and mobiles inspired by this book, and many Spanish speaking children who read books in Spanish have mentioned in their letters that this is their favorite book.

One of the most moving moments in my career as a children's book author happened while I was visiting the Coral Way Elementary School in Miami, Florida, during the Miami International Book Fair. This extraordinary school has been a pioneer in bilingual education for many years. It is a school where all children, regardless of their home language background, become fully bilingual and biliterate in both English and Spanish.

My day-long visit was filled with wonderful expressions of the students' responses to my books. Instead of writing a biography about the author, as is more common, some of the students had written my "autobiography." In those pre-internet times I could not believe all of the intimate details about my life they were mentioning in their first-person accounts, and I had to ask what sources they had used. Gleefully, the students told me that they had read all of the dedications of my books to learn the names of my friends and relatives. They had concluded that, if I had dedicated my books to these people, they must be important to me and incorporated them in their "autobiographies".

Later that day, a group of children read aloud the story of *El pañuelo de seda*, and it was evident that the story had moved them. After the reading, one of the students presented me with a beautifully wrapped box containing a silk scarf. "Instead of white like in the book," he told me very seriously, "we chose a blue one. That way, the next time you find a bird that needs help, it won't be so hard for you to see the scarf getting stained." It was clear that they had identified me with the protagonist of the story.

It would be hard to imagine a more thoughtfully chosen gift. My joy is enormous to know that children were moved by the values of kindness and personal sacrifice that are portrayed in *El pañuelo de seda* and saw them as life actions to be repeated. Many children have written to say that they appreciate that the story "makes me feel happy and sad at the same time." They have also said that the story makes them cry, or "almost made me cry."

While the text of this book is brief, it seems to invite attention to details. Often children mention in their letters what they liked best about a book or their favorite part of the story. I have been surprised to see that, with regard to this book, the responses have been quite varied. Many children focus on the relationship between the child and the injured bird *(a mí me puso muy, muy, muy, muy feliz que Anita salvara a la grulla que estaba herida .../ it made me very, very, very, very happy that Anita saved the injured crane...)*.

Yet I have received letters that refer to almost every other aspect of the book, even to the fact that the girl enjoyed looking up at the sky! It is wonderful to know that children today still feel that it is important to find joy in looking up at the sky, as does Anita, the young protagonist of this book.

The World of Fantasy

It may seem odd to create a section for the world of fantasy, since fantasy is present in so many of the books that have already been mentioned. Yet 1 would like to honor the books that have been born solely from the simple desire to tell a good story.

I must thank Olmo, the oldest grandson of my good friend Viví Escrivá, for two of these books. Olmo was barely four when I was visiting Viví and her family in the enchanting village of Polop de la Marina in Alicante, Spain. One afternoon, Viví asked me to babysit Olmo while she went off to a doctor's appointment. Both stories were born that afternoon.

Olmo was a bright and beautiful child and I was delighted to take care of him, but I soon discovered that he held the firm belief that one's feet should never, ever, touch the ground. As he climbed and jumped and ran, with me following along behind him, out of breath and worried that he might hurt himself, I decided to use the best magic I knew to quiet down a child: I asked Olmo if he wanted to hear a story.

Olmo's reply was instantaneous. Yes, he wanted a story, a story about rabbits. His aunt, Ana López Escrivá, today a children's book illustrator, had just given him a little bunny. So I sat down with Olmo trying to decide on a good rabbit story, when he added, "About rabbits and trains!" I was startled for a moment, yet his request led me to come up with the story later published as **Serafina's Birthday**, illustrated by Louise Bates Satterfiel. This story has become very meaningful to me, as it is a celebration of the storyteller.

The story begins when Serafina's good but forgetful friend Sebastian is about to miss the train that would allow him to attend Serafina's birthday party. Having forgotten her present in his rush to catch the train, Sebastian experiences numerous misfortunes in his attempt to find a new present. He finally decides that it is better to show up even without a present. His arrival fills Serafina with joy, since she had been afraid that her best friend had forgotten her party. She is already feeling a disappointed, as her grandfather is sick and there will be no storytelling. When Sebastian sits in grandfather's chair and tells all that happened to him and why he is arriving late and empty-handed, everyone agrees that he has brought the best present of all, the gift of a story.

Sebastián: *(Está saliendo y regresa a cepillarse los dientes.)* ¿Cuándo se ha visto que un conejo salga de casa sin cepillarse los dientes?

(Se oye el silbato del tren.)

Sebastián: *(Corriendo.)* No puedo perder ese tren.

The original story is out of print, but there is a dramatized version magnificently illustrated by Claudia Legnazzi, in the anthology ***Teatrín de don Crispín - Scenes from Roll'n'Role.***

Olmo had listened enraptured to the story of Sebastian and Serafina, yet I did not forget his initial display of momentum. When Viví returned, I suggested to her that we create a book to celebrate Olmo's energy. This was the origin of the picture book ***Olmo y la mariposa azul***. In English: ***Olmo and the Blue Butterfly***

Olmo awakens to find a blue butterfly in his room. When the butterfly flies out the window, Olmo follows. He will pursue it in skateboards and bicycles, scooters and cable cars, boats and helicopters. Finally, as he travels on a spaceship, he realizes that the butterfly has quietly settled on his helmet.

Is the purpose to engage children in reading the vivid images, predicting the next vehicle hinted in the illustration? Is it to celebrate the many modes of travel, or the fascination with movement and speed? Is it to convey the message that each of us have our own blue butterfly to pursue?

Some scenes of Olmo and the Blue Butterfly

Perhaps the real message that what we are seeking is already with us?

It was a joy for me to leave this book so open-ended that each reader can choose his or her own answers to these questions!

Teachers and Librarians' Ideas

Creating a Blue Butterfly

Teachers have used *Olmo and the Blue Butterfly* or *Olmo y la mariposa azul* as an inspiration for many diverse activities. I have been delighted to walk into classrooms where all of the children had made their own butterflies, which hung on the walls or from the ceiling. The outline of a butterfly traced on poster board can become a beautiful butterfly by covering the wings with crumpled tissue paper.

This activity becomes more meaningful when teachers and librarians invite students to talk about the dream that each butterfly represents.

Making Their Own Books

One frequent response to a book is to create another. The structure of this story invites children to create, individually or as a group, their own version of what it might be like to follow a butterfly.

Children have also retold Olmo's journey in a first-person narrative, describing the places and people they see when they run, jump on a skateboard, ride a bicycle, etc.

In Search of Identity

The process of defining one's identity is a universal human experience, but for some individuals it becomes a very poignant search. Questioning my identity has been a constant in my own life. As a child, I grew up in an unconventional family who did not share the same faith as most of the people in my hometown, and I was always in the perpetual role of new student as I attended a different school each year during my elementary education. As a teenager, 1 had several experiences as a foreign student in the United States and in Spain; later, as a young woman, I experienced the challenges of being an immigrant, first in Perú and later in the United States.

As I observed my own children grow, as well as the many children of diverse backgrounds I have encountered over the years, I have seen how crucial it can be to be able to define one's self and how one fits in with others. Thus, it is not surprising that this theme comes up frequently in my writing.

From the various stories in which issues of identity plays a central role, I will mention three. The first is the bilingual book *El cuadradito azul - The little blue square*, illustrated by internationally acclaimed Ulises Wensell. The extraordinary illustrations succeed in giving distinct personalities to the members of a family of squares. With  minimal text, the story tells about a little blue square who does not like being a square and dreams of being something different, like a circle or an oval. His grandmother explains that a square is full of potential and that by folding himself carefully he can become many things, including a paper boat... a bird ... or any of the other origami figures shown in the illustrations.

The story originally appeared in **Exploramos**, one of the books in the **Hagamos caminos** reading series. The enthusiasm with which children and teachers received this story lead to its publication as a bilingual picture book.

One of my books about identity, **The Unicorn of the West** [in Spanish **El unicornio del oeste**] illustrated by Abigail Pizer,

began as a bedtime story: One evening when I was visiting three of my great-nieces, I offered to tell them a bedtime story. When I asked them what they wanted the story to be about, they immediately asked for a story about unicorns. Having never told a story about unicorns before, I began to let the words flow and started to spin a tale about a unicorn who did not know who he was, since he had never seen another being that resembled him. The "unicorn who does not know that he is a unicorn" is befriended by a bird, a squirrel, and a butterfly, all of whom want to help their friend discover who he is, and they set forth in search of other beings like him. While friendship is a strong element in this story, this book is clearly about identity. In due time, the unicorn does find out who he is, as one hopes we all will, and discovers that his mission is to ensure that love continues to live in the world.

Children have written to me about how much they enjoyed the story. As one of my more personal expressions, it continues to be one of my own favorites. It is one of the books I often choose to give as a gift to someone special.

The third picture book that I will mention here is **Bernice the Barnacle** [in Spanish **Más poderoso que yo**]. This is not an original story, but instead a creative retelling of the traditional fable about the little mouse and the mountain. I have set the story in the underwater world of the ocean, where a small barnacle seeks to discover who the most powerful being of all is. Encountering one powerful being after another, he finally discovers that the largest one of them all, the blue whale, considers barnacles to be more powerful, since she cannot prevent them from adhering to her skin.

Viví Escrivá's beautiful illustrations of the many wonders of marine life have made this book a favorite with many children, who delight in the fact that a little tiny barnacle turns out to be such a powerful protagonist, and with teachers who find it a good resource to show ocean life and the progressive size of its creatures.

Teachers and Librarians' Ideas

Más poderoso que yo or **Bernice the Barnacle** has seemed particularly suited for retelling. Among the examples I have seen or that have been sent to me are:

Retelling the Story with Other Characters

After introducing the traditional version of the story and explaining how a story can be told in a variety of different settings, teachers have often encouraged children to retell the story in a new setting with different characters.

Retelling the Story from another Point of View

Some teachers have asked their students to tell the story as a father or mother barnacle would tell it to their children, describing the adventures they experienced while meeting the various ocean dwellers. This kind of retelling could also serve as a creative culminating activity for a science unit on ocean life.

The Promise of Transformation

In my own journey through time, I have learned to see life as a constant process of becoming. I owe much to Paulo Freire for having helped me to see the significance of praxis, or action that arises naturally from the attempt to understand more deeply the circumstances of our lives and which is, in turn, followed by further reflection and action. My life work has become an effort to promote education as an opportunity to awaken each person's desire to create a better world and thus an opportunity for both individual and social transformation. It is therefore no surprise that the theme of transformation appears frequently in my stories.

As mentioned earlier, my first children's book in the trade market published in the United States was **The Gold Coin** [in Spanish **La moneda de oro**], illustrated by Neil Waldman, and published by Atheneum.

The Gold Coin continues to be one of my most widely read books. Since many of the stories I had written earlier were retellings of folktales, it is not surprising that this original story also reads like a folktale. People sometimes mistakenly refer to it as such, which to me is an honor, since I have great admiration for folktales. At the same time, this is a good place to set the record straight. While I have had many moments of inspiration in my life, I have never again had an experience quite like the one that gave birth to **The Gold Coin** and **La moneda de oro**.

I was living in San Mateo, California, and traveling once a month to the Salinas Valley to work with migrant farm working parents at the Pájaro Valley School District. With the support of Alfonso Anaya, then Bilingual Director for the district, we had organized a family literacy project based on children's literature. We would read carefully chosen picture books aloud to parents, and invite them to explore the connections between the stories in the books and the stories in their own lives. This project was quite successful and has been written about extensively (Ada, 1988, 1990, 1997, 2003; Zubizarreta, 1996).

On summer evenings we held the meetings late, since the work in the fields does not stop until sunset. Thus, it was past midnight as I was returning home one night, driving alone through the fields. My thoughts returned to the parents. During the sessions, I had been humbled by seeing how these parents, who had so little by way of material things, were so willing to help others. I was deeply moved by all that I had witnessed— the quiet dignity, the enormous sense of responsibility, the willingness to sacrifice themselves for their families, the generosity of spirit. Beneath the sadness and anger at the unjust conditions these parents face, I also felt a deep sense of gratitude for the work they did, the work that feeds us all. And I wondered whether their closeness to the earth had something to do with all of the wonderful qualities I had seen.

At that moment, a story began to unfold in front of me. The story of **The Gold Coin** was first conceived in images: I saw Juan roaming the countryside, looking for something to steal, all hunched over and afraid of people, then, the figure of Doña Josefa emerged and he began to follow her, wanting to rob her of her gold. As scene after scene unfolded, it felt as though this story had been hovering over the fields, only waiting to be told. Needless to say, I cried the rest of the way home.

When I arrived, I went straight to my desk and wrote down the entire story. The next morning, I thought it had all been a dream, until I went downstairs and found the entire hand-scribbled manuscript right where I had left it.

This book has given me multiple moments of joy as I receive letters from teachers and students who have found inspiration on it. To complement their experience while reading the book I have recorded it, both in English and Spanish, and added some personal comments about the process of creating the book and its significance. The recording is published as a CD in the series *On the Voice of the Author/ En la voz del autor.*

Of all of my picture books, another personal favorite is **Jordi's Star,** illustrated by Susan Gaber. This story tells of a lonely shepherd who lives a bleak life on a very dry mountain. The shepherd struggles to dig a well that will provide him with some water. Although he never finishes the well, the large hole he has dug fills up with water after a storm. Gazing down at the water, Jordi is surprised to find the reflection of a star. The star becomes a

companion and source of inspiration. For the star's sake, Jordi begins to beautify the small pond and its surroundings.

In a similar manner to **The Gold Coin,** this book also reads like a folktale. When children ask about the origin of the story, I explain that the inspiration came as I traveled along a road in northern California where one can see forested mountains on one side of the road and very barren on the other. This in turn reminded me of the striking landscape of the Callejón de Huaylas in Perú, the path between the Cordillera Blanca, the White Range, and the Cordillera Negra, the Black Range. These two mountain ranges lie next to each other, but they have very different appearances and ecosystems, as one of them receives a large amount of water in the form of snowmelt and the other does not. I also tell children that, in another way, this story has always been growing in me, along with the knowledge that what we see in life depends on what we choose to notice, that beauty is hidden in the smallest details, and that love can truly transform our world. While I cherish each of the books I have written, it is also true that **Jordi's Star** holds a very special place in my heart.

The story behind the writing of **The Malachite Palace**, illustrated by Leonid Gore and translated by my daughter Rosa Zubizarreta; is multifold. I am glad to be able to tell it here.

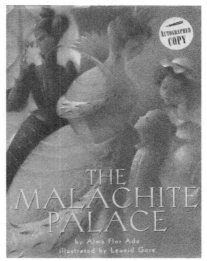

As a child, I was a lover of poetry. Few poems delighted me as much as *"A Margarita Debayle"* by the great Nicaraguan poet Rubén Darío; I memorized this long poem at a very young age. Dario's modernist verse is very sonorous, and its images are filled with sensory delights. Among the many wonders that comprise the king's possessions—a crystal palace, a tent made of daylight, a herd of elephants—there was one that particularly intrigued me: *"un kiosko de malaquita"* (a kiosk made entirely out of malachite).

At the time I did not know what malachite was, yet that did not matter: it sounded quite magical. When I later learned the meaning of the word, it added yet another level of visual and tactile delight to the poem.

Many years later, during a visit to the Hermitage Museum in Leningrad, I wandered off from the guided tour and found myself in a huge room where the only piece of art on display was a life-sized malachite kiosk! My surprise was enormous, as I had assumed that such a wondrous object was only possible in a poem.

The mystery remained unsolved in my mind. . . Had Dario, a Nicaraguan poet who lived part of his life in Spain, heard of the existence of this life-sized malachite kiosk? Or did his imagination as a poet create such a marvel on its own? Is it possible that Dario's poetry inspired this amazing work of art? Or was it the other way around?

As I mused about the powerful relationship between literature and life, I picked up a pencil and wrote: 'There once was a princess who lived in a malachite palace. . ." and thus, a story was born.

When the story was to be published, a surprising coincidence occurred. My editor at Atheneum, Jonathan Lanman, was

selecting an illustrator for the story. Completely unaware of my visit to the Hermitage, Jonathan chose Leonid Gore, an artist who had recently emigrated from Russia. The delicate translucence of Leonid's pictures, which the Kirkus Review called "stunning" and "evanescent," created an ideal visual environment for the story.

Three stories **The Malachite Palace, Jordi's Star** and **The Unicorn of the West** have been recorded by me in one CD with personal comments about the books.

Some people see **The Malachite Palace** as a book of friendship, and while unquestionably, friendship plays a very important role in the story, in my mind, the essence of the book is formed by the little princess's growing awareness of the restrictions imposed by prejudice, as well as her determination to take responsibility for her own actions, and pursue the friendship she so much value.

Teachers and Librarians' Ideas

As *The Gold Coin* is one of my most well-known stories and has been read by children at various grade levels, I have seen many different kinds of projects created in response. I will mention below some of the most exciting ones. Both *Jordi's Star* and *The Malachite Palace* had short lives on bookstore shelves, as they went out of print after their first edition. However, they have captured the imagination of many children and the interest of many teachers. Both of these books can still be obtained through Del Sol Books.

The Malachite Palace has also been included in a reading series. My granddaughter Cristina Isabel told me very excited that her class had read the story. And at a book signing, a second grader enthusiastically informed me that her class had voted this story as their favorite story of this year. What more could an author want!

My Treasures

One of my favorite activities, after reading *The Gold Coin* with students of any age, is to invite students to reflect on why Doña Josefa felt as though she was "the richest woman on earth" when she lived in a humble cottage in the countryside. Once students identify the nature of Doña Josefa's wealth (being kind to others, being able to help others, having useful skills, being able to heal, feeling appreciated and loved), I invite students to think about what makes each of them "the richest person on Earth"

Before inviting them to tell me about their "wealth," I explain that the rule of the game is to not repeat what someone else has said. Then I write their various contributions on chart paper or type them into the computer. Students usually begin by mentioning that their wealth is their family, their parents, their friends, their school, their pets. When they run out of ideas, I encourage them to also think about more abstract kinds of wealth, such as health, kindness, love, and friendship. Sometimes children begin to spontaneously include the realm of nature as a kind of wealth, recognizing that the earth, clean water, clean air, and sunlight are also things that we can treasure.

A next step can be to invite students to create books, either individually or collectively, about their sources of "wealth." Depending on the age of the students, the pages can consist of simple words and pictures, longer sentences and paragraphs, or complete essays on the subject. Sometimes teachers add an extra touch by helping students publish the final book in the shape of a treasure chest or pot of gold.

My Own Gold Coins

I treasure every book I receive from a classroom. Sometimes I am given a handmade book when I visit a school. Other times, I receive them as a surprise in my mailbox. These books comprise the most beloved section of my library, and each of them is special in its own way.

One particular book that I will describe now is in the shape of a gold coin. Inside, each page is written by a different person. All of the book's authors have been asked to complete the sentence, "If I had a gold coin ..."

While everyone has chosen to give their gold coin to someone, each page is different. A few are more general, such as, "*I would give my gold coin to a poor person, because they don't have clothes or toys.*" Many others chose to offer their gold coin to people they know well: "*to my grandmother, because she is poor,*" "*to my Mom, sometimes she gets sick and I want to help her,*" "*to my Dad, because he has no coins to give my Mom,*" "*to my aunt, she doesn't have a job, and she has a daughter,*" "*to my uncle, he doesn't have a car, and needs money for his family.*"

In some cases, the gold coin seems to have become imbued with Doña Josefa's healing arts: "*to my abuelita, she is a little sick and I want her to get well.*" One child wrote with a very touching mixture of verbal tenses, love, and wistfulness: *"If I had a gold coin I would give it to my grandmother. She needs it more than me and this is why I gave it to her, so that she will not die. Thanks for receiving my gold coin."*

Creating a Mural

The Gold Coin, Jordi's Star, and **The Malachite Palace**, have served as inspiration for murals. Students selected moments from the story in order to depict them in a large painting. One very original mural of **The Gold Coin** depicts the various scenes from the story as part of a larger circle.

Turning a Story into a Play

The Gold Coin.

Several years ago, Dr. Nancy Jean Smith, one of my former doctoral students, later a professor at California State University in Stanislaus, designed a unique program designed to offer educators from the United States the opportunity to study transformative literacy, while also learning about indigenous cultures in Mexico, by living for a month in the homes of indigenous families in Teotitlán del Valle, Oaxaca, a village of weavers.

Isabel and I had the opportunity to participate the first summer the program was offered. One of the participants, Silvia Dorta Duque de Reyes, invited local middle school students perform *The Gold Coin* as a play. The students chose to create a circular stage in the center of the town plaza. They built doña Josefa's hut and brought in different plants to represent the various stages of her circular journey and created an extraordinary performance.

Jordi's Star

Never would I have thought of *Jordi's Star* as a story that could be dramatized, since it does not have the usual characteristics one would think a story needs in order to be turned into a play. While Jordi is a rather poetic tale, it has only one character, little action, and no dialogue! Yet one should never underestimate the creativity and imagination of a teacher. During an author's visit to a school, I was quite surprised to see a very engaging dramatization of Jordi.

One young boy had been chosen to play Jordi. While a narrator read the story and Jordi acted out his part, other children waved different pieces of cloth to create the storm, the night, the blue sky. In a simple but effective manner, Jordi moved very realistic papier-mâché stones to create the border of the pond and brought pebbles and wildflowers to decorate it. His various physical expressions were so convincing... tiredness, awe at the beauty of the star, puzzling over what to do next, joy at the results, that I was left afterward with the feeling that I had met the real Jordi.

The Malachite Palace

I have yet to see *The Malachite Palace* as a play, yet I am delighted to say that it has been transformed into a ballet.

The magic of this story was revealed in a unique way. A young Canadian girl found the book in her local library in Cape Breton, Canada. She liked the story so much that she was able to convince her mother, the director of the Ballet Bras d'Or, to stage the story as a ballet.

The choreography set to a combination of Spanish and Russian classical music, with over 40 dancers, both adults and children, was amazingly beautiful.

While I will always regret not having been able to see this amazing production on stage, I'm thankful it was recorded.

It can now be seen in YouTube by searching for **The Malachite Palace performed by Ballet Bras d'Or.** https://www.youtube.com/watch?v=DF-p_iftLME&t=62s

Performed by Ballet Bras d'Or

Based on the story by
Alma Flor Ada
with illustrations by
Leonid Gore

Recorded at
Strasthpey Place
Cape Breton, NS
June 13 , 2008

The Princess Jessy Watson
The Bird Rachelle Aucoin
The Malachite Leah Lamble, Brianna Covey,
Cassie Ehler
The Queen Anastasia Feigin
The Governess Jeannie Becks
Ladies in Waiting Laura Peart, Sheryl Peart
Court Ladies Anita MacIver, Julie Bartlett,
Danielle Knott, Rina Baker,
Michelle Kahoe, Sarah
O'Halloren
The Vines Erika Leblanc, Brielle Doucet,
Ashley Aucoin, Anastasia Feigin
The Little Maidens Annika Becks, Catherine
MacDonald, Mia Nishi Gorshi,
Molly Peart, Allisson MacLean,
Kayli MacLean, Haley Fraser
The Children Sadie Beaton, Robin Jessome,
Jasmine Chisholm, Rebecca
Clark, Lynn MacKinnon, Ginette
Michaud, Deardre Elyse Fraser,
Mac Lafort, Zoey Lafort, Tessie
Doyle, Jenna MacKinnon,
Chantelle Marie Walsh, Maggie
Power
The Birds Joelle Larade, Taylor Deveau,
Leah Burns, Megan Burns, Kyerra
Doyle, Julia Curley, Emma
MacKinnon, Jesse MacKinnon

Artistic Director and Choreography
Diana Lamble
Sound and Media Direction
Robert Lamble

© 2008
Ronald Newcombe
Commercial Art
902 563 6111
ron.newcombe@ns.sympatico.ca

DVD
VIDEO
NTSC

The Vast Heritage of Folktales and Legends

Among its many gifts, our complex history as Latinos has given us a very rich folklore. The diverse areas that are now South America, Central America, and Mexico all had rich indigenous cultures before the Spanish conquest. But what is less well-known is that Spain itself is not a monolith. The diverse regions of Spain—the Basque country, the Galician area of the northwest, the Catalonian provinces, the southern lands of Andalucía, and the central plateau—all have very distinct geographies and traditions, and even different languages that are unintelligible in other regions. Eusquera, the language of the Basques, is not even related to any other European language, Spanish included. In each of these various areas, new stories were created and borrowed ones were modified until they took on a distinct regional flavor.

By the end of the seventh century, the Arabs, aiming to expand the Muslim faith, had conquered all of the lands in North Africa along the Mediterranean coast. In 711 C.E., they reached the Iberian Peninsula. Overcoming the weak resistance of the fragmented Visigoth kings who fled to the north of the peninsula, the Arabs settled in most of what is today Spain and Portugal. The Visigoths retained strongholds in the Cantabrian Mountains in the north. The mountainous Basque region remained autonomous, as it had during all earlier invasions.

For more than seven centuries, Arab caliphates and kingdoms flourished on the Iberian Peninsula. In many aspects, the culture of the Arabs was far superior to that of medieval Europe. Their cities were cleaner, with an abundance of gardens and fountains, and their knowledge in mathematics, astronomy, chemistry, and medicine was highly evolved. It is due to their leadership in these areas that words such as *algebra, chemistry,* and *alcohol* are all derived from the Arabic language. Indeed, 20 percent of all Spanish vocabulary is of Arabic origin, particularly in the fields mentioned above, as well as in the areas of government, architecture, and agronomy. The Arabs creation of the numeric system we use today [0, 1, 2, 3, 4...] which substituted the Roman system [I, II, III, IV...] facilitated the development of mathematics, particularly with the creation of the numeral 0, a concept that had been known to older civilizations, but which was absent in the Roman system. Arab contributions in other areas were also substantive. The Mezquita in Córdoba, the Torre del Oro in Seville, and the Alhambra in Granada are only a few examples of the splendor of their cities. The guitar, that universal instrument, was born in Spain from Arabic influences.

A culture with a great love for stories, many Arabian contributions to the art of storytelling are still alive today, including *Las mil y una noches,* which in English is best known as *The Arabian Nights.* This masterpiece was the inspiration for similar collections of stories in medieval Castilian; among the best known and most influential of these are *Calila e Dimna* and the stories of *El Conde Lucanor.*

When the Spaniards crossed the Atlantic to the Americas, they brought their stories with them to a world that was already very rich with its own people, culture, and mythology. The invasion and conquest of the Americas by Europeans brought about much destruction of the indigenous civilizations. The Christians —whether Catholics or Protestants— were much less tolerant of other cultures than Islam had been. Nonetheless, a new culture was born in the Americas with elements of both the indigenous and the invading cultures. Stories from both worlds mixed and combined, and new ones were born to tell of new developments. The people brought in as slaves from Africa were unable to carry many material possessions, but they did bring with them the rich lore of their own lands. Their cultures influenced the growing new culture as well, and the stories continued to evolve and change.

My childhood was blessed with many of these traditional stories. Some were brief with cumulative lines of rhyming verse that I loved to memorize and recall. Others were long, filled with details and descriptions that made it hard to discern the story line. All these stories sparked my imagination and dreams, filling me with wonder and awe as well as nostalgia for bygone eras.

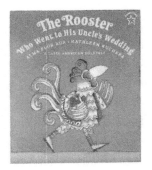

For a brief period between adolescence and motherhood I forgot about these stories, but when my children were born I found renewed delight in them. One of my children's favorites later became ***The Rooster Who Went to His Uncle's Wedding: A Latin American Folktale***, illustrated by Kathleen Kuchera, with an introduction by Tomie de Paola. It continues to be a story I love to tell. There is a more recent version published by Frog Street.

I have already mentioned that my first book for children that I compiled for my daughter Rosalma was a collection of these

traditional tales, together with some of the poems I had loved in my childhood. One of the stories in this book was that of the rooster who goes to his uncle's wedding, which became the favorite of my son Alfonso. Much later in life, when he had already grown up to become a successful engineer, he called me one day with the news that he had been offered a new position. His first sentence was: "I'm like the rooster who went to his uncle's wedding; I can't quite decide what to do." Once again, the lasting influence of folktales became apparent to me!

Two things were remarkable about the way my grandmother told this tale. The first is that she would tell the cumulative part very fast, increasing her speed as the list of beings who refused to help the rooster became longer and longer. When I tell the story I like to do this too, and I enjoy watching young children hold their breath as they wonder if I will make it to the end of the list before running out of breath myself.

The other remarkable thing is how my grandmother would adapt the story each time as she was telling it. While we sat on the porch as I listen, she would be looking around for things to include that might give it a flavor of immediacy. Across from our house there was, an open field where animals grazed. Depending on what animal was there that evening, it would be a cow, a horse, a donkey, or a goat that appeared in the story... and, as she pointed to the animal, I could just see the rooster approaching to ask for help. As I have often mentioned, my grandmother's willingness to pass on as well as adapt the traditional folktales gave me permission to see folklore as a living, changing form.

There are different versions of the popular tale story of *Mediopollito* I chose the one my grandmother told for the book ***Half-Chicken/Mediopollito,*** illustrated by Kim Howard. The news of a newly hatched chicken with only one wing, one leg, and one eye spreads quickly throughout the countryside, and he is soon given the name "Half-Chicken." Convinced by all this attention that he is quite special, Half-Chicken decides to visit the King's court. Along the way, he meets Water, Fire, and  Wind, who are all in need of help. Here the story takes different turns in the various versions I have encounter. In some versions, Half-Chicken is vain and insensitive and does not offer any help when asked, something that proves disastrous for him in the end, when he finds himself thrown into a pot by the King's cook. In my grandmother's version, Half-Chicken is willing to stop and help, and, in return, when he later lands in the pot, Water helps by pouring itself over Fire, who gladly accepts being put out. When the King's cook returns to find the fire out, he tosses the chicken out the window, where Wind rescues him by lifting him up to stand tall on the highest turret. From there Half-Chicken can watch the court to his heart's content, and, as the first weather vane, can continue to play with the Wind.

One of the most compelling characters in our folklore is Blancaflor. There are many tales about this lovely girl, who is always wrapped in mystery as the daughter of a giant or the victim of a sorcerer. Her stories were told in the evenings in that innocent time before television. I heard many different versions from the various women who sometimes worked in my grandmother's house, helping with the cooking, cleaning, or laundry. I was a constant beggar for their stories, and they were often willing to comply, weaving yet one more shroud of mystery around beautiful and willful Blancaflor.

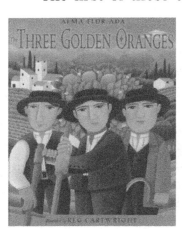

The first of these tales that I have retold, ***The Three Golden Oranges***, illustrated by Reg Cartwright, tells how, after being trapped inside an orange, Blancaflor is rescued by the youngest of three brothers. Because he only partially follows the instructions he has been given, Blancaflor is at first not completely rescued, but is instead transformed into a white dove. With her kindness, the dove endears herself to the young man's mother, until at last the young man and his mother are able to help her regain her true form.

Reg Cartwright created vibrant and exquisitely stylized illustrations, which portray the Spanish landscape in bold colors while conveying the magic and mystery of the tale.

Another Blancaflor story appear in a collection of Hispanic folktales rewritten by Isabel Campoy and myself, and illustrated by various illustrators, ***Tales Our Abuelitas Told***, in Spanish ***Cuentos que contaban nuestras abuelas***, both published by Atheneum.

My connection with Mexico began when I was a young girl. From the perspective of a Cuban child, Mexico was a fascinating land. My father would not let me listen to the soap operas that were so popular on Cuban radio at the time, because he disapproved of their vulgarity. One of the few shows I was allowed to listen to was *Cri-cri,* a Mexican program for children by Gabilondo Soler that combined stories, poems, and songs. Some of my mother's magazines also came from Mexico, as did many of the movies I  saw, particularly those about the *charros*, or Mexican cowboys. Furthermore, my aunt Mireya Lafuente went to Mexico City to study with the Ballet Folklórico de México and brought back wonderful music and costumes and exquisite handcrafts, as well as a deep love for the country.

Thus, whenever I found a Mexican folktale I read it with particular interest. One of my favorites was the story of the little lizard who was able to find the Sun after everyone else had given up the search. The retelling of the story resulted in *The Lizard and the Sun / La lagartija y el sol*, illustrated by Felipe Dávalos.

My own love for lizards may have contributed to my appreciation for this tale, but certainly the lizard's persistence, her willingness to continue on what seemed to be an impossible quest, makes her one of the characters in my books with whom I most closely identify. The illustrations by Felipe Dávalos, who is extremely knowledgeable about the ancient cultures of Meso-America, are the perfect complement to the text.

Much of Felipe's initial artwork was created in connection with archeological research and has been published by Yale University Press and National Geographic. His willingness to dedicate both his archeological knowledge and his art to a young audience fills me with hope. Felipe now lives in Sacramento, California, where he has seen firsthand that very few Latino children have the opportunity to learn about their rich cultural heritage. He is committed to creating art that can inspire our young people and fill them with pride.

It has been an enormous satisfaction that Felipe Dávalos would be the artistic director for the series Puertas al sol / Gateways to the Sun co-authored by Isabel Campoy and myself. His own knowledge and aesthetic values and the respect he commands among Latin American illustrators allowed him of these books authentic gems.

Teachers' and Librarians' Ideas

Writing Folktales

Children gain great satisfaction from writing their own books, and folktales are a great starting point for creating their own original stories. Here are some tips you can share with children to guide them in the process:

1. **Read**

   We learn to write by reading; thus it is important to encourage children to read extensively. If they are planning to write a folktale, it will serve them well to read as many folktales as possible.

2. **Decide on the Topic**

   What will the story be about? Many folktales are *Porquoi pas?* stories, that is, stories that explain why or how something came to be. For example, they may explain why elephants have trunks, why turtles have shells, or, as with my beloved *Half-Chicken,* how the first weather vane came to be. A folktale may also convey a message. In *The Rooster Who Went to His Uncle's Wedding,* the message is the importance of being willing to help others. A story may also offer both a message and an explanation. *The Lizard and the Sun,* for example, gives a clear message about the value of persistence and not giving up, while also explaining why the Aztecs held yearly musical festivals to help keep the sun awake.

3. Imagine a World

Stories occur in specific times and places. Once they have an idea for a story, invite the students to imagine the world where it will take place.

Is it a real world or an imaginary one? What is it like? Encourage students to describe the setting with colors, smells, and sounds. Have them describe how something tastes or how it feels to the touch. These details will make the world become real to the readers.

4. Research the Time and Place

Gathering information about the time and location in which they want to set their story provides students with a number of authentic details they can then use in their writing. These details might include, for instance, the plants and trees that grow in that area, as well as typical foods, celebrations, and other activities. These authentic and accurate descriptions will add to the quality of the story.

5. Create the Main Character

Invite children to imagine all the details concerning their characters, whether they are human, animal, or other. Some students may find it helpful to make drawings of their characters, while others may prefer to write lists of their characteristics. For example:

> *External:* tall or short; heavy or light; young or old; athletic or weak; strong or slight; also, color of eyes, hair, skin, or fur.

> *Internal:* brave or timid; courageous or fearful; outgoing or shy; kind or mean; generous or selfish.

> What is the character known for? How will his or her personality affect the story?

6. **Plan the Plot and Pacing**

   A good story will need:

   - an interesting, engaging beginning;
   - a conflict or moment of tension: a question to be answered or something that needs to be resolved;
   - an ending that feels satisfying because the conflict has been resolved or the question has been answered.

   The pace at which the story moves—not too slow, not too fast—will affect how engaged readers will be. Remind children to not rush the ending.

7. **Use a Traditional Pattern in Your Story**

   Many folktales start with phrases like *Había una vez,* "Once upon a time...," *En un lugar muy lejano,* "In a faraway land...," or *En la tierra de Irás y No Volverás,* "In the land of make-believe..." Students can also use rhymes or repeated phrases to maintain a sense of continuity and anticipation. You can point to the ones I used in *Half-Chicken* as an example:

   > I have no time to lose!
   > I'm off to Mexico City
   > to see the court of the viceroy!

   > *No tengo tiempo que perder*
   > *Voy a México*
   > *a ver la corte del virrey.*

   You might also remind students that folktales are meant to be told out loud. If they are having difficulty writing, encourage them to write their story as if they were telling it aloud to a friend.

8. **Allow the Reader to Experience the Story**

   Good writing often "shows" things, rather than "telling." In this way, the reader feels like seeing the story taking place. One way to achieve it is to use dialogue, which allows the characters to speak for themselves, instead of the writer telling what the characters think.

So, for example, rather than writing:

Pedro told his father he wanted to go to town.
He tried to convince him to let him sell the
oranges.

you might try this instead:

"Father, let's go to town," said Pedro.
"I'm sure I can sell all the oranges in the
market. I will get a good price!"

9. Conquer the Fear of the Blank Page

Staring at a blank page can be terrifying. Encourage students to start writing about anything, including how they are feeling right now. Often, the more one has already written, the easier it is to keep going. Of course, some of what one writes at first won't make it to the final version, but it can serve as an important stepping stone.

10. Revise

Explain to students the value of the process of revision. Students can help one another by reading each other's stories, but first encourage personal revision. Ask them to:

- Read your story aloud to yourself. Pretend it was written by someone else. Does it make sense? Is anything missing? Does it flow well? Are there any repeated phrases that will help readers remember the story?

- Pay attention to the dialogue. Do the words fit the character? Each character needs to have a different way of talking, just as actual people do!

- Read your story aloud to a friend or family member. Ask them to just listen the first time around. When you finish, ask them to tell you three things they liked about the story. Then ask them if you can read your story again to them. This time, invite them to stop you and let you know whenever they don't understand something. Each time they ask you to stop, think about what you really want to say. Is there something missing that you could add right there, so the reader will understand more of what you mean? Or, maybe you want to shorten something, or leave something out entirely. Is that part really important? If so, is there an easier and simpler way to say what you really mean?

Wearing the Author's Shoes

As I was writing the book you are now reading, I received a very engaging request. A student who has read *Half-Chicken* wrote me asking if I would send her an old pair of shoes. The accompanying letter from the teacher explained that, in order to create a special writing atmosphere, her students were asking for authors' old shoes to wear as they write.

This is certainly the most surprising request I have ever received. On my trip to the post office, to mail the original manuscript to the editor, I also mailed a pair of used shoes to the students!

A Giant Half-Chicken

Many teachers have made half-chicken silhouettes by enlarging an illustration from the book, which their students then cut out and glue onto a stick. Adding colored feathers makes these chickens very lively. Two of them grace my studio and always draw a smile when I look at them.

During an author's visit to a school in the California Central Valley, I saw that the students had created a giant half-chicken for display in the cafeteria. Instead of feathers, the very large half-chicken silhouette had smaller half-chickens of many different colors pasted all over it, for a very striking effect.

Dramatizing a Folktale

When visiting schools, one of my favorite activities has been to tell the story of *The Rooster Who Went to His Uncle's Wedding*. Since it lends itself well to a simple dramatization, when Isabel and I are visiting together, she will frequently encourage the children, and occasionally the parents and teachers, to volunteer to play the roles of the different characters. It's a real pleasure to see how much fun this can be!

I have also seen several more elaborate productions. Some teachers were able to obtain help from parents in order to create full costumes. Others have used simpler resources. For example, in one performance, the children who played the rooster and the sun wore special headdresses designed to represent their character. The children who had other roles, such as the lamb, the dog, the stick, the fire, and the water, each wore a poster board hung around their neck with a drawing of the character that he or she was portraying.

Regardless of whether the production is sophisticated or simple, children still benefit from the experience of being on stage, learning to project their voices, and having the experience of being listened to and recognized.

In the section *It's Play Time* I explore in further detail the value of children's theatrical productions and offer some suggestions for their successful implementation in the school or library.

Traditional Characters in Contemporary Settings

In an earlier mention of my grandmother Lola's gifts as a storyteller I told about how she made her stories come to life by incorporating elements from the real world around us. Perhaps that is what gave me permission to tell the story of the great-great- granddaughter of the well-loved Cucarachita Martina.

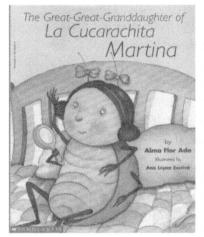

In **The Great-Great-Granddaughter of Cucarachita Martina**, in Spanish **La tataranieta de Cucarachita Martina**, illustrated by Ana López Escrivá, as in the story of her illustrious great-great-grandmother, the young protagonist of our story is wooed by many different suitors: a cat, a dog, a horse, a rooster, a bull.... In a departure from the traditional story, each of them invites her to live with him in a different place: New York, Arizona, Texas, Mexico, Puerto Rico.... She refuses them all, and instead chooses Ratón Pérez, a college student who shares her interests in music and science. Together, they set out for the university....

Another different presentation of traditional characters in found in the book **One, Two, Three. Who can it be?** in Spanish **Uno, dos, tres. ¡Dime quién es!** is co-authored with Isabel Campoy and illustrated by Viví Escrivá. The predictable format of this book invites children to guess who the next character will be based on the clues that are given in each page. The various storybook characters speak in the first person, offering previously unrevealed insights about their lives that children delight in discovering. This book was born from the longing familiar to every reader, of wanting to learn more about their favorite characters!

We also learn more about the lives of well-loved characters in the book ***A New Home for the Seven Little Kids***, in Spanish ***La casa nueva de los siete cabritos***, illustrated by Viví Escrivá.

To her family's good fortune, Mother Goat has found a pot of gold at the end of the rainbow. Since she wants to build a new house for herself and her seven little goats, she obtains the services of Pig Three, a well-known master architect. As Mother Goat travels through town, shopping for furniture for their new home, she is being followed by the shadowy Big Bad Wolf, who dons different disguises to remain in hiding while he is pursuing his prey. But not to worry—Mother Goat is more than a match for him!

Another book based on fairy-tale characters is ***Happy Birthday, Little Red Riding Hood***, in Spanish ***¡Feliz cumpleaños, Caperucita Roja!*** illustrated by Ana López Escrivá. Little Red Riding Hood is helping her mother plan her birthday party; they are creating a guest list, sending out invitations, deciding on the menu and looking forward to the celebration as a time to enjoy all of their wonderful friends!

Teachers and Librarians' Ideas

Retelling Folktales in a New Setting

After reading ***The Great-Great-Granddaughter of Cucarachita Martina***, children can be invited to rewrite a favorite folktale in a new setting. All of the suggestions given earlier for writing a folktale can be useful, but you may want to precede them with the following questions: What favorite story would you like to retell? In what new setting would you like the story to take place? What changes will take place in the story now that the setting has changed?

Writing "I am" Books

After reading ***One, Two, Three. Who can it be?***, in Spanish, ***Uno, dos, tres, ¡dime quién es!***, students have used the book as a framework for writing their own first-person accounts about who they are, what they like to do, and what they would like others to know about themselves.

Ideas for varied formats for the I AM books can be found in the Authors in the Classroom book or in the website, which features many books created by teachers, children and parents: www.authorsintheclassroom.com

Folktale Quilts or Wall Hangings

A favorite activity is to respond to literature by creating quilts. I have been the fortunate recipient of several, which I treasure, some made from fabric, others, with paper.

Sometimes they are focused on a single folktale, and children have drawn different characters or scenes from the story in each square. Other times, the quilt includes scenes or characters from different folktales in each of the squares.

Part V: Writing in Multiple Genres

The Richness of Multiple Voices

As an author, one of the most difficult questions for me to answer is "What genre do you write in?" Many authors do specialize in a few specific genres, so it could sound pretentious for me to say that I write in all genres. Yet, as I explained earlier in my own case becoming an author was something that developed naturally over time, as a part of living. Writing was not a profession that I consciously chose nor the fulfillment of a life plan. And just as I did not consciously set out to become an author, I did not choose a particular genre in which to specialize.

In my most inspired moments I write poetry. I don't usually think of it as something that will eventually become a book, but instead as something that I need to put on paper in order to not lose the flash of inspiration. Later, I may toy with a poem and work on it, but it always begins as a gift. Stories for picture books also have a way of appearing surprisingly and unexpectedly, triggered by something visual, a memory, or just the sound of a word or phrase. Memoirs, longer narratives, plays, and non-fiction each have their own way of coming into form; I will describe those in detail in the relevant sections. For me, all of these genres are important. They are all means of fulfilling my desire to enrich the lives of children and adolescents, and I feel immense gratitude to all of the people who participate in the process of turning my words into a book, a CD, or a video, a play, or a ballet.

Poetry and I

Books of Original Poetry

A la sombra de un ala
Una vez en el medio del mar
Minuto eterno

Books of Original Poetry with CDs of poems turned into songs by Suni Paz

Abecedario de los animales
Arrullos de la sirena
Canción de todos los niños del mundo
Coral y espuma. Abecedario del mar
Gathering the Sun. A Bilingual Alphabet of Poems
Todo es canción

Poetry Anthologies in Spanish

Días y días de poesía
Caballito Blanco y otros poemas
El gato de trapo y otros poemas

Book of Original Poetry Bilingual co-authored with Rosalma Zubizarreta Ada

Arenas y trinos. Abecedario del río/Sand and song.
The ABCs of the River

Poetry Anthologies in Spanish co-authored with F. Isabel Campoy

Programa **Alegría: Poesía cada día**
Programa ***Música amiga***
  Música amiga - 10 books and 10 CDs with music and voice by Suni Paz
Colección ***Cielo abierto***
  Gorrión, gorrión
  Verde limón
  La rama azul
  Dulce es la sal
  Nuevo día
  Huertos de coral
  Ríos de lava

Books and CD - Frog Street
    Salta, saltarín
    Poemas con ton y son
Books - Houghton Mifflin Harcourt
    En los montes, monte soy
    Superlibro de Rimas – K
    Superlibr de Rimas — 1

Poetry Anthologies in Spanish and English co-authored with F. Isabel Campoy

Gateways to the Sun/Puertas al sol series
    Pimpón/Dreaming Fish
    Antón Pirulero/Laughing Crocodiles
    Mambrú/Singing Horse
    Chuchurumbé/Flying Dragon

Multicultural Poetry Anthology

A Chorus of Cultures (co-authored with Lee Bennet Hopkins and Violet Harris)

TO POETRY
Sounds
  sh... sh... sh...
Words
  flower
    family
      friendship
each with its own color
      dawn
its own fragrance
    forest
its own taste
      ocean.
I take a pencil
  write one
    joy
  two
    girls, boys
  three
    play, learn, dream
  many
    always, here, there,
      everywhere
each word different
  unique
and yet
  each one happy
to be on the page
  to create
    together
a gift for all
    peace, solidarity
in a poem.

A LA POESIA
Sonidos
  sh... sh... sh...
Palabras
  flor
    familia
      amistad
cada una con su color
      amanecer
su fragancia
    bosque
su sabor
    mar.
Tomo un lápiz
  escribo una
    alegría
  dos
    niñas, niños,
  tres
    juegan, aprenden,
      sueñan
  muchas
    siempre, aquí, allí,
    en todas partes
cada palabra distinta
  única
y, sin embargo,
  contentas todas
de estar en la página
  de formar
    juntas
un regalo para todos
    paz, solidaridad
en un poema.

Poetry has been a presence in my life since my earliest days. My maternal grandfather, was a poet and my maternal grandmother, a lover of poetry. Rhymes and songs were all around me. My mother sang me old romances, the Spanish medieval ballads. My grandmother sang me José Marti s'verses, set to tunes she herself composed. Even my loving father, who lacked any great musical talent, sang old traditional songs or created simple lullabies for me:

> *Si mi niña quiere la luna*
> *al cielo yo subiré*
> *y en bandejita de plata*
> *a mi niña la luna traeré*

"If my daughter wants the moon / I will go up to the sky/ and in a silver platter/ I will bring her the Moon'

The rhymes included bringing a lucero, or bright star, on a golden dish or even a comet on a diamond platter. Later he would share his love for astronomy with me and those celestial bodies that had lulled me to sleep became fascinating even if distant realities.

I was barely three years old when my grandmother began to teach me poems that I would recite for my parents and other family members. She scorned the conventional practice, prevalent in that time and place, of teaching children trivial rhymes that they would repeat without much understanding. She believed that children, who are immersed in the daily process of discovering a new world, are particularly capable of connecting with poetry, which is a new way of looking at the world. As a result, she taught me José Marti's verses and my grandfather's poems, which I delighted in reciting and whose meanings I intuited, more than understood.

THE RICHNESS OF CHILDREN'S FOLKLORE: TRADITIONAL NURSERY RHYMES AND CHRISTMAS CAROLS

My childhood was blessed with the richness of folklore. During my first seven years of life, when I was an only child in a home full of adults —grandparents, parents, aunts, and uncles— every evening at around 5 o'clock, without any formal summons, a group of children would spontaneously gathered on the large porch of our old house, the Quinta Simoni, on the outskirts of Camagiiey. A few came out from neighboring houses, nicely dressed and accompanied by a parent or a grandparent who would return a couple of hours later to pick them up. Most came from the poorer houses further away from the town, many times barefoot and poorly dressed. Yet, we all knew the same songs, and as we held hands in a circle for a round or lined up across from each other for a game, we

followed the same patterns other children had followed for generations before us. We had a common heritage, and it was our bond.

Those songs and games were a gift from centuries past we cherished and enjoyed. These childhood experiences are recounted in **Pin pin sarabín** [Childhood games], illustrated by Pablo Torrecilla, one of the seven books in the collection *Cuentos con Alma*, and alter included them in **Island Treasures**, in Spanish, **Tesoros de mi isla**, in the section *Días en la Quinta Simoni* or *Days at the Quinta Simoni*. I have treasured these memories, and the songs and rhymes, throughout my life.

In my numerous travels, I have heard the same songs, or regional variations of them, sung by children in humble rural schools in Mexico, Ecuador, and Perú, as well as in affluent urban schools in Mexico City, Bogotá, and Caracas. I have heard these same songs sung in warm Caribbean islands beneath the blooming flame trees of Puerto Rico and the Dominican Republic, as well as on cool autumn afternoons among the falling leaves of rural Castilian towns.

These songs are not only sung in the Americas, from Argentina to New Mexico; once, while teaching at the University of Guam, I discovered that on that Pacific Ocean island they still sing the beloved *"Tengo una muñeca vestida de azul / con zapatos blancos y velo de tul'* [I have a doll all dressed in blue / with white shoes and a lace veil]. In the local version, these first two lines are sung in Spanish, while the rest of the song is sung in the vernacular language, Chamorro.

In addition to having had such a long and extended life, this storehouse of folklore is even richer as a result of its diversity. In the course of centuries of limited communication, varying versions and offshoots of the same rhymes and songs have evolved in the different communities throughout the vast areas of the world where Spanish is spoken. Each and every version is to be treasured, and one of my dreams is to see them all compiled and made available to all children.

The bilingual anthologies of nursery rhymes *¡Pío Peep! Nursery Rhymes in Spanish and English; MooMuu Animal Nursery Rhymes* and *Mamá Goose. A Latino Nursery Treasury*, prepared in collaboration with Isabel Campoy, have given us the opportunity to offer these well-loved verses to Spanish-speaking children living in the United States and, at the same time, also make them available to English-speaking children. What a joy it is, not only to preserve these beloved rhymes but also to extend the range of their audience!

Due to the large number of existing rhymes, these three books are just an initial glimpse of the much larger treasure trove that needs to be preserved and shared. *¡Pío Peep!* and *MooMuu* feature warm full-page illustrations by Viví Escrivá, and we were fortunate to have the collaboration of Alice Schertle in creating the English version of *¡Pío Peep!*

For the more extensive collection *Mamá Goose, A Latino Nursery Treasure* Maribel Suárez created the whimsical illustrations: "The playful and perky watercolor illustrations, featuring small-eyed assortments of families and friends (both human and animal) work in harmony with the text, balancing the poems without overtaking the space" *(The Bulletin of the Center for Children's Books* 58, no. 9, May 2005). *Mamá Goose* was recognized as Book of the Month by the excellent website *Colorín Colorado,* the Spanish site of *Reading Rockets.*

Merry Navidad, a collection of *villancicos* or traditional Christmas carols, was published by HarperCollins in a bilingual edition. Christmas carols are abundant in Hispanic culture and highlight various aspects of the season. Therefore, Isabel Campoy and I decided to organize our selections into several sections: *On the Road to Bethlehem, The Posadas, Christmas Eve, The Shepherds, Christmas Lullabies, Saint Joseph, The Christmas Tree, Aguinaldos,* and *The Three Wise Kings.* Each section begins with an introduction that explains the significance of that particular theme in Hispanic culture and includes a few representative carols.

My daughter Rosalma Zubizarreta created a poetic rendition in English for each carol, as well as the musical transcriptions that appear in the book. Viví Escrivá's art reflects the diversity of the many lands in which these *villancicos* are sung, as well as the diversity of the people who sing them.

Isabel created a new version of the popular children's song, *Diez perritos*. In the original version the ten puppies disappear, one at a time, under non auspicious circumstances, and the child who sings the song ends up without any puppies at all. In our version the puppies leave for fun reasons and one remains to be the child's best friend forever. Our dear friend Ulises Wensell created the illustrations of the ten darling puppies and again, my daughter, Rosalma Zubizarreta, was able to create an English version that retains the same musical quality of the original.

POETRY ANTHOLOGIES

Poems are gems, and collecting them is a passion that began in my childhood. I filled many notebooks with poems written by the poets I loved, copying a poem carefully was a pleasurable way to overcome my dyslexia.

The first time that the tiresome drills of my after-school English lessons changed from *"Tom is a boy. Mary is a girl. This is a pencil. That is a chair"* to *"In Winter I get up at night / And dress by yellow candlelight / In Summer quite the other way / 1 have to go to bed by day* what had once been a boring task was now filled with new and exciting discoveries. For a child living in a tropical country, where there is no winter to speak of and the days are always the same length, there were many foreign concepts with which to grapple in this poem, and yet how wonderful it was to savor the words in my mouth and to let them come back again and again into my memory. I practiced saying them slowly at first, then more rapidly, searching for the right cadence, knowing that I was not to chop them up at the end of each line but instead find a way to make them into a harmonious whole—that the rhyme would be more powerful if I treated it with subtlety. Once I was able to enjoy poetry in English, I knew that I could enjoy studying that language forever.

Collecting poetry for children has also been a constant joy. I started copying poems for my own children, and eventually in 1967 some of those collections were published in Perú by Editorial Arica, later Editorial Brasa, as part of a series that I called Edad de Oro [Golden Age] in honor of José Marti, whose magazine for children, which was later compiled into a book, bears the title *La Edad de Oro*. These four books, *Poesía menuda* [Tiny Poems], *Poesía pequeña* [Small Poems], *Poesía alegre* [Joyful Poems], and *Poesía infantil* [Children's Poems], were the first of many anthologies.

As bilingual programs developed in the United States in the 1970s, it became apparent that there was a dire lack of materials in Spanish for both Spanish-speaking children as well as for those learning Spanish. Some federally funded programs attempted to address the need, but it was obvious that the production of sufficient appropriate materials required commercial publishers to join in the venture.

The treasure trove of poetry in Spanish-speaking countries is enormous. While economic conditions in many of these countries have restricted development in areas that require financial investment, such as science and technology, nothing can restrict the soul of a poet. Thus, our poets have composed innumerable verses, both orally and in writing, many of them addressed to children.

As a lover of poetry, I felt called to share this heritage with children from Spanish-speaking families in the United States, as well as with all of the children in this country.

The title of the reading series ***Hagamos caminos*** [Creating Paths] was inspired by lines of a poem by Antonio Machado *"Caminante, no hay camino, se hace camino al andar"* [Fellow traveler, there are no roads; we make the roads as we walk]. Creating this series afforded me the opportunity to showcase the work of poets who at the time were not very well known in this country; Mirta Aguirre, Julia Calzadilla, David Chericián, Jaime Ferrán, Isabel Freire de Matos, Gloria Fuertes, Fernando Luján, Fernán Silva Valdés and María Elena Walsh. Others, such as Juan Ramón Jiménez, Nicolás Guillén, José Martí, and Francisco Matos Paoli, were well known among adult students of Spanish, but had not been made accessible to children in mainstream publications.

What a joy it has been to see that from then on, these poets and others whose work I helped publicize—Dora Alonso, Arturo Corcuera, and Washington Delgado, among many—have begun to be included in educational materials for children published in Spanish by several other publishers. Hampton-Brown was one of the publishing houses that were beginning to produce more educational materials in Spanish, and I was very pleased when they embraced my idea of a poetry anthology that included a poem for each day of the year.

Días y días de poesía [Days and Days of Poetry] is structured like a calendar with a poem for each day, related to the day, the month, or themes related to each season. It features poets from Spain and Latin America, and early authors to write poetry for children in Spanish in the United States. I was glad to feature Ernesto Galarza's wonderful books of poems in Spanish, in English, and in bilingual editions. His published books are brief and sparse, often illustrated with black-and-white photos taken by the author himself or with simple line drawings. They almost look handcrafted, and what wonderful poems they contain! To share his work with others throughout the United States by means of my anthologies has given me great satisfaction.

Of course, while developing ***Días y días de poesía*** there were many holidays and significant moments of the year for which no appropriate poem in Spanish existed at the time.

This offered an opportunity to write poems for Martin Luther King Jr. Day, César Chávez, St. Patrick's Day, Easter, Fourth of July, Halloween, Thanksgiving, and Christmas, among others. There are a total of 55 of my original poems included in this anthology.

Numerous teachers have shared that the recipe of "a poem a day" transformed their teaching. The success of ***Días y días*** led to the publication of A ***Chorus of Cultures***, a parallel multicultural anthology which I had the pleasure of coediting with Lee Bennett Hopkins and Violet Harris. I could not have anticipated that this would be the beginning of a delightful friendship with Lee Bennet Hopkins. With great generosity Lee invited me to collaborate in several anthologies that he edited. A list of the poems I created for those anthologies can be found in the bibliography at the end of this book.

Both anthologies are accompanied by oversize charts depicting poems with full-color illustrations. The message given by these charts is one I have always wanted to convey: **Poetry importance cannot be overstated. It deserves to be highlighted in the classroom. Together, poetry and art offer a special message that enriches each day.**

After ***Días y días* de poesía** had been used so successfully in classrooms for over twenty years, Hampton-Brown decided to publish an updated version. It took some time for this to happen, but now, ***Alegría: Poesía cada día***, co-authored with Isabel Campoy with an astonishingly beautiful design by National Geographic offers teachers poetry for every day. The teacher's anthology, with close to 400 poems, is lavishly illustrated in color with magnificent photos from National Geographic. The poems in the three oversized books are illustrated both by drawings and photographs.

The audio component of the program, to be accessed through its website, includes the reading of each of the poems, either by Isabel or me. Before and after reading each poem we make brief comments to foster greater understanding of the poems meaning and intent. For many of the poems there are musical versions in the voice of Suni Paz.

The website offers pedagogical suggestions for the exploration of the poems in class as well as additional resources. One specific aspect of the website gives me great joy: teachers will be able to print copies of the poems for their students that
will be able to create and keep their own personal anthologies.

Isabel Campoy and I have developed together many other Spanish poetry anthologies. There are seven anthologies in the series *Cielo abierto* [Open Sky] produced by Harcourt: *Gorrión gorrión* [Sparrow, Sparrow], *Verde limón* [Green Lemon], *Dulce es la sal* [Where Salt is Sweet], *La rama azul* [The Blue Branch], *Nuevo día* [New Day], *Huertos de coral* [Coral Gardens], and *Ríos de lava* [Rivers of Lava]. Our aim for these anthologies was to collect the best poems written in Spanish for children throughout the Spanish-speaking world.

To the previously mentioned poets, we added others such as Rafael Alberti, Tomás Allende, Elsa Isabel Borneman, Morita Carrillo, Rodolfo Dada, Ester Feliciano Mendoza, Emilia Gallego, Marta Giménez Pastor, Horacio Guillén, Floria Jiménez, María Hortensia Lacau, Gabriela Mistral, Carlos Murciano, Amado Nervo, Antonio Ramírez Granados, Gilda Rincón, Marina Romero, Fryda Schultz de Mantovani, Javier Sologuren, José Sebastián Tallón, María de la Luz Uribe, and Celia Viñas. These anthologies also contain many original poems written by Isabel Campoy as well as others of which I am the author.

It has been a source of constant sorrow for me to see that children with a Spanish-speaking background frequently feel ashamed of their language. Somehow, society has succeeded in persuading them that the language of their parents and grandparents is an inferior language, not worth learning and speaking, and reflecting only a culture of poverty. More than once, children have told me directly they don't want to speak the "language of the poor," "the language of losers."

It is certainly true that due to the unjust prevailing social inequality many of the people who speak Spanish in this country live in very difficult economic circumstances. At the same time, there is much to be admired in the dedication, hard work, and courage so prevalent among these immigrants whose home language is Spanish.   And we could say that Spanish is the language of unsung heroes.

In addition, I want our young people to learn that Spanish, the language of their hardworking immigrant parents, who came here dreaming of a better life for their children; is also the language of some of the World's most admired writers, like Cervantes, Santa Teresa de Jesús, San Juan de la Cruz, Sor Juana Inés, José Martí, Pablo Neruda, Gabriela Mistral, and Gabriel García Márquez, but also of some of the World's most admired artist like Diego Velázquez Pablo Picasso, Fryda Kahlo, of musicians like Pablo Casals and Plácido Domingo, scientists like Carlos Finlay and many other creators, scientists, and visionaries who

have enriched the world for all people.   This has become a life mission for both Isabel and I.

The dual language collections *Gateways to the Sun* and *Puertas al sol,* published by Santillana, have been artistically designed by Maestro Felipe Dávalos using the work of more than 50 Latin American and Latino artists, as well as reproductions of the best Hispanic art. These series aim to convey to Latino children as well as to all children in the United States, a vivid presentation of the rich culture of Hispanic Americans.

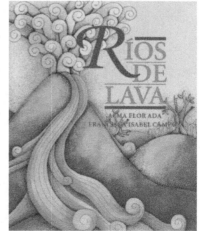

One of the series of this collection is devoted to poetry, it includes four anthologies published in separate editions, in English and Spanish **Pimpón/ Dreaming Fish; Mambrú/Singing Horse, Antón Pirulero/Laughing Crocodiles**, and **Chuchurumbé/Flying Dragons**.

Instead of grouping the poems by dates or by themes as we did in other anthologies, in these, we have taken a unique approach and grouped the poems by the authors' countries of origin and gave special relevance to the author by writing poems about the author and the country.

We wanted to emphasize that poems do not appear out of thin air, but are instead the expression of a particular poet. By inviting children to learn about the poets who created each poem, we hope to convey the message that they, too, can write poetry. This message is supported by the four journals that accompany these books: **Letras**, **Palabras**, **Rimas**, and **Poemas**, in English, **Letters**, **Words**, **Rhymes**, and **Poems**. The journals guide the children through the process of discovering their own poetic voice.

Each book is divided into sections devoted to individual poets, and each section begins with a poem celebrating that poet's native country. By connecting the poets

to their own countries of origin, whether México, Cuba, or Puerto Rico, Guatemala or Nicaragua, Argentina or Spain, we seek to convey the message that as Latinos, we not only partake of the heritage of the country of our ancestors, but we can also partake in some measure of the heritage of the entire Hispanic world. The initial section of each book is devoted to a Latino poet living in the United States. For those sections, rather than writing a poem to a country, we have written a poem about the experience of being a Latino or a Latina in this county.

In each section, the opening poem is followed by another poem, written by either Isabel or myself, to the poet whose work is showcased in that section. The "poem to the poet" may play with the language and metaphors used by the poet or focus on one of their literary or personal qualities. In all instances, it is an expression of admiration and gratitude, for we want children to witness our respect for other poets. We want our open admiration of these poets to awaken their own sense of appreciation, as we feel that appreciating others helps to develop one's sense of self-respect. *"Honrar, honra,"* wrote José Martí. This succinct phrase means "when we honor others, we act honorably," and this is the message we want to pass on.

Following our introductory poems, each section includes several poems by the featured poet. Three of the books conclude with a section on popular folklore, for which we have written poems dedicated to the anonymous poets who created these verses and where we acknowledge all of the parents and grandparents who were the first ones to recite these verses to their children and grandchildren, and who are our earliest teachers.

The birth of a child is an occasion for anticipation and hope. At the time two of my daughters-in-law were expecting my heart swelled with feelings for those future babies. In the peacefulness of a retreat, that I was attending with one of the mothers to be, I let my feelings become words on the paper. The poems wrote at that time became significant to me,  because they expressed my love for those two granddaughters a love that has only increased through the years. I thought of them as something very personal, and it took many years before I shared them. What a joy it is, that now that those poems have become a book many mothers and grandmothers see their own feelings reflected in them, and, what a treasure the delightful music created by Suni Paz for **Arrullos de la sirena**! [The Mermaid's Lullabies].

POEMS SET TO MUSIC

When the inherent musicality of a poem is set to a melody, the poem will not only sing on the page but can also become a beloved song. Having the excellent composer Suni Paz write music for my poems included in *Hagamos caminos* was one of the greatest gifts I have ever received. She also sung and recorded the poems turned into songs in her own voice, which has been recognized by the Smithsonian Institute as one of the most significant voices of the twentieth century.

After **Hagamos caminos** was no longer in print, and the rights have reverted to me, my generous son Alfonso Zubizarreta, always so supportive of my work, created Del Sol Publishing to produce Suni's recordings, of the songs, which included not only my poems but also a few poems written by others, as well as many traditional pieces of folklore. Isabel Campoy agreed to write a number of poems for this project. These ten anthologies and their accompanying CDs, comprising 120 songs, have been published under the collection title of **Música amiga**. Individual titles are:

> **¡Qué rica la ronda**! [The Joy of Rounds]
> **Canta la letra** [Words that Sing]
> **Canción y alegría** [Songs and Joy]
> **Corre al coro** [Join the Chorus]
> **Con ton y son** [Singing With Rhythm]
> **Caracolí** [Seashell]
> **Sigue la música** [Follow the Music]
> **Do, Re, Mi, ¡Sí, sí!** [Do, Re, Mi, Yes, Yes!]
> **El camino de tu risa** [Following Your Laughter]
> **El son del sol** [Song of the Sun].

To facilitate making the best use in the classroom of these songs, Isabel and I wrote the book **Música amiga Aprender cantando** which offers reading strategies as well as specific activities to promote language development, initial reading strategies, critical thinking skills, and creative attitudes, in accordance with the Creative Reading Methodology.

Suggestions on the use of all our other songs as well as of pairing songs with children's books make this book a rich tool.

For several years Suni Paz and I offered in multiple conferences the presentation *Aprender cantando*. Because many of the participants wanted a recording of the session,

I wrote and recorded the text and inserted professional recordings of Suni's songs. Originally published as a cassette, **Aprender cantando** is now published as a doble CD. The text appears included in the first part of the book **Música amiga: aprender cantando.**

Teachers and Librarians' Ideas

Children's and Family's Own Anthologies

Folklore can serve as a welcome opportunity for creating a stronger connection between children's homes and the school or library. Sometimes it can be difficult to engage parents with books. They may feel intimidated by their lack of formal education, especially if they never had the opportunity to receive any.

Cinco pollitos

Cinco pollitos
tiene mi tía:
Uno le canta,
otro le pía
y tres le tocan la chirimía.

Letting parents and relatives know that the songs and games familiar to them are considered valuable by teachers and librarians, and are even collected in beautiful books, can be a way of encouraging family members' self-esteem and highlighting the significance of their contributions to their children's education.

Due to the vast territory in which Spanish is spoken and the many cultures that have contributed to it, Latino oral folklore is quite rich. Inviting children's families to contribute a song, a rhyme, or a verse in order to create a classroom anthology is a process that often reveals some beautiful gems.

To help every child feel included, it's important to make sure that every member of the class or group is represented in the anthology with a contribution provided by a family member or family friend. Each page can include the name of the child as well as the name and ancestral home of the adult who contributed the piece.

Children can also create individual anthologies with their own favorite songs and games as well as other family favorites.

Books of Original Poetry in ABC Format

In addition to the poems included in the various anthologies just mentioned, I have also written many other poems. Some are as yet unpublished; others have been published in book format. While I do not like to admit to having any favorites among my books, I do feel a special place in my heart for my books of poetry.

Gathering the Sun, an alphabet book of poems celebrating farmworkers, is one of the books that I love best. When I first wrote the poems in Spanish many years ago, I never imagined that one day they would be translated by my daughter Rosalma Zubizarreta into English, and published as a beautifully illustrated bilingual picture book. These poems reflect my profound appreciation for farmworkers—for the value of their backbreaking work on which all of our lives depend; for their courage and their dedication to their families; their sense of honor and dignity, based not on material possessions or achievements but on a life devoted to work; their adherence to solidarity and friendship; their sense of hospitality and caring for one another; and the sincerity of their words.

The poems were shortened substantially since we needed to allow enough room to present the poems in both languages and to showcase Simón Silva's bold and striking illustrations. Silva, himself a child of farmworkers, brought his own authentic experiences and memories to the pages of this project, in addition to his enormous artistic talents.

This book has given me great satisfaction. People often ask me to autograph it as a gift for a child who is being baptized, for a First Communions, a Quinceañera, a golden wedding anniversary, or for a baby who is not yet born. It gives me great joy to have helped create a book that has become a symbol of cultural pride, affirmation, and community for so many Latinos.

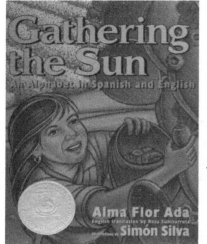

There are many moving anecdotes connected with this book. Once, a teacher in San Diego told me I had "put her in my book." Showing me the illustration of a young girl and her father that accompanies the poem "Islands," she told me that as a child she had looked just like the girl in the illustration and had a basket just like hers, which her father would fill with asparagus each afternoon when she met him in the fields. Then, sobbing, she added, "And this man is my father. What a pity he died before he could find himself dignified in a book."

Another time, after a parents' meeting, a woman waited until everyone had left to ask me to sign two books. One was a book that had been given out to all of the parents at the meeting, and she asked me to dedicate that copy to all her five children. The second book was a copy of *Gathering the Sun,* which she had purchased for herself and wanted me to dedicate to her. "I don't know how to read," she told me. "I have tried to learn several times, and never could. But I know this book will teach me how, because this book is about me. This is my life.

I have experienced so many moving moments in connection with this book that it would be impossible to share them all here, yet 1 will close with one more. Once Isabel Campoy and I were offering an all-day presentation to more than five hundred teachers in New York City, on the subject of encouraging the authorship of teachers, students, and families—the process we describe in our book, ***Authors in***

the Classroom. The assistant superintendent opened the meeting by asking everyone to open their copy of ***Gathering the Sun*** (unbeknownst to us, she had earlier decided to give each participant a copy of this book as a gift) and to read aloud, all together, the poem "Honor." Anticipating our surprise—after all, we were in New York City and this was a book about farmworkers—she introduced the reading by saying, "Do not be surprised that I have chosen a book about farmworkers. It is important for us to remember where the children we teach come from, or where their parents come from, or where their grandparents come from. At some point, we all come from the land."

She added that she uses this poem every year when she meets with the new principals in her district, because she wants to emphasize the importance of remembering that all honest work, no matter how humble, is honorable. Too often children are not given this important message, even though it may be very relevant to their own family situation and speak to their parents' livelihoods. I must confess that tears were streaming down my face as I once again realized the power of the published voice, and how necessary it is that we dedicate that power to the benefit of all.

Of course, sometimes we write books just to celebrate the playful side of life as well. One of my first books of poems was ***Abecedario de los animales***, an ABC book with two poems for each letter of the alphabet. One poem is about an animal whose name begins with that particular letter, while the second poem in each set is about the letter itself. This book had a surprising genesis. My very dear friend Kuki Miler used to travel to the United States to visit us from Venezuela, where she lived for several years during the time that she was exiled from her native Argentina. Once the Junta's

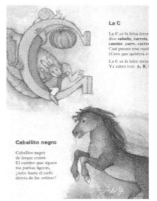

dictatorship ended and she was about to return to her native country, she came for a final visit and this time brought her young son, Emilio. It was an important moment. It would not be so easy for Kuki to come again from Argentina. Yet, when they arrived, I was in bed, with a horrible cold. I was extremely disappointed to not be able to meet Emilio, and at the same time, I did not want to risk him catching my nasty cold. So instead, I decided to write him a series of poems, and thus the *Abecedario de los animales* was born.

It has been fun to play with the coincidences between the shapes of some letters and words beginning with those letters. In Spanish many of names for vehicles with wheels begin with the letter C *(carro, carreta,carretón)*. The word for "horse" *(caballo)* and the verb "to run" *(correr)* also begin with the letter C, whose shape almost resembles that of a wheel. Maybe the letter C would like to run? By adding a few more alliterations, the following poem was created:

La C es la tercera letra	*The third letter is C.*
dice caballo, carro,	*It says* caballo, carro,
carrera,	carrera
casi parece una rueda	*It looks almost like a*
creo que quisiera correr.	*wheel,*
La C es la letra tercera	*I think it would like to run!*
ya sabes tres: A, B, C.	Now you know three: A, B, C.

Alma Flor Ada / Vivi Escrivá

CORAL Y ESPUMA

ABECEDARIO DEL MAR

Ever since Suni Paz set these poems to her delightful music, the enthusiasm they awaken in children has been heightened. What a joy it is to visit classrooms where children know these songs by heart!

The success of **Abecedario de los animales**, which has had multiple reprints, including a Big Book Format and a posters format, led its Spanish publisher Espasa-Calpe to publish **Coral y espuma. Abecedario del mar**, a collection of poems about the ocean.

The exquisite musical renditions created by Suni Paz add a special dimension to this book.

As an island woman, this book is also very dear to my heart. Now, I'm in the process of having this book published in a new edition with amazingly beautiful illustrations by Cuban artist, Samantha San Roman, the daughter of my cousin Leana Labrada. I am delighted to show a couple of them here.

A very young artist, Samantha is developing her own style, to some extent inspired in "Art Noveau"

Uva caleta and Coral y espuma by Cuban artist Samantha San Román

Another ABC book is **Abeceloco**, published by Frog Street Press. In this whimsical book the animals representing each of the letters, introduce the one corresponding to the next letter giving a clue to the reader to guess what the next animal would be. **Abeceloco** was originally part of the *Hagamos caminos* reading series.

During most of my life I have written without even considering the possibility of publishing, just because I have felt the call to convey thoughts of feelings unto written words. Of course, I have been delighted when some of the things I have written with no publication in mind have been published, sometimes a long time after, as it happened with **Arrullos de la sirena**, which I have already mentioned

Just now, as I am finishing this book, a set of poems I wrote while on a magical camping trip with my daughter Rosalma has been published as a book by Arte Público Press. Those days and nights on a sandy cove by the river Yuma, brought up emotions that I put into paper right there. Later, I savored the simple poems for years, as reminders of the joy of those moments. Now many years later they have been published in a bilingual book **Arenas y trinos. Abecedario del río. Sand and Song. The ABC's of the River.**

Fue una alegría compartir con Rosalma la creación del libro, igual que habíamos compartido la experiencia que le dio origen. Y estoy muy agradecida a Arte Público Press por haber convertido esos poemas en este libro y a Gabhor Utomo por las delicadas ilustraciones que capturan la esencia de los poemas.

STORIES RETOLD AS POEMS AND SONGS

Retelling stories is one of my favorite genres, and retelling Stories in verse (whether they are my own stories or traditional ones) always delight me.

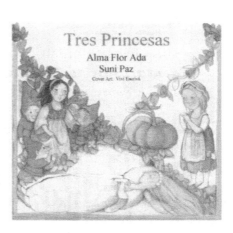

Gifted Suni Paz has created some extraordinary compositions for my retelling in verse of *Cenicienta*, *Blancanieves*, and *La bella durmiente* [Cinderella, Snow White, and Sleeping Beauty], published in the CD **Tres princesas.**

In the CD **Cuéntame un cuento**, the stories in verse form are *Los tres cerditos*, *Las semillas mágicas* and *Caperucita* [The Three Little Pigs, Jack and the Beanstalk and Little Red Riding hood]. It also includes my poems, *Cuéntame un cuento* [Tell Me a Story] and Los *libros son mis amigos* [Books Are My Friends], which Suni Paz has also turned into songs.

After I rewrote in verse form the 12 Spanish stories in the collection *Cuentos para todo el año / Stories the Year 'round* Suni Paz recorded her musical creations, with favorites like **No fui yo** [It Wasn't Me], **La hamaca de la vaca** [In the Cow's Backyard], **La piñata vacía** [The Empty Piñata], and **No quiero derretirme** [I Don't Want to Melt]

The CD includes my reading of the 12 original stories, with some comments about how they came to be, as well as Suni's performance.

The five Spanish books of the collection **Libros para contar/Stories for the Telling: Amigos** [Friends], **El canto del mosquito** [The Song of the Teeny-Tiny Mosquito], **Una extraña visita** [Strange Visitors], **¿Quién nacerá aquí?** [Who Will Hatch Here?], and **Me gustaría tener** ... [How Happy I Would Be!] have also been recorded as songs.

Responses from Teachers, Librarians, and Children

I. A Poem a Day

Some of the most meaningful responses to my anthologies and books of poems have come from teachers who have accepted the invitation to enrich their students' lives with "a poem a day." They have come up with such diverse metaphors and/or mottos to describe their success as

"A poem a day keeps minds alert."

"A poem a day makes my classroom a happy place."

"A poem a day is my long-lasting gift to my students."

"A poem a day creates a robust vocabulary."

"A poem a day is a powerful classroom management tool."

Most of these teachers take a few minutes at a specific time each day to teach a new poem. Sometimes they use it as their handwriting, spelling, and/ or vocabulary-building time. Teachers often mention that reviewing a poem presented on a previous occasion not only helps children remember the poems, but also works as a classroom management tool. When children are tired, bored, sleepy, hyperactive, or noisy, reciting or singing a well-loved poem can serve as a way of bringing their minds back to receptive alertness.

2. Connecting Poetry and Art

Poems can be illustrated by children and can also serve as the starting point for nonrepresentational artistic expression using watercolors, clay, or collage.

3. Modifying or Expanding a Poem

Inviting children to expand or modify a poem can be a good way to help them feel more comfortable with poetry and to discover their own creativity. For example, teachers have invited students to add their own personal lines to my poem "Orgullo"/"Proud" from **Gathering the Sun**:

Orgullosa de mi familia	*Proud of my family*
orgulloso de mi lengua	*Proud of my language*
orgullosa de mi cultura	*Proud of my culture*
orgullosa de mi raza	*Proud of my people*
orgullosa de ser quien soy	*Proud of being who I am*

Children can add lines such as "proud of my parents ... my teacher ... my school ... my grandparents ... my siblings ... my friends ... my work ... my art ..." and so on.

Teachers have also encouraged their students to modify the poem "Abuelito" [Grandfather] from **Días y días de poesía** and now, **Alegría, poesía cada día.**

Dime una cosa, Abuelito,	*Tell me something, Grandpa,*
pero dime la verdad.	*But, please, tell me the truth:*
¿Siempre te portabas bien	*Did you always behave well*
cuando tenías mi edad?	*When you were my age?*

Students can modify the poem by substituting *Abuelito* [Grandfather] with another person of their choice—*Abuelila* [Grandmother], *Mamá* [Mom], *Papá* [Dad], *Tía* [Auntie]—and changing the third line to include some other form of behavior: *¿Comías toda la comida? ¿Te acostabas temprano? ¿Hacías toda la tarea?* [Did you always eat all your food ... go to bed early ... complete all your homework?]

4. Creating their own ABC Books

The ABC is an excellent format, with endless possibilities to encourage creating self-published books, since it provides a

structure to follow. This bilingual ABC, was created by a family under the direction of one of my former doctoral students. Her intention was to raise the family's awareness of their strength as a family.

She invited all to dialogue in order to choose meaningful words, related to the family experiences. Then she took a photo to illustrate that word for the English page, while the Spanish pages were illustration with drawings made by the children.

The text for the letter V is a testimonial to the pain suffered by families when some of their members are forced to leave the country. It says: VERÓNICA. *"V" is for Verónica. I chose Verónica because she is my older sister and I love her very much; I miss her greatly because I have not seen her in two*

years. When she and Hermelinda, mi little sister had to leave, they told me they loved me very much. And they left crying.

5. Becoming Poets

Children are drawn to poetry and have a natural ability to express themselves using original metaphors, since in their ongoing explorations of the world they are often finding unsuspected connections.

Sometimes the topics of the poems can be left to children's free choice; other times, the teacher may propose a theme. One teacher asked her students to write *I Am* poems, and relate their poems to the ocean, which they were studying. The children created images to describe themselves based on animals or plants found in the sea. The I Am format is described at length in the book *Authors in the Classroom* and in www.authorsintheclassroom.com

One of the children described herself with images related to different sea creatures finishing with the wonderful metaphor:

> **I am like a star fish**
> **always ready**
> **to give more than one handshake**.

A book co-authored with F. Isabel Campoy, and recently published by Santillana, provides suggestions to explore the potentials of Spanish poetry. The structures and the richness of poetry writen in Spanish as well as activities for its best implementation in the classroom, with specific suggestions for the various levels, are the focus of *Está linda la mar.*

Curtains Up!

Anthologies in Spanish: *Colección Cielo abierto* series, co-authored with F. Isabel Campoy:

Primer acto
Escenas y alegrías
Risas y aplausos
Actores y flores
Saludos al público
Ensayo general
Acto final

Anthologies for *Gateways to the Sun/Puertas al sol* series, co-authored with F. Isabel Campoy

Teatro del Gato Garabato
   Rat-a-tat-Cat
Teatrín de don Crispin
   Roll'N'Role
Escenario de Polichinela
   Top Hat
Tablado de doña Rosita
   Curtains Up

Theatre and I

In the provincial town where I grew up, my only encounters as a young child with full-scale dramatic productions were the few glimpses afforded in an occasional movie. Of course, I attended some events at our local theatre, such as the end-of-the-year student talent shows, yet live theatre remained something foreign, fascinating, and alluring.

Our local theatre house, the Teatro Principal, had been built in the 1800s. When I knew it as a child, it had lost much of its original splendor, yet it still remained a majestic structure, and it has since been renovated.

In "Gilda" a chapter of **Under the Royal Palms** [in Spanish **Bajo las palmas reales**, also included in **Island Treasures**, in Spanish **Tesoros de mi isla**] I share an experience that took place when I was about nine years old. I was able to be backstage during the rehearsals for the end of school performance of the small ballet academy I was attending. It was a memorable experience. The cavernous space seemed huge to my young eyes. How many dressing rooms there were! Who were the actors and actresses who had used these rooms to change into their costumes? In the films of the '40s and '50s, there were often scenes set in actors' dressing rooms, so it was easy for me to imagine these now-empty rooms lined with brightly lit mirrors and filled with bouquets of flowers.

Having watched several movies along the lines of *Red Shoes* and *The Unfinished Dance,* I knew that the behind-the-scenes innards of the building where I now stood had seen their share of real-life drama. But I had no inkling as yet of the nature of the dramas that were presented on the stage. Finally, when I was in sixth grade and about ten or eleven years old, my father took me to the theatre to see three plays that, together, left a lifelong impression on me.

While Camagüey was only the third-largest city in Cuba and was by no means as well known internationally as La

Habana, due to its geographical location it had an international airport. Transcontinental flights from New York to Mexico City, Caracas, Lima, Sao Paulo, and Buenos Aires would often stop in Camagüey for refueling. As a consequence, world-renowned artists who were touring Latin America could often be persuaded to offer a performance in our city. And we had the privilege of enjoying among other luminaries concerts by Jasha Heifetz, Andrés Segovia, Alicia de la Rocha, Arthur Rubinstein, Claudio Arrau and the soprano Victoria de los Ángeles.

On this particular occasion, a Spanish theatrical company was in town for three performances of García Lorca's plays. My parents never let pass any opportunity for my cultural enrichment. When we attended concerts, my mother who took me; for these plays, my father did. Each night the company performed a different play by García Lorca. While the plays may not have been quite so appropriate for a child my age, they made a profound impact on my soul.

First we saw *Bodas de sangre* [Blood Wedding], and I was deeply moved by the destructive power of jealousy. The second night we saw *La casa de Bernarda Alba* [Bernarda Alba's House], and I was frightened by a new awareness of the shadows that can lurk in the depths of the human soul. But it was the third play, *Yerma* [Barren], that shook me the most. This yearning for motherhood, the pain of a loveless marriage, and the destructive force of a judgmental society in those preadolescent days frequently kept me awake with questions I struggled to answer.

Yet beyond the individual impact of each play, I experienced an even greater revelation: the power of theatre itself. The fact that such strong emotions could be generated within the confines of a stage kept me dreaming about the possibilities.

Earlier in this volume, when I wrote about my school years in the section "Becoming an Author," I mentioned my extraordinary sixth-grade teacher, Dr. Rosa María Peyrellade. Her sensitivity to each of her students was a key part of the way that she taught, so of course she noticed that something was going on in me.

Years later, she told me that when in response to her inquiries, I told her about my fascination with the theatre, she was somewhat taken aback as this she knew nothing about incorporating theatre in her teaching. However, she did not feel that she could disregard my interest, and so she encouraged me to write a play and stage it.

Both the play, which I wrote with great enthusiasm, and the performance were rather naive, yet they brought me great joy and became an opportunity for all the students in the class to partake in the experience of staging and performing a play. The principal character was Amalia Simoni, a significant and patriotic figure in the history of my hometown during the struggle to gain independence from Spain. Amalia was very dear to me, as the house where I was born had previously belonged to her family, and she was also grown up there. The plot of my play was based on stories I had often heard at home, and on a long ballad written by my maternal grandfather, Medardo Lafuente.

I no longer have a copy of that play, nor remember many of the details. I do remember that it consisted of three acts: the opening act showed the heroine as a young woman filled with patriotic feelings, falling in love with Ignacio Agramonte, a young lawyer who would later write the Cuban Constitution and command a group of patriots in the Ten Years' War of 1868. In the second act, Ignacio leaves for the countryside to lead his troops and Amalia insists on accompanying him. She lives in a secluded hut where she bears her two children. The last act shows the moment when Amalia is taken prisoner by a Spanish general who offers freedom for herself and her children if she agrees to write a letter asking Ignacio to surrender. She of course refuses and the play ends with her proud exit from the stage as a prisoner.

While my maternal grandmother's family had been Cuban for many generations, [I have recently been able to trace the ancestry of my grandmother Lola all the way to 1714 in Camaguey] both of my grandfathers were Spaniards, proud of their origins and yet fervent lovers of Cuba. Because of this, I learned very early on the difficulty of negotiating identities and how one's national origin could be a complex phenomenon. Both of my grandfathers were pacifists and each of them had a very strong sense of social justice. They deplored colonialism and were very critical of the role Spain had played in history, acknowledging both the negative and the positive outcomes, condemning some acts and approving others. They taught me— not intellectually, because I was too young to put the concepts into words, but experientially—to stay away from stereotypes, to recognize the importance and responsibility inherent in each individual action, and to understand that each person has the ability to act according to his or her own conscience, regardless of circumstances of birth. I also learned that one did not have to adhere to any particular set of values, just because one happened to belong to a particular group of people. It was an enormous gift of freedom for which I have been grateful all my life.

Our secondary education in Cuba, modeled after the Spanish system, was very different from the high school experience in the United States. I described my high school years in some detail in the earlier section, "Becoming an Author." During those years, the Batista dictatorship had an effect on students' lives. Many students were politically active and thus, it was common for classes to be interrupted, sometimes because the students went on strike, at other, the government closed the schools in order to prevent protests.

During my 4th and 5th years, since the Instituto was closed for long periods, some professors suggested that we could design independent study projects in order to make up for the lost time, something we had not been invited to do before. This was a perfect opportunity for my love for theatre to resurface. I wrote three plays, which we rehearsed in the open air at the Casino Campestre, a large public park next to the Institute, since we had no other space available.

The plays were quite a success, and I was very moved emotionally by portraying a variety of different heroines: the unfortunate Juana, known unjustly by history as "Juana, la loca" or "Crazy Juana " the daughter of Isabel and Fernando who was distraught by the grief of losing her husband and being robbed of her throne, first by her father Fernando and later by her son, Carlos; the brave Agustina de Aragón, who faced the invading Napoleonic troops in Spain; and the brilliant Sor Juana Inés de la Cruz, who found refuge in a convent, the only place where she could lead an intellectual life, and yet who even inside the convent experienced persecution as the powerful men of her time could not accept a woman with so much talent. These plays had only a brief life, performed once, one at a time, on the stage of one classroom, yet they led to the idea of staging a play as part of a graduation party for our professors.

While there was no precedent such a party, the fact that my father taught at the Instituto allowed us to invite the faculty as well. All were delighted by this unusual opportunity in our rather traditional town, and every single one showed up.

Professors from the Instituto de Segunda Enseñanza de Camagüey.
Extreme left my father Modesto Ada Rey.
At, the entrance of our home "La Quintica".

My classmates and I had improvised a rustic stage in our garage [we never realized how poor it was until we saw the photos] and had rented folding chairs to place on the lawn. After everyone had the opportunity to mingle and to help themselves from the buffet that my parents had provided for our guests, they all sat down to watch the play.

Opposite to me, playing the role of the protagonist, is Severo Sarduy who would later become a remarkable author.

Instead of a dramatic historical play, what I had written for this occasion was a simple comedy, *La sonámbula* (The Sleepwalker) about a girl at a boarding school who, thanks to the collusion of the friendly sister of the principal, is enjoying a late-night conversation with her boyfriend.

When the girl is caught in the parlor by the school principal, she pretends to be sleepwalking. In her sleep, she is reciting her Latin lesson on syllogisms: *Barbara, Celarent, Darii, Feri, Cesarent, Camestres....*

The comedy has a happy ending that implied a certain amount of criticism of an educational system largely irrelevant to young people's life issues; but since there was only a minimal amount of critique that we could interweave into the story without ruining its effectiveness as a play, we had decided to follow the performance with a roundtable discussion.

We chose the tiniest of round tables—actually, a flower pot stand—and sat around it still wearing the costumes and makeup we had on during the play. Then we began to lash out with our pedagogical critiques of the system that we had just experienced during the last five years, and we bolstered our case by citing the statistics on the high percentage of our classmates who would not be joining us for the graduation ceremony as the system had not been designed to help them succeed.

Needless to say, our presentation was not very well received by all faculty members. Some felt betrayed precisely because we, who were the cream of the crop, had dared to criticize the system that we had so successfully managed to survive. It might have been easier for them to accept some criticism from the discontented ones, the "failures," but not from us, the successful ones. Of course, the "failures" would never have had the opportunity to have their voices be heard.

It was a somewhat difficult situation for my parents, since they had had no clue as to what the content of our performance would be. Yet they were the ones who had taught me to be analytical and both of them were strong believers in a more humane educational system.

Furthermore, they knew that I was following in the footsteps of my maternal grandparents, who had been very innovative educators. Therefore, they did their best to stand by us and attempted to persuade the faculty that not only had we meant no disrespect, but also that our ideas should be given a fair hearing.

Their soothing words had a positive effect on some of the faculty, although there were a few who were not willing to forgive what they felt had been an affront. The reality is that most faculty members were highly qualified and had the best of intentions, but they were restricted by a system that forced them to teach too many students, of which probably more than half were not meant, by their families own limited economic situation, to continue and graduate.

The upheavals the country would go through shortly afterward made this incident pale in light of the serious events that would radically change the life of every Cuban forever. Yet, many years later, after many of these teachers had left Cuba and were living in the United States, some of them were still commenting on the shock they had received that afternoon when their traditional modes of teaching were publicly questioned by their students.

After that first performance, so many people in town got wind of the play and wanted to see it that we were encouraged to rent the Teatro Principal and present the play as a fund-raising event for Catholic Youth Action. Thus, we experienced the joy of packing the colonial Teatro Principal for a performance of *La sonámbula* [The Sleepwalker]. Severo Sarduy, the young man who played the leading male role of the young girl's boyfriend, grew up to become a highly acclaimed writer, who regrettably died while still quite young. As for myself, this has been my sole experience as an actress and playwright for the general public, but it left me with even greater love for the theatre than before.

High school students at the Colegio Abraham Lincoln, staging Cinderella, following their own script. The staging was also created by them.

Later, in my early twenties, when I taught at the Colegio Lincoln in Perú, I invited my high school students to put on a play. They wrote and performed, very successfully, their own version of Cinderella. Not having many resources for decoration and prompts, the students enthusiastically created the necessary atmosphere with some details made by construction paper, showing that it is enough to give the imagination a little suggestion and allow it to do the rest.

Their enthusiasm, the level of collaboration, the positive effect that being on stage had on some of the more timid students, and the surfacing and blossoming of many unsuspected talents, contributed to strengthened my conviction that theatre can be one of the most significant media for creating community in the classroom and for education and personal growth.

All of this inspired me to begin writing plays for children. As in the case of my picture books, which I have discussed previously it was not easy for me to imagine that I might create my own story lines. Thus, my first plays, published in Perú, were adaptations of well-known stories.

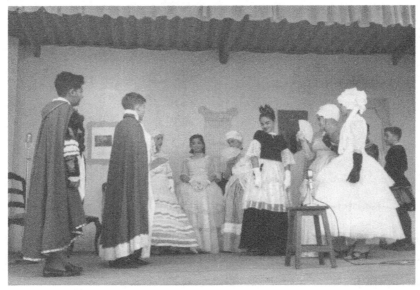

Colegio Bilingue Abraham Lincoln, Lima, Peru

As a teacher, my students; commitment and enthusiasm were a gift. Enjoying today the friendship of wonderful human beings who were my students more than half a century ago is indeed a blessing I cherish.

Plays in the Classroom

In 1970, I moved to Atlanta, Georgia, where I was an Associate Professor at Emory University. My mother, Alma Lafuente de Ada, was also living in Atlanta. She was in charge of a television project for the Dekalb County Office of Education that was part of a larger program called Foreign Languages in Elementary Schools (FLES).

She had conceived the idea of creating simple 15-minute TV programs in Spanish, for which she wrote delightful scripts using simple language that reinforced the lessons the students were learning. At the same time, the programs offered students rich cultural experiences. The scripts incorporated a number of different songs, and were performed by students from a different classroom each week. At any one time, there were a number of different programs at various stages of production: some were still being rehearsed while one was being taped. By always including scenes where a chorus could act or sing she ensured that all the children from a given classroom could be involved.

The enthusiasm that the children and teachers showed for this work was an inspiration to me, and an additional confirmation of my belief in the unlimited potential of theatre.

Later, I had the joy of having my mother join me in offering teacher training courses at the University at El Paso, Texas; in Philadelphia, Pennsylvania; and in Puerto Rico. Together, we taught bilingual teachers the value of bringing theatre into the classroom, the multiple possibilities of its use, and how to stage different kinds of improvised or scripted plays. We always ended by staging a classic example of a well-written play, the excellent *La historia de una muñeca abandonada* [The story of an abandoned doll] by the Spanish playwright Alfonso Sastre.

In each production, we made sure that every teacher in the course would be on stage, by adding a chorus of children singing nursery rhymes to the script. We also invited each group to design their set in whatever manner they chose. It was fascinating to witness how the infusion of local elements altered each version of the play—and how powerful every version was!

One summer while teaching a course in Chicago for the Associate Colleges of the Midwest, I suggested the participating teachers to stage *La historia de una muñeca abandonada*. They did such a great job that it seemed a pity not to have children enjoy it, so I made arrangements for the teachers to present the play at a summer school for inner-city children.

The unique experience of seeing a live performance is one, alas, that many Spanish-speaking children in the United States will never have. The surprise in the children's eyes, the glow on their faces, the anticipation in their bodies as they leaned forward to catch every single movement—these are the priceless rewards for all the effort that goes into putting on a play. During the performance in this inner-city Chicago school, one could have heard the flapping of a butterfly's wings, so great was the silence.

Upon leaving the auditorium, the children were lined up to shake hands with the cast of teachers who had performed the play. At the end of the line stood a kindergartner who had caught my eye because of the way she had followed the performance, almost in tears. When her turn came to say good-bye, she stood silently in front of the young teacher who had played the role of Lolita, the spoiled girl who abandons her doll. Then, to everyone's astonishment, she raised her little foot and we heard her say in a most reproving tone, "*¡Mala!*" (bad person), as she proceeded to kick the teacher. Despite the momentary pain the poor teacher must have felt,

I believe that having a character of his denounced so vehemently as "Bad!" was one of the best compliments that Alfonso Sastre could have received.

It is also a powerful argument in favor of engaging our students in theatre. By allowing children to enter an
unknown world, to have new experiences that are powerful yet nonthreatening, to make judgments and act on them, and to exercise their imaginations as they transform the stage into another world, children's theatre can help youngsters play their own roles better on the grand stage of life—*el gran teatro del mundo.*

PUBLISHED PLAYS

As part of the *Cielo abierto* collection, Isabel Campoy and I compiled a series of seven anthologies of theatre for children, all in Spanish. In several of the books, we have included plays that we ourselves have written, either individually or jointly.

Gateways to the Sun/Puertas al sol gave us the opportunity to publish theatre anthologies for children in separate editions in Spanish and in English. Again, some of the plays are our original creations. Under the direction of Felipe Dávalos, several Latin American artists have contributed vibrant illustrations that not only enhance the plot but also offer clues for possible staging and characterization.

RESPONSES FROM TEACHERS, LIBRARIANS, AND CHILDREN

1. Transforming a Well-Known Story into a Play

A good way to bring theatre into the classroom is to allow children to dramatize a story they know well. They can either improvise the dialogue or write it out beforehand.

2. Performing a Play

An enriching performance does not have to be extraordinarily elaborate in order to be meaningful. While it is a wonderful experience for children to participate in a fully staged play with sets, props, costumes, and makeup, it is also possible to experience some of the magic through a simple dramatic reading or an impromptu performance in a comer of the classroom. I have visited classrooms where teachers use the overhead projector as a stage light, or have the students draw the background for a set on butcher paper or even on the blackboard. The true gift of theatre lies in having the freedom to imagine, and become, another character; while sets, costumes, and props can often serve to enhance that experience, we have seen that in the realm of the imagination, much can be done with very little indeed.

Part VI: Telling my Own Life Stories

CHILDHOOD MEMORIES

Where the Flame Trees Bloom
   Allá donde florecen los framboyanes
Under the Royal Palms
   Bajo las palmas reales
Island Treasures
   Tesoros de mi isla

Pregones
Barquitos de papel
Barriletes
Pin-pin-sarabín
Días de circo

Young Authors Fairs can be wonderful experiences for mature authors as well as for the children for whom they are intended. I am indebted to students at an extraordinary young Authors Fair in Saint Helena, California, for encouraging me to write about my childhood memories.

During the fair, 1 was speaking with a group of students about what a privilege it was to have a school library as wonderful as theirs. I explained to them that, like most of the world's children, I never had access to a library when I was a child. None of the schools I attended had a library, nor was I encouraged to read books in school. As I spoke with the children about how different my school experience had been from theirs, the students became very excited and told me these were the stories I should be writing, the real stories of my own childhood.

I had never intended to write about my own life, but the children's invitation was so sincere that I began to search for those experiences that could be shared. I wrote five vignettes that I originally submitted as a book to Alfaguara in Spain, who then offered me a contract. However, Sam Laredo had just concluded his many years as president of Santillana USA to start a new venture, Laredo Publishing. Santillana had been the first to publish my work in the United States, with the publication of **Friends** and the collection **Stories for the Telling / Cuentos para contar**. Now they had begun to publish the twelve-title collection **Stories the Year 'Round / Cuentos para todo el año**. When Sam expressed interest, I decided to give him and his new company the option of publishing the vignettes I had written.

Sam decided that the stories deserved to be printed as five individual books in a new collection he called **Cuentos con Alma** (Stories with Alma). In Spanish, the title has double meanings, since *alma* in Spanish means soul. Sam asked the talented artist Pablo Torrecilla to illustrate these books. This was Pablo's first assignment as an illustrator, and he brought immense dedication to his work. His creativity reached beyond the reality I had described, in order to evoke the underlying feelings I had only hinted at. For that reason, his art is truer in some ways than a more realistic depiction might have been. I

Alma Flor Ada

Pregones

Ilustraciones de Pablo Torrecilla

love how Pablo captured my experience as a young child filled with awe at the wonders that surrounded me. At the same time, I must acknowledge that in reality, my childhood circumstances were not nearly as wealthy or fanciful as the illustrations might lead one to believe.

There are no real plots to these books; instead, they depict characters and experiences that for me embody a particular moment in time. **Pregones** (Vendors' calls) shows the rhythm of daily life being marked by the calls of the various vendors who peddled their merchandise through the streets of my small town. It allows me to share the pride of the Chinese man who brought fresh vegetables to our door each day, on the day he also brought along his young son. Recently arrived from China, his son had been growing as healthy and strong as the colorful vegetables in his father's circular flat baskets.

Barquitos de papel (Paper boats) is a reflection on the special days brought about by the torrential tropical rains and how a girl who lived mostly outdoors managed to endure those rains. The change in weather meant a change in pace. A wise father's treasure drawer, from which one object, and only one, could be retrieved on a rainy day, was both a source of marvels as well as a lesson in choosing.

Barriletes (Kites) depicts other kinds of entertainment that also depended on the weather. The winds brought kite season along with them. How many wonderful rituals preceded the moment in which dreams could take flight! First, we had to gather all of the materials and implements needed to make the kite. My father would sharpen his special knife so that it could

cut the dry bamboo shoots with total precision. He would make glue by carefully boiling and constantly stirring the pearls of Arabic gum until they dissolved into an amber- colored liquid. The brightly colored China paper was placed smoothly upon the large dining room table so that no crease would mar the kite's perfection. Meanwhile, my mother and I would search through her bag of scraps for the right material to make a long tail. Soft, light material was preferred, and it was particularly important that all the strips be of similar weight and carefully tied together.

How fastidiously my father worked, and with such precision! He would cut the exact amount of string and make the knots just right. Then he would patiently help me fly the kite higher and higher, until it was only a speck of color high up in the sky!

Of these books, **Días de circo** is the one that most closely approximates a story. Every year a traveling circus camped on

the empty land across from our house. My father had agreed to let them use water from a tap on the side of the house, since they had none available. In thanks, they would give us some tickets for the show and the rides. For me it was one of the highlights of the year.

Among the circus troupe there was a girl a few years older than I who worked as a contortionist. I was full of admiration for her skills and her life, which seemed to be so full of adventure. One year, we chanced to talk. She had come for water and had decided to practice in the shade of our porch. I was beside myself with awe, but to my surprise she was the one full of questions. What was it like to live in a house, to have your own bed, to be in the same place,

to go to school? More surprising yet was her revelation that while I had been admiring her adventurous life, year after year she had been gazing with longing at our old, big house as the perfect place to be, a place where one could have roots, make friends, and count on knowing what each day would bring.

As books sometimes do, these went out of print after a few years. It has been a joy to incorporate them in **Island Treasures**, and its Spanish version **Tesoros de mi isla**, on a brief collection called *Days at the Quinta Simoni* or *Días en la Quinta Simoni*.

The books **Where the Flame Trees Bloom** [published in Spanish as **Allá donde florecen los framboyanes**] and **Under the Royal Palms** [published in Spanish as **Bajo las palmas reales**, winner of the 2000 Pura Belpré Medal of the American Library Association] were also written in response to requests, although of a different nature.

An editor from *The Hungry Mind* asked me to submit for publication a real-life story that I first heard in childhood. I was so intrigued and excited that in response, I wrote "The Teacher," "Choices," and "The Surveyor." Not knowing which one to choose for submission, I sent in all three. I will always be grateful for the warm letter in which the kind editor, while explaining that they would only be able to use one story, added that the stories were so interesting that if I were to write a few more, I would have a book. This encouraged me to search my memory for other moments worth sharing, and **Where the Flame Trees Bloom** was born.

Having my friend Antonio Martorell illustrate one of my books had been a long-time dream of mine, and I was very moved when I saw his illustrations for *Flame Trees.* He had captured my grandmother, my grandfather, and the other characters in the book without ever having seen them. Since Antonio is Puerto Rican, he understands very well the Caribbean world I depicted in my stories. Even so, it was astonishing to feel as though he were seeing my world through my own eyes!

A few years after the publication of the book, Antonio called to wish me a happy New Year. I was surprised when during the conversation he asked, "And where is the next book you promised?" When I expressed my puzzlement he scolded me. "Don't you keep the promises you make?" he asked. "At the end of *Flame Trees,* you said that these stories are only a few of the many hanging from the branches of your childhood. You owe your readers another book."

Again, receiving an invitation to write proved to be a great stimulus, and *Under the Royal Palms* was born. Jonathan Lanman, my Atheneum editor at that time, chose to have this book illustrated with real-life photographs to emphasize its autobiographical character.

The greatest satisfaction the books have given me has been to allowed me to honor the people to whom I owe everything, beginning with my life, and whose own lives deserve recognition.

One of the most meaningful moments I have experienced with respect to these books took place during an unscheduled school visit, as we happened to stop by the classroom of a teacher who had a copy of *Where the Flame Trees Bloom* on her desk. She was a first-year teacher, and had no idea who I was. When I asked her if I might see the book, I realized by the inscription in it, that someone had given it to her as a graduation present. She confided, "This book has been such an inspiration to me. It has a story in it about an extraordinary teacher." She was referring to the
vignette "The Teacher," which I had written about my grandmother. Then she added, "I would like to become that kind of teacher"; so, whenever I encounter something difficult

or challenging, I ask myself, 'What would Dolores Salvador do?'"

She was extremely surprised when she realized that her classroom visitor was none other than the author of the book she was reading! Yet her surprise was matched by my own profound emotion at hearing that now, in California, there is a young teacher who takes as her model my grandmother, who died in a remote city in Cuba more than 75 years ago.

This moving incident reinforced my determination to continue spreading the message that Isabel Campoy and I present in *Authors in the Classroom,* encouraging all of us, and in particular all teachers and librarians, to recognize the unsung heroes in our own lives, and to take the time to share their lives, their efforts, and their inspiration with others.

An immense joy has been Atheneum's decision to unite **Where the Flame Trees Bloom** and **Under the Royal Palms** in one volume **Island Treasures** in Spanish **Tesoros de mi isla** adding the re-written stories originally published as *Cuentos con Alma* in a third section of this new book. **Island Treasures** has also been published by Recorded   Books, in a two CDs set, narrated by Trini Alvarado.

ADULT MEMOIRS

The books of childhood memories lead to me writing my memoirs for adults. It was a long process of reflecting and recognizing the many people that have contributed in multiple ways to enrich my life.

Recognizing the importance of bilingualism in my life, as student and teacher, as well as in my advocacy of linguistic human rights, I chose as a title ***Vivir en dos idiomas*** [Living in two languages]. A deeper reading of this title comes from acknowledging that *I live in the language.* Words are my environment, my support, my way of understanding, where my own being resides, concurring with Heidegger statement that "Language is the House of Being." Many friends have asked me to create an English version of the book, but so far, I have not been able to do it.

Recently, at the request of my son Miguel, I wrote and publish another memoir, this time in English, and focused on my life as an educator. ***A Lifelong Journey: Becoming a Teacher.*** My value and respect for education has led me to try to become each day a better teacher. And as the title says it has been a lifelong journey.

Nothing would please me as much than having these books becoming an invitation to write your own journey, kind reader. Every life deserves to be told and that can only be done in full by the person who experienced each moment, who felt the emotions, who valued those who were part of the journey.

No book is written in its entirety on one sitting. One writes sentences that become paragraphs, that turn into chapters, who create a book.

Because I was helped by the encouraging of others to write, and aware of today's possibilities of self-publish, and knowing how enriched you will be by the process, I must tell you that your life story deserved to be told!

Teachers and Librarians' Ideas

Children's Authentic Writing

Throughout the years, multiple teachers have told me that these books have inspired upper elementary as well as middle and high school students, to begin writing about authentic moments in their lives.

By sharing daily experiences rather than momentous events, these books show how attention to feelings, details, sensory experiences, and feelings can make any topic relevant and interesting, no matter how simple it may be. Through their encounter with these vignettes, many children have realized that they do not need to have something extraordinary happen in order to have good material to write about.

I. Writing a Poem to "A Person in My Life"

Students can write a poem to an important person in their lives by following the process below:

1. First, create a poem of your own using the same process you will be presenting to your students, so that you can share an authentic example with them as a model.
2. Invite the group to close their eyes and sit quietly, with paper and pencil ready, and to be prepared to write after each of your prompts.
3. Invite them to reflect on how much we owe the people around us who have helped us to survive, who support us and celebrate who we are. Then ask them to think about one of the many persons in their lives who are important

to them. Emphasize that it could be anyone—a grandparent, a parent, a brother or sister, a relative, a neighbor, a teacher, a friend....

4. Read the first of the prompts below slowly. Offer your own response to the prompt as an example; then pause to give your students time to come up with their own responses, and to write. Repeat this process successively for every prompt.

A person in my life	*My grandmother*
I hear	*I hear her steps as she enters my room.*
I feel	*I feel her take me in her arms.*
I smell	*I smell her soft fragrance of talcum powder and ilang-ilang.*
I pretend	*I pretend to be still sleeping.*
I experience	*I experience her brisk steps as she takes me out to the fields.*
I suffer	*I suffer knowing not every child has experienced this kind of love.*
I wish	*I wish my children would get to know who she was.*
I decide	*I decide I will try to share what I learned from her.*
I hope	*I hope her dreams for justice, equality, and peace will come true.*
I believe	*I believe in life and the power of love.*
I am	*I am a grateful granddaughter*

You can find numerous examples of these poems turned into books in www.authorsintheclassroom.com

2. Writing Childhood Memories

The fact that my childhood memoirs have been written as collections episodes, many teachers have used them as examples when inviting their students to write their own books of memoirs.

While writing an entire book or autobiography can feel like a daunting task, writing a short episode or a portrait feels doable. Yet by writing these briefer texts, one at a time, a whole book can be created.

Some teachers have analyzed the two books with their students, looking for themes. For example, in ***Where the Flame Trees Bloom*** there are vignettes devoted to a grandmother, a great-grandmother, a grandfather, an uncle, an animal, a storm, a surprising event that happened to a friend of the family.... Can the students identify similar themes in their own lives?

Other teachers encourage all of their students to write about a given topic at the same time. Others allow students to select their own topics. Likewise, some teachers have encouraged students to organize their stories in chronological order, while others have allowed students to create their own order.

Regardless of these different approaches, all of these teachers have shared how meaningful the project has been for their students, and how becoming authors of their own books has helped them to feel proud and confident!

A middle school student in Miami, Florida, who shared his book with me, affirmed: "After writing this long book," he said, "I know I can accomplish anything I want in life!"

Part VII - Creating Non-Fiction Books for Children

Non-fiction books
co-authored with F.Isabel Campoy

Art

Gateways to the Sun/Puertas al sol
Blue and Green/Azul y verde
Brush and Paint/Brocha y pincel
Artist's Easel/Caballete
Canvas and Paper/Lienzo y papel

Biographies

Gateways to the Sun/Puertas al sol series
Smiles/Sonrisas (Pablo Picasso, Gabriela Mistral, Benito Juárez)
Steps/Pasos (Rita Moreno, Fernando Botero, Evelyn Cisneros)
Voices/Voces (Luis Valdez, Judith Baca, Carlos Finlay)
Caminos/Paths (José Martí, Frida Kahlo, César Chávez)

Culture

Yes! We Are Latinos: Poems and Prose about the Latino Experience
¡Sí! Somos latinos
Gateways to the Sun/Puertas al sol series
The Quetzal's Journey/Vuelo del quetzal
On the Wings of the Condor/En alas del cóndor
Eyes of the Jaguar/Ojos del jaguar
Colección Cielo abierto series
Ecos del pasado
Recuerdos del pasado

Celebrations

Stories to Celebrate/Vamos a celebrar series
[Combining fiction and non-fiction in each book]

Celebra el día de Martin Luther King con la clase de la Sra. Park

*Celebrate Martin Luther King, Jr. Day with Mrs. Park's
    class*
Celebra el Año Nuevo Chino con la familia Fong
    Celebrate Chinese New Year with the Fong Family
Celebra Mardi Gras, con Joaquín, arlequín
    Celebrate Mardi Gras with Joaquin, Harlequin
Celebra el Día de San Patricio con Samantha y Lola
    Celebrate St. Patrick's Day with Samantha and Lola
Celebra el Cinco de Mayo con un jarabe tapatío
    Celebrate Cinco de Mayo with the Mexican Hat Dance
Celebra el Cuatro de julio con Champ, el campeón
    Celebrate Fourth of July with Champ, the Scamp
Celebra un Powwow con Sandy Starbright
    Celebrate a Powwow with Sandy Starbright
*Celebra Halloween y el Día de Muertos con Cristina y su
    Conejito Azul*
    *Celebrate Halloween and the day of the Death with
    Cristina and her Blue Bunny*
Celebra el Día de Acción de Gracias con Beto y Gaby
    Celebrate Thanksgiving Day with Beto and Gaby
Celebra Hanukkah con los cuentos de Bubbe
    Celebrate Hanukkah with Bubbe's Tales
Celebra Kwanzaa con Botitas y sus gatitos
    Celebrate Kwanzaa with Boots and her Kittens
Celebra Navidad y Reyes Magos con Pablo y Carlitos
    *Celebrate Christmas and Three Kings Day with Pablo
    and Carlitos*

Language

Colección Cielo abierto
Sigue la palabra

While the books that I most enjoyed as a child and adolescent were literary works of fiction and poetry, I was also attracted to books that provided other information I
craved. In our small city there was no public library; therefore, the only place where I could borrow books was the library of the U.S. Information Service. Aware of my thirst for knowledge, my generous parents, who ran a jewelry and gift store at the time, allowed the representative of Jackson Publishing Company to exhibit books in our store. In exchange, we became the proud owners of two sets of encyclopedias whose tides, loosely translated from the Spanish, were something like "The Wonderful World in Which We Live" and "The Animals That Surround Us." My father built a beautiful cabinet with glass doors to protect the volumes, and the time and care he spent crafting that cabinet was a powerful statement that these were books to be treasured.

Each volume, with black-and-white photographs showing the various countries of the world as well as the variety of animals that inhabited each one, was a constant source of wonder for me. I returned to their pages again and again to satisfy my curiosity. While my own city was a microcosm, and I delighted in discovering the variety of the people in it, these books helped me realize that diversity was more prevalent than I had ever imagined. Perhaps my conviction that the most representative characteristic of our planet is its diversity and that consequently, the most basic norm is a respect for uniqueness, was born on those long, hot afternoons that I spent making new discoveries through the pages of those dear books.

Yet, like many children who grow up in third-world countries, or in households outside the majority culture, a great deal of what I found in books had little to do with my own reality. In *Reading, Writing, and Leaving Home: Life on the Page,* Lynn Freed contrasts her own South African childhood with the world she found in children's books. She recounts how books told her that snow fell at Christmastime, that there were fires rather than flower arrangements in fireplaces, and that

314   Part VII: Creating Non-Fiction Books for Children

hedgehogs, toads, foxes, and moles—not monkeys, snakes and iguanas, the animals of her childhood—were the sort of creatures which, in fiction, would stand up on their hind legs, don clothing, and sally forth into a story.

More significantly books managed to convince her that those customs and creatures so far from her reality, were more real than those in the world she lived in. By not finding her real world in the literature available to her, she became convinced that such world was not worthy of fiction.

While the realities that have historically not been included in children's books are many and diverse, the disorienting experience of not seeing oneself and one's immediate environment reflected in the books one reads as a child has been expressed numerous times. This has been a driving force in my own motivation to create books for all children that reflect the richness of Hispanic culture.

Isabel Campoy and 1 are very grateful to SantillanaUSA for welcoming our proposal to create *Gateways to the Sun/Puertas al sol,* a collection of oversize books lavishly illustrated by numerous Latin American artists under the artistic direction of Maestro Felipe Dávalos. This collection is dedicated to sharing some of the treasures of our rich culture with both students

and teachers, in Spanish and English, and inviting our readers to continue exploring that vast wealth.

ART

From the early paintings covering the walls of the Altamira caves in Northern Spain, to the extraordinary artistic creations of the ancient cultures that inhabited the Americas, Hispanic/Latino people have a powerful artistic legacy to offer the world.

The collection *Gateways to the Sun/Puertas al sol* includes a series on art that is focused on painting. The four volumes within this series offer a glimpse of some of the many remarkable painters from Spain and Latin America, as well as Latino painters.

The set of four book covers reflects the inclusive spirit that inspired the collection. The first book cover showcases a painting by a classical Spanish artist, Velázquez; the second, a painting by a renowned Guatemalan artist, Paniagua. The third, highlights the work of an anonymous indigenous painter from Mexico; and the fourth, features a painting by Simón Silva, a contemporary Latino painter born into a family of farmworkers.

These book covers portray that as Latinos, we have a heritage that transcends the boundaries of our families, neighborhoods, and ancestral places of origin. Our larger heritage begins with our particular origins, and we need to celebrate those roots. Yet like the branches of a tree, our roots extend far beyond our immediate vicinity, and connect us with all of the other branches.

It is our hope that Latino children will come to see that, in addition to the culture of the barrio, and the various birthplaces of their parents, grandparents, and ancestors, they also have a share in the culture of every Spanish speaking country in the world. In addition to the murals that brighten so many of our barrios in the United States, we also want them to recognize, as part of their heritage, the murals of the great Mexican muralists Rivera, Orozco, and Xiqueiros, Picasso's *Guernica,* and the Altamira caves. Full-color paintings are displayed on each of the odd- numbered pages of the books, inviting readers' contemplation. This invitation is enhanced by the books' design, which includes on each even-numbered page a small black-and-white portion of the larger painting—a subtle suggestion for the reader to find that smaller portion in the full painting on the facing page. The paintings are complemented with brief texts or poems, whose language has been purposefully kept simple so they can be enjoyed by young children and English learners as well as by readers of any age.

In the opening book, **Blue and Green/Azul y verde,** the first text found alongside Velázquez's painting of *Las Meninas,* reads:

> *The painting is the artist's masterpiece.*
> *You, are life's masterpiece.*

This affirmation of the uniqueness and intrinsic worth of each individual embodies the overarching philosophy of **Gateways to the Sun/Puertas al sol**

Responses From Teachers, Librarians, And Children

Librarians have acknowledged enthusiastically the value of having these accessible books on Hispanic/Latino art in their collections. Teachers have welcomed the idea of experimenting with new possibilities for sharing art with children. The guide for the series created by Alfaguara/SantillanaUSA is filled with suggestions for using the books in the classroom or library. I will only mention one outstanding example.

A Classroom Gallery

Sometimes great ideas can be very simple, such as the one that two teachers from Micronesia showed me. "When our students create art, we always wish we could frame it," they told me. "Since that is not possible, now we always make a frame as part of the painting."

- Give each student a poster board, preferably a thick one. Have them use a pencil and a ruler to draw a frame anywhere from 1½ to 2 inches wide. This area will be left unpainted until the painting is finished.
- Invite each student to choose a painting from one of the four art books. Before they begin drawing, ask them to write a few sentences about the piece and why they have chosen it.
- You can encourage students to copy the entire painting within the frame, or alternatively, allow them to focus on only one section of the painting.
- Once students have completed their initial sketch, have them add color to their drawing with whatever medium is available to you. (The Micronesian teachers had their students use oils, after covering the floor with newspapers, and instructed students to begin painting from the center of their drawing outward.)
- When students' paintings are complete, invite them to paint the frames in a dark color that will complement their artwork.
- Invite students to complete their writing by explaining what their piece means to them now.
- Now you are ready for an art gallery display where the students take turns talking about their artwork and/or reading aloud what they have written.

BIOGRAPHIES

Gateways to the Sun /Puertas al sol also includes a biography series, consisting of four titles, in separate editions English and Spanish with three biographies apiece.

> *Smiles /Sonrisas:* Pablo Picasso, Gabriela Mistral, Benito Juárez
> *Steps/Pasos:* Rita Moreno, Fernando Botero, Evelyn Cisneros
> *Voices/Voces.* Luis Valdez, Judith Baca, Carlos Finlay
> *Caminos /Paths.* José Martí, Frida Kahlo, César Chávez

It was indeed quite a challenge for us to choose from among so many interesting lives which ones to include in these books. As we wanted to portray a diversity of artists, scientists, and activists, we chose painters Picasso, Botero, and Khalo; authors Martí and Mistral; social and political leaders Martí, Juárez, and Chávez; and artists Valdez, Cisneros, and Moreno.

With regard to the scientists, we were particularly interested in including Carlos Finlay, the Cuban doctor who discovered how malaria, or yellow fever, is transmitted. Finlay devoted much of his life to the lengthy and difficult process of determining that only the female mosquito of a particular species, *Aedes Aegypti,* is capable of transmitting the disease, and that she is only able to do so during a very specific moment in her life. At the time, no one knew that mosquitoes could transmit illness. Finlay came from a tiny country, Cuba, and had a speech impediment. As a result, he was laughed at and dismissed when he delivered his findings in Washington, D.C. Yet without his discovery, the construction of the Panama Canal, where workers were dying of yellow fever in alarming numbers, would not have been possible. Finlay's contributions continue to be credited to others, and outside of Cuba and Panama his work has not been sufficiently recognized. However, a school in Miami, Florida, was named after him, maybe signaling the beginning of wider recognition. We chose to write about him, as well as the other noteworthy individuals featured in these books, to offer children not only fascinating histories but also messages of hope and possibility.

RESPONSES FROM TEACHERS, LIBRARIANS, AND CHILDREN

I. Write a Biography as an Autobiography

A natural follow-up to reading these books is inviting students to write a biography. One interesting twist is to encourage students to write the biography in the first person, as if they themselves were the person they are choosing to write about. The value of this activity is that it allows students to imagine themselves in the role of another person and to explore that character's feelings, emotions, thoughts, and reflections. It also gives them the opportunity to imagine themselves acting in ways that would lead to strong feelings of accomplishment.

2. Recognize a Hero in Your Live

Reading about famous historical figures can be an excellent opportunity to reflect on the lives and struggles of those people around us who may never become famous and yet whose lives are nonetheless deserving of acknowledgement.

When I speak to parents from low socioeconomic groups I often tell them, quite sincerely, that I see them as heroes; what they do on a daily basis—working odd shifts; holding two and sometimes three jobs, all of which may lack adequate support and protection; working hard to keep their children in school, that they might have a brighter future; and despite their exhaustion, attending an evening meeting to learn one more way to help their children succeed in school—all that is truly heroic.

Children may not always understand the value of their parents' and grandparents' struggle. Encouraging them to write or speak about their family stories in the classroom can be a powerful opportunity to help strengthen children's appreciation of and connection with their families.

CELEBRATIONS

One of the greatest riches of the United States is the diversity of its people, which resembles the diversity that nature constantly offers us: not *one* flower but lilies and daisies, orchids and roses; not *one* fish but tiny minnows and powerful sharks; not *a* tree but oaks and sequoias, palms and willows.

In the field of multicultural education, we have insisted that multiculturalism must go beyond heroes and holidays, that it is not something to be acknowledged only at a given moment of the year and forgotten the rest of the time, and that we need to focus not only on the external aspects of culture but also on values and worldviews. At the same time, celebrations are a significant part of each culture's traditions, and need to be honored as such.

The series of twelve books, *Stories for Celebrations / Cuentos para celebrar* (Alfaguara 2006), focuses on celebrations that take place in the United States. The overall message is that, while the external aspects of celebrations may be diverse, their spirit—appreciating the power of life, the value of family and friends, the desire to express joy and thankfulness—is shared across cultures.

Addressed to young children, these books are a combination of fiction and non-fiction. Each book begins with a story that portrays real-life characters who reflect the multicultural population of the United States. The second half of each book explains, with photographs accompanied by brief texts, the origin of the celebration, its different expressions, and its significance within the United States. The various celebrations featured include Martin Luther King Day, Chinese New Year, Mardi Gras, St. Patrick's Day, Cinco de Mayo, Fourth of July, Powwow, Halloween, Thanksgiving, Hanukah, Kwanzaa, Christmas, and Three Kings Day.

Many of the fictional stories portray true multicultural experiences, with characters from different backgrounds interacting with one another. It is our hope that these books will serve as mirrors for many children, allowing them to see images of their own families and communities, while also offering windows into the lives of members of other communities.

Responses from Teachers, Librarians, and Children

Children can use the same pattern found in these books to create their own book, first writing a fictional story about a traditional celebration in their own family, and then offering some non-fiction facts about that celebration. Teachers and librarians may also choose to use the information offered in the books to enhance their own celebrations of these cultural events.

The Santillana website (www.santillanausa.com) offers free activities for K- 2 and 3-6 students to accompany all the books of this series. They are available at

http://www.santillanausa.com/cuentosparacelebrar.htm.

CULTURE

The land of Latin America, home to millions of Spanish speakers as well as speakers of other languages, is vast, diverse, and full of great contrasts, such as warm rivers surrounded by harsh deserts and majestic snow-capped mountains alongside lavish tropical forests dense with flora and fauna. In order to sustain themselves, the original peoples of the western hemisphere developed cultures that were closely tied to the land. Inspired by their surroundings, they created beautiful objects making use of stone, clay, metal, precious woods, shells, seeds, and feathers.

They were inspired by nature's beauty to be creative with jade. with gold. with feathers.

Three of the books from *Gateways the Sun/Puertas at sol* are devoted to the rich contributions of the numerous indigenous peoples living south of the Río Grande/Río Bravo. Their extraordinary illustrations were carefully designed for historical accuracy by a team of Mexican illustrators under the expert guidance of Maestro Felipe Dávalos, who brought his extensive archaeological background and profound knowledge of ancient indigenous cultures to this project. Published in separate editions in English and in Spanish, these books are titled:

> *The Quetzal's Journey/Vuelo del quetzal*
> *On the Wings of the Condor/En alas del condor*
> *Eyes of the Jaguar/Ojos del jaguar*

The extraordinary art of Felipe Dávalos contributes to highlight the richness and diversity of our culture.

A combination of prose and free verse allowed Isabel and myself to present major moments in the history and evolution of Latinos in the United States in the book:

> ***Yes! We Are Latinos***
> ***¡Sí! somos latinos***

Two other books on Latino culture, co-authored with Isabel Campoy, are:

> ***Ecos del pasado***
> ***Imágenes del pasado***

These anthologies of indigenous legends re-told by either Isabel or myself also include some informational pieces, such as "*Y florezca la luz,*" a narrative about the Teatro Campesino [the Farmworkers Theatre] of San Juan Bautista, California.

Brothers Santa Cruz

Responses from Teachers, Librarians, and Children

I. Discussing the Content

Many of the questions that you can ask students after reading these books will be appropriate for readers of any age, just as the books are. The answers will vary, of course, reflecting the age and maturity of the students.

- What new things have you learned about the land and geography of Latin American? What has been most surprising to you?
- What have you learned about the various indigenous peoples who inhabit these lands?
- What has been most interesting to you?
- How do you feel about beauty? What are the sources of beauty in your own life? How important is it to you that everyday objects be beautiful? In what ways do you help create beauty around you?
- Indigenous peoples have contributed many different food products to the world, including potatoes, corn, tomatoes, coffee beans, and the cacao beans that are used to make

- chocolate. How have these foods affected the history of the world? How can indigenous peoples be recognized for these contributions?

---

2. Reading in Two Languages

Just as I was completing the manuscript for this book, I received an e-mail from the director of a Spanish literacy center thanking me for these books on culture, which she has been using with adults at the center. She said that adults were enjoying the books because the language, while clear and simple, is not condescending and the text is rich with information that can be appreciated by readers of any age. She found that the adults with whom she works were highly motivated to read a page in Spanish and then read the same page in English, as a way of developing their English language and reading skills.

LANGUAGE

In my life of frequent up rootedness, of living in many different places, Spanish—my first language, my mother tongue—has been my personal abode, my most permanent home, and my constant companion. Language in general has been a tool for me to earn a living and an instrument for questioning and understanding life. It is also the source of the great joy that I derive from reading, and even more so from writing.

It is not surprising, then, that all of my life I have been fascinated with the history of the Spanish language. I have coined the word *matria* [motherland] as distinguished from *patria* [fatherland] to refer to the role of Spanish, my mother tongue, as the nurturing reality that has sustained my life. As a high school teacher in Lima, Perú, I wrote a version of the history of the Spanish language for my students. It was published in the book *Castellano, Tercer Curso* (Editorial Arica, 1965, multiple editions). Many years later, I was surprised to find that a history of the Spanish language had yet to be published for young people. At that time, Isabel

Campoy and I were creating the series *Cielo abierto,* which seemed an appropriate place to publish such a story. Therefore, we gave new life to that earlier text, enriching it with sections on the presence of Spanish in the United States and enlivening it with striking photographs from all over the Spanish speaking world.

While I always have difficulty choosing when children ask me what my favorite is among all of the books I have written, as each of them is special to me, there is no question that *Sigue la palabra* (Harcourt) holds a very dear place in my heart.

Now Isabel and I are delighted with the forthcoming publication of **La fascinante historia de la lengua española** (Velázquez Press) an enriched version of this theme we have cherished and studied for so long.

It feels very appropriate to end this section on culture with this note of anticipated joy!

RESPONSES FROM TEACHERS, LIBRARIANS, AND CHILDREN

I. Discussing the Content

Many of these questions will be appropriate for readers of any age. The answers will vary, of course, reflecting the age and maturity of the students.

- What are the things that language help you do?
- Can language be hurtful? When?
- Can language he healing? When?
- What things would be impossible to do without language

I. Strengthening the Home-School Connection

- Encourage students to make lists of 10 favorite words of each member of their family. Create a display to share in the class.

Part VIII: Preserving my Ancestor's Voices and History

Throughout this book, I have made frequently mention of my admiration and gratitude towards my grandparents, my parents and my aunts and uncles.

A way to honor them, and express my gratitude, has been to try to keep their voices alive.

Medardo Lafuente Rubio and Dolores Salvador Méndez

My maternal grandparents were both educators and writers. On the section about Letters I recounted the significance that the letters my grandfather wrote my grandmother had in my life and shared that I had published those letters.

My grandfather was an accomplished poet. During his life, his poems had been published extensively in journals and newspapers, but never in a book. At his death my grandmother wanted to honor his memory publishing them in a book, *Jornadas líricas*. It was but natural that I would have the book reprinted.

Finding his articles in century old newspapers in Cuban libraries has been a major task, and I am indebted to the several friends who helped me find many of them, published in *Páginas rescatadas* [Rescued pages], now in a third extended edition.

It has only been very recently that I was able to find several of my grandmother's writings. So, I added to her published short-stories and her handwritten comments on a notebook, newspaper articles written about her by her daughters and others who admired this extraordinary woman.

The book is entitled *Dolores Salvador: Maestra de maestras*. [Dolores Salvador: Teacher of teachers] In recognition to the many of her students, at the night school for working women, first ever in our city of Camagüey, that she initiated, who became teachers with her encouragement inspiration and support.

Alma Lafuente Salvador, my mother

My mother wrote constantly. Even during her very busy life as a coordinator of Foreign Language in the Elementary Schools of Atlanta during the day, and a night teacher of English as a Second Language, having become a widow after the untimely death of my father and the sole supporter of my youngest daughter, she found time to write.

I have inherited numerous boxes of her writing, some final products, plays, poems, other unfinished novels for adults and children, numerous pedagogical and curricular suggestions, many she managed to implement or gave other teachers to apply. Many are profound reflections about life and teaching that I hope to be able to compile. From that treasure I have published three books so far:

My father was not a writer. He was a fascinanting speaker, a doer who built us a house with his own hands. As a surveyor he could create precise maps, so neat and beautifully design I would have loved to frame them, as a professor in the School of Surveying he was both eloquent and clear. But, as much as he loved to read and valued language, writing was not a task he would particularly practice.

On birthdays, and ocassions that invited his reflections, he would write carefully drafted messages. But when, after leaving Cuba, he found himself separated from my mother when he went to work on different states, and from me, who was living in Perú at the time, he poured his heart into loving letters.

His letters would probably be meaningless to others. For me they were my only connection with him during the last four years of his life. Hurridly written most of the time, because his life was consumed trying to reconstruct what had been a succesful and very satisfying life, where his knowledge and advise were seeked by many, in a new reality, in a language he did not know. While he had taught students that would become surveyors, here he had to carry the instruments and do the heavy task, as a poorly paid assistant to others, who once they found his knowledge made him do all the work for which they would get the creadit and monetary reward. He had no time to complain, nor was that in his nature. When he was not working, supporting my mother, taking care of my sisters, he was studying, until he was able to master the language, the different processes and legislations, and was able to pass the Board to be cerutified as a Surveyor. So his letters were written many times in haste, but the thoughts that inspired them, reflecting what he instill in me during my childhood and adolescence, have been my guidance all my life. I published them in a simple edition, in profound gratitude to this man who lived his life never expecting to receive reward or repraisal, committed to do what's right and good only for the sake of goodness itself.

My aunts Virginia and Mireya Lafuente Salvador

The family inclination to write extends also to my aunts. **Virginia Lafuente Salvador** was a teacher educator, beloved by her students, who initiated her career as a rural teacher in Cuba. This book collects some of her experiences as well as some of her memories, and poetry.

Mireya Lafuente Salvador, also an educator, relates her life combining enliving details, nostalgic memories and an incomparable sense of humor. Written to be shared with the family I could not but publish this book which gives an insight on her rich live and a picture of Cuba between the 30s to the 50s.

My mother's younger sister **Lolita Lafuente Salvador** was a gifted composer who created numerous memorable songs, some of which have been recorded.

La Quinta Simoni, the magnificent Colonial house where I was born and where I spent the initial part of my childhood, together with parents, grandparents, aunts and uncles and young sister and cousins is very significant for Cuban history, as the home of Amalia Simoni, born into a family of Cuban patriots and married to the one of the most important leaders of the struggle for Cuban independence from Spain.

This book shares about the house and the two luminous families who inbahited it, the Simoni-Argilagos and the Lafuente-Salvador, both contributors in different times to the civic life of Camagüey.

Ancestors of the Lafuente-Salvador Family

The ancestors of my grandmother Dolores Salvador Méndez extend to the founders of the city of Camagüey, and through them to both indigenous and Spanish roots. In this book, **A orillas del Tínima**, created after a careful genealogic research I share what I have been able to learn about our ancestors, and the reflections about the deep emotions evoqued by the discovery of the diversity of our roots, that include both indigenous and slaved people as well as those who colonized their lands and include some surprising historical figures.

My own children: Rosalma, Alfonso, Miguel and Gabriel Zubizarreta

Although I have focused extensively in the past, I can't but celebrate my own children and grandchildren.

I had nothing to do with the writing of my daughter' Rosalma's first book, **Dynamic Facilitation** but I was happy to help her with the translation when she was asked to teach in Chile, and was pressed by time and it was a joy to help get it published.

She has continue to publish and an outgrowth of this book was published in German in Germany. The success of the first edition led to a second German edition, enriched and expanded.

I have already mentioned having written this memoir of my children's childhood as a gift for my grandchildren. It was very significant for me to relive the days of their childhood.

And now the youngest published author in the family, my grandfaughter Collette, youngest daughter of my son Gabriel, has written a collection  of short stories, which I was delighted to translate.

The backcover *of A Little Bit Creative* reads: *"As suggested by the book cover, the short stories in this book are particularly brief. Thei magic consists on creating intriguing plots, believable settings and unforgettable characters with a minimum amount of words.*

Adding to the particular charm of the book is the author's invitation to the readers to be willing to enhance or transform the stories' endings with their personal imagination.

Two freestyle poems shiw the author's innermost thoughts and her ability to delight readers in yet another genre."

In Closing

It has been a pleasure to share with you some of the "stories behind the stories," as well as the many creative ideas that teachers and librarians have used to enrich the magical encounter between children and books. My wish for you is that the experience of introducing these stories and poetry to children will be as satisfying for you as it has been for me to write them.

And may the reflections on my life be an invitation to you to write your own life journey whichever your focus, efforts and experiences may have been.

Epilogue: The Transformative Power of Language

The Transformative Power of Language: Alma Flor Ada's Gift to Her Readers
by Janet Hill and Anthony L. Manna

Alma Flor Ada lives by the profound belief that words have the power to define and shape human experience, identity, and society. This is a major theme in her autobiographical works, in her scholarly work, and in her bilingual books for children. In April 2003, we had the pleasure of first getting to know Alma Flor Ada when she was a featured speaker at the Virginia Hamilton Conference on Multicultural Literature for Youth at Kent State University in Ohio.[1] In a very sensitive presentation about her life, her art, and her views of the world, she told stories that illustrated the ways language and literature could have a profound impact on people's lives. We believe that the stories she told us at the conference reflect and enhance the works that are highlighted in this volume.

Alma Flor Ada is a storyteller who motivates her readers to develop their own voices and claim their own place in the world. Ada told us a story about a kindergarten boy whose language helped shaped his own fate, illustrating one of the ways that language, as Giroux says, "allows people to be active authors of their own world." As a result of problems at home, the boy was going to be removed from his school and transferred to another school more convenient to a foster home. In a simple statement, written in a personal poem, the boy declared that he was happy. This single piece of writing convinced a social worker the boy needed to remain in his school and among his friends where he was comfortable and happy.

THE POWER OF LANGUAGE

Language, when controlled by the dominant culture, limits people's ability to claim their place in the world. Misused language marginalizes people because it generates the assumption that everyone shares the same language, culture, and experiences. Those who do not fit into the dominant culture are placed in a passive position that robs them of their power to speak for themselves. By reclaiming their own language, they are able to develop their own voice. One very accessible way to respect multiple languages is to provide bilingual texts that not only preserve native languages but also honor cultural iden- dty and support the development of voice. Alma Flor Ada empowers children through her bilingual texts. She told us that she believes "language is one of the most important creations of the human spirit ... and that it is essential for understanding the world."

In her speech at the Virginia Hamilton Conference, Ada related a story of an adult reader who experienced a personal and cultural reawakening when she was introduced to Ada's bilingual books. The reader wrote to Ada, saying, "The colors, the words, the pictures, the language, so beautiful. Where had I been? Where had I lost myself? Where was that little Mexican girl that left her country sixteen years ago and never got a chance to be embraced by the beauty of her poetic Spanish?" After years of living in a cultural void, the young woman discovered how much of her culture she missed and how essential it was to reclaim that part of her life. "Being surrounded with so much Spanish was overwhelming. I remember walking on air as I looked from one side of your display to another. And everywhere I looked, I could identify myself, everywhere I turned I found something that spoke to my experience." This experience was one of many that helped this young woman believe in herself as a Latina educator with something important to communicate.

This same tribute to cultural identity is seen in Ada's picture book, **_Gathering the Sun_**, a bilingual alphabet book that honors Hispanic farmers and their traditions. Words that are chosen for each letter of the alphabet are meaningful in a very ordinary way and yet they represent a kind of authority in that they distill cultural experience. By honoring the language and values that are deeply rooted in the hearts and lives of the farmers, Ada is drawing attention to the contributions they are making to the well-being of society.

Alma Flor Ada's belief in the power of language to transform people's lives is also at the heart of an educational philosophy that awakens people to their own abilities to define the events in their lives, their relationships, and their responsibility to the larger community. Ada and her co-author F. Isabel Campoy have named this philosophy "Transformative Education" and have provided illustrations of the concept in their book,

Authors in the Classroom. A Transformative Education Experience releases teachers, students, and parents from the fears of expressing themselves in writing and rekindles writers' true voices. Through Transformative Education, the classroom community is enriched with an atmosphere of equality, justice, and peace. Through very personal writing activities and experiences, community members acquire the tools that help them to draw on their individual life experiences and put them in touch with their own personal power and identity. During the activities described in the book, participants share and analyze photographs and other artifacts that have given their lives meaning.

From these activities come rich autobiographical writing that validates the lives and life events of the authors. It is the recognition of their own language, their own story, and their own wondrous unique experiences that gives them the power to speak and be heard.

THE MEMOIRS

Through her two autobiographical narratives, ***Where the Flame Trees Bloom*** and ***Under the Royal Palms***, Ada has shared her own personal journey of rediscovering her childhood experiences and the fascinating people that surrounded her as she was growing up in her native Cuba. Through her crystal- clear memory of the fine details of her childhood, she draws connections with larger themes that speak to universal experiences. The stories of Ada's childhood resonate with a range of human feelings and wonderful insights into the human condition. For instance, in **Where the Flame Trees Bloom**, she relates a story of Félix Caballero, a surveyor who worked with her father. One day in the mountains, Félix became stranded on a railroad bridge when a train carrying sugar cane approached. As there were no walkways or handrails, Félix placed his surveyor's poles below the tracks to hang from them to escape injury or death. Alma Flor, as a young girl hearing this story, was awed by this event. In her book, she ends the story with, "If there was so much courage, such an ability to calmly confront danger in the quiet, aging man who sat rocking in our living room, what other wonders might lie hidden in every human soul?"[4]

Ada's memoirs demonstrate how language can become a medium for exploring an emerging identity. As she recounts the details of a childhood filled with memorable people, she reveals how these people shaped her sense of self and her sense of the world. The stories serve as insights into her own character and perspectives on what it is that makes people who they are. In her case, Ada's own political views were nurtured by family members who were teachers, political journalists, and radical political reformists.

Through gentle stories about the common experiences in her own life, Ada encourages her readers to find their own vital stories in everyday incidents of growing up, of mishap, of perseverance and hardship, and of respect for family and heritage. Her meticulous attention to detail and her appreciation for the small things in life have inspired both children and adults to open their eyes to the need for sharing their own personal narratives. She told us of one child, deeply moved by her memoir, *Under the Royal Palms,* who wrote to Ada to tell her how much she appreciated the vivid descriptions that helped her look into her own life. By using the same kind of telling detail, this girl was able to gain an understanding of her own stories and the important meanings they held.

Ada believes in the power of literature to invite reflection and encourage an understanding of how one fits into the world. At the Virginia Hamilton Conference, she talked about the far-reaching possibilities of multicultural literature.

We know that books can be mirrors and we know that they can be windows and all children need them both. They also need the encouragement to know that their stories, their own personal stories, are so important to tell.

Ada also talked about people who have not been able to realize their own stories, and consequently have not been able to claim their own cultural identity. In one scenario, she described the story of one of her graduate students who grew up in a migrant family. Their only shelters were the shacks provided for the workers in the fields. They felt privileged that they owned a truck and were able to travel in their own vehicle and stop by the side of the road for a meal under a billboard. For this student, that meal, that truck, and that billboard represented "home." However, when she went to school, she was expected to conform to the traditional concept of home and was reprimanded when she didn't. Therefore, this young woman learned early on to hide her true identity. It is through Ada's sharing of her own personal memoirs that she helps people like her graduate student understand how the many stories in their own lives can help them realize who they are in relation to the world. This process allows her students to reclaim their own humanity; to uncover their potential, their goals, their own value as a person, and, ultimately, their power to speak for themselves.

Ada recognizes that one way to become fully human is to know oneself and recognize one's responsibility to the world. Ada serves as a model for others' attempts at self-awareness because she is not afraid to look inward and reveal with honesty the parts of her life that have made lasting impressions. She is willing to risk being vulnerable to her readers to encourage them to tell their own life stories and to risk honestly revealing intimate experiences that explore the depths of their identities. Her remarkable recall of the detailed emotions and responses she experienced as she was growing up in Cuba give an authenticity and a very personal voice to her work.

THE IMPORTANCE OF NAMES AND NAMING

Alma Flor Ada gives names the status that they deserve. Names are symbols of identity; they suggest a very personal culture, a uniqueness and personal history as well as a commonality in that everyone has a particular attachment to their own name. A name provides an anchor that stabilizes one's individuality and one's relation to the community.

The way names are perceived is another indication of how language can either control or empower personal and cultural identity. Ada's attention to the language of naming has taken on a very significant role in her life, as well as in the life of her main character in **My Name is Maria Isabel** Alma Flor was a name created by her loving grandmother and she has always had a difficult time convincing people that *Alma Flor* is really her first name. Likewise, the multiple names of the character Maria Isabel Salazar Lopez are a vital link to her Hispanic roots as they provide a blend of both sides of her family. When her teacher Anglicizes her name, calling her "Mary Lopez," Maria Isabel is robbed of her identity. Without a name, she has no voice. And without a voice she feels excluded and marginalized. When she is reprimanded by her teacher for not answering to "Mary," the name her teacher has given her, "Maria Isabel slumped down in her seat. She didn't know how to tell the teacher that she just didn't recognize herself in that strange new name."[5] Maria Isabel communicates her frustration and her hurt feelings through a writing assignment. Again, it is language that helps Maria Isabel regain her voice. In her assignment, Maria Isabel takes the risk of standing up to her teacher and reclaiming an identity that reflects pride in her family and her heritage. In this story, Ada is drawing on one of Paulo Freire's most powerful ideas about language. "To speak a true word is to transform the world."[6] Freire also said, "To exist humanly is to *name* the world, to change it."[7] Ada told us that she believes that "naming a ... problem is necessary for transformation to occur." Just as Maria Isabel defends her right to her name, oppressed people must use language to defend their rights in order to break "the cycle of oppression."[8]

In his research, Freire worked with oppressed people of Brazil, giving them the tools of language as to uncovered the meaning of their own words and to identify for themselves the realities that shape and influence their lives and culture. Similarly, Alma Flor Ada believes that while language bears the weight of social identity and control, it can also serve to liberate as well as to oppress. In her presentation at the Virginia Hamilton Conference, she spoke of the sanctity of words.

Words can take on a very profound meaning from the experiences of the people who have used them, and words are associated with the struggle and the efforts, the sacrifices, the dreams, and the thoughts of people.

For Ada, language brings people of diverse backgrounds together through the recognition of basic human experience. We see this in *¡Pío Peep!*, Ada's folklore project of Hispanic nursery rhymes. Ada gives nursery rhymes the power to not only preserve Hispanic cultures but also to offer these cultures to the world as a shared experience of childhood and parent-child relationships.

THE VALUE OF SHARED EXPERIENCE

In Ada's own childhood world, she was surrounded by people who shared a vision of how to make the world a better place. From a very young age, she witnessed a community of family and friends who were politically aware and actively supported one another in their efforts to do something for the good of the people. She saw them building homes, creating schools, and visiting orphanages out of an honest concern for others.[9] These influences from her childhood have led her to a lifelong exploration of the value and richness of shared experiences. We find that this notion of shared experiences is a major theme that permeates all of her work. Ada's picture books communicate a sense of community and solidarity.[10] Her translated books create a bridge that connects shared experiences in two languages. Her memoirs celebrate a respect for those who cross the boundaries of culture to create an inclusive world. In her work with teachers, Ada has emphasized the ways in which story can unite people from diverse cultures and backgrounds.[11] Ada told us, "Everyone can resonate to the human experience that belongs to all of us. But it's only through the particular that we can come to understand what unites us all."

For Alma Flor Ada, people who come together for the common good create a common voice. And it is this common voice that builds personal and collective power and enables political and social change. People are energized by their own language, their own story, and their own words. What that ultimately leads to is individuals and communities affirming their right to social justice, freedom, and equality, and creating a world that "works well for everyone without resorting to the mistreatment of any group or class."

Conclusion

Ada trusts that story will help us get through. She believes that story is one of the ways we make sense of ourselves, the world, and ourselves in the world. She urges us to claim the right and the power to narrate our lives in order to realize a sense of pride and self-respect. When people tell stories to one another they create an inseparable bond that transports them to a comforting place from which they can draw strength and courage. In **Under the Royal Palms** she writes, "I hope that you will see my stories as an invitation for you to discover the many stories in your own life, and the meaning that they hold for you."[12] This idea of passing on the power of the storyteller is at the heart of her work for children. "When we write with honesty, our work is open for everyone. I want you to know that words are very powerful and we need to give our children the ownership of their words from the very beginning."[13]

Notes

1. Alma Flor Ada, presentation given at the Virginia Hamilton Conference on Multicultural Literature, Kent State University, Kent, Ohio, April 4, 2003.
2. Henry Giroux, "Theory and Resistance in Education: A Pedagogy for the Opposition"; quoted in Donaldo Macedo, *Literacies of Power: What Americans Are Not Allowed to Know* (Boulder, CO: Westview, 1994), 133.
3. Alma Flor Ada and F. Isabel Campoy, *Authors in the Classroom: A Transformative Education Process* (Boston: Allyn & Bacon, 2004).
4. Alma Flor Ada, *Where the Flame Trees Bloom* (New York: Atheneum, 1994), 24.
5. Alma Flor Ada, *My Name Is Maria Isabel* (New York: Atheneum, 1993), 12.
6. Paulo Freire, *Pedagogy of the Oppressed* (New York: Continuum, 2000), 87.
7. Ibid., 88
8. Ada and Campoy, 24.
9. Alma Flor Ada, *Where the Flame Trees Bloom* (New York: Atheneum, 1994), 24; Anthony M. Manna, Janet Hill, and Kathy Kellogg, "Alma Flor Ada and the Quest for Change," *Language Arts* 82, no. 1, 2004.
10. Janet Hill and Anthony L. Manna, "A Promise for a Better World" in *Alma Flor Ada and YOU, Volume 1* (Westport, CT: Libraries Unlimited 2005).
11. Alma Flor Ada, presentation given at the Virginia Hamilton Conference on Multicultural Literature, Kent State University, Kent, Ohio, April 4, 2003.
12. Alma Flor Ada, *Under The Royal Palms* (New York: Atheneum, 1998), 6.
13. Alma Flor Ada, presentation given at the Virginia Hamilton Conference on Multicultural Literature, Kent State University, Kent, Ohio, April 4, 2003.

Bibliography

Ada, Alma Flor. Presentation given at the Virginia Hamilton Conference on Multicultural Literature for Youth, Kent State University, Kent, Ohio, April 4, 2003.

Ada, Alma Flor, and F. Isabel Campoy. *Authors in the Classroom: A Transformative Education Process* (Boston: Allyn 8c Bacon, 2004).

Freire, Paulo. *Pedagogy of the Oppressed* (New York: Continuum, 2000), 87.

Giroux, Henry. "Theory and Resistance in Education: A Pedagogy for the Opposition"; quoted in Donaldo Macedo, *Literacies of Power: What Americans are Not Allowed to Know* (Boulder, CO: Westview, 1994), 133.

Hill, Janet, and Anthony L. Manna. "A Promise for a Better World." *Alma Flor Ada and YOU, Volume I* (Westport, CT: Libraries Unlimited, 2005).

Manna, Anthony M., Janet Hill, and Kathy Kellogg. "Alma Flor Ada and the Quest for Change." *Language Arts* 82, no. 1 (2004).

PUBLICATIONS

I

LITERATURE FOR CHILDREN

by Alma Flor Ada

Original Poetry for Children

Bilingual Poetry Books

Arenas y trinos. Abecedario del río. Sand and song. ABCs of the river. English versión Rosalma Zubizarreta. Illust.by Gabhor Utomo. Arte Público Press. 2020

Gathering the Sun. Illust. Simón Silva.
Once Upon A World Award [*Museum of Tolerance*]
Notable Book in the area of Language Arts
Best Books of the Year. [Kirkus Review]

Poetry Books in Spanish

A la sombra de un ala. Illust. Ulises Wensell
Madrid: Escuela Española. 1988.

Abecedario de los animales. Illust. Viví Escrivá.
Madrid: Espasa Calpe. 1990

Abeceloco. Illust. María de Jesús Álvarez. Dallas:
TX: Frog Street. 2010

Arrullos de la sirena. Illust.
Bogotá, Colombia: Panamericana. 2015.

Canción de todos los niños del mundo. Boston:
Houghton-Mifflin. 1993.

Coral y espuma. Abecedario del mar. Illust. Viví
Escrivá. Madrid: Espasa Calpe. 2004

Cuéntame un cuento. Illust. Viví Escrivá. Madrid:
Espasa Calpe. 2004

Tres princesas. Illust. Viví Escrivá. Madrid:
Espasa Calpe. 2004

Todo es canción. Illust. María de Jesús Alvarez.
Miami, FL: Alfaguara. 2011.

Una vez en el medio del mar. Illust. Ulises
Wensell. Madrid: Escuela Española. 1988.

Anthologies in Spanish

Días y días de poesía. Hampton Brown. 1992

El cuento del gato y otras poesías favoritas. Hampton Brown. 1992

Caballito blanco y otras poesías favoritas. Hampton Brown. 1992

Cinco pollitos y otras poesías favoritas Hampton Brown. 1992

Individual Poems in Spanish
included in Anthologies or Magazines

Bilingüe in **Great Morning! Poems for School Leaders to Read Aloud.** S. Vardell and J.Wong Eds. Pomelo Books.2018 p. 98

Bilingüe in **The Poetry Friday Anthology for Celebrations.** S. Vardell and J.Wong Eds. Pomelo Books. p. 66

Bilingüe [Poem] **Iguana. Revista para niños**.feb. 2014

Durazno, César Chávez, Pájaro in **A pocketful Voices/Un bolsillo de voces.** The Best of Poetry Inside Out. Canada. 2009. Pages 98-100

La H, La S, La W, La Z in **Cuentaquetecuento**. Revista latinoamericana de literatura para niños y jóvenes. Vol III, Año 3, no. 1, págs. 57-59

Voy a ser químico: Mario José Molina in **The Poetry Friday Anthology for Science. K-5 Teacher's Edition**.   S. Vardell and J.Wong Eds. Pomelo Books.2014 p. 260

Fifth Grade Student Edition, p. 41

included in Educational Materials

Amigos **En busca de amigos**. SRA. P. 26

Animales domésticos. Nuevos Pasos 2.1
Lectura. Scott Foresman 2000

Canción de todos los niños del mundo
Juegos y fiestas 1-4 **¡Vamos de Fiesta!** A
Harcourt Spanish Reading/Language Arts
Program Harcourt 2000

Diego Rivera. **¡A girar, girasol!** 3
Macmillan McGraw-Hill, 1993

En el país de las maravillas **Literatura Abremundos**
Colección de lecturas,   colección 2, libro 1
Silver Burdett Ginn, 1997

Hipopotamito. Cantos y Fiestas 1-3. **¡Vamos de
Fiesta!** A Harcourt Spanish Reading/Language
Arts Program. Harcourt 2000

Hipopotamito. Aquí y Allá 1-3. **Trofeos.** Un programa
de lectura y artes del lenguaje Harcourt 2003

Honor. ¿Te lo imaginas? 3.1. **Lectura**
Scott Foresman 2000

Horizonte. **Mundo Ortográfico 2**. Editorial
Barcanova. Spain. p. 73

Invierno. **Sol, solecito 1**
Macmillan/McGraw-Hill, 1993

Lo que vamos a ser **Horizontes en ciencia** 1
Silver Burdett & Ginn 1991

Los libros son mis amigos. **Literatura Abremundos**
Colección de lecturas, colección 5
Silver Burdett Ginn, 1997

¡Manzano, manzano! Disfraces y fiestas 1-5
¡Vamos de Fiesta! A Harcourt Spanish
Reading/Language Arts Program. Harcourt 2000

Mi amiga la sombra. **Puerta del Sol,** 2
Macmillan/McGraw-Hill, 1993

Mi amiga la sombra. Un pequeño ruido 1
¡Celebramos la literatura! Programa de lectura
Houghton Mifflin 1993
Orgullo. Descubro al mundo 2
Estudios sociales. Harcourt Brace, 2000
Regar. ¿Te lo imaginas? 3.1
Lectura. Scott Foresman 2000
Regar. Encuentros maravillosos 2.1
Sigamos juntos. Serie de español para la
escuela elemental. Pearson Education Caribean,
2004
Surco. ¡Que sorpresa! **Lectura**
Scott Foresman 2000
Velero **Mundo Ortográfico 2**. Editorial
Barcanova. Spain. p. 50

Poetry for Children in English
Poems included in Poetry Anthologies

"*A Sunday Trip to Chinatown*" in
Amazing Places Lee Bennet Hopkins Ed. Lee
&Low
"*Bilingual*" in **Great Morning!** Poems for School
Leaders to Read Aloud. S. Vardell and J.
Wong Eds. Pomelo Books. p. 97
"*Bilingual*" in **The Poetry Friday Anthology for
Celebrations.** S. Vardell and J.Wong Eds.
Pomelo Books. p. 67
"*Chirstmas in Summer*" in **Christmas is Coming!**
The Metropolitan Museum of Art. Abrams.
2019 p. 123
"*Dancing*" in **World Make Way. New Poems
Inspired   in Art from The Metropolitan
Museum of Art**. Ed. Lee Bennet Hopkins.
Abrams. 2018, p. 14

"*Farmworkers in the Field*" in **The Poetry of Us**
    J. Patrick Lewis. National Geographic p. 117
"I Will Be a Chemist Mario Molina" in **The Poetry**
    Friday Anthology for Science. S. Vardell and
    J.Wong Eds.   Pomelo Books. p. 260
"*Llama*" in **Manger.** Lee Bennett Hopkins. Ed.
    Grand Rapids, MI: Eerdmans 2014 p. 28
"*Spanish Teacher*" in **School People** Lee Bennet
    Hopkins Wordsong 2018 `p. 14

Anthologies co- authored by Alma Flor Ada, Lee Bennet Hopkins & Violet Harris

A Chorus of Cultures. Carmel Valley, CA. Hampton
    Brown.
I Love Your World. Carmel Valley, CA. Hampton
    Brown.

Narrative

Bilingual Books

Daniel's Mystery Egg + El huevo misterioso
Daniel's Pet + Daniel y su mascota
El árbol de Navidad + The Christmas Tree
El cuadradito azul + The Little Blue Square
Let Me Help! + ¡Quiero ayudar!
Medio pollito + Half-chicken
    AEsop's Accolade [American Folklore Association]
The Lizard and the Sun + La lagartija y el sol
    GoldMedal [Folkore category] National Association
    of Parenting Publications

English and Spanish Parallel Books

Colección Libros para Contar / Stories for the Telling
Illustrated by Viví Escrivá.   Santillana/Loqueleo/Vista
<u>Books in Spanish</u>
Amigos
El canto del mosquito
Me gustaría tener
¿Quién nacerá aquí?
Una extraña visita

<u>Books in English</u>
Friends
How Happy I Would Be
Strange Visitors
The Song of the Teeny-Tiny Mosquito
Who's Hatching Here?

<u>Book in Haitian Creole</u>
Zanmi [Amigos]

Colección Cuentos para todo el año / Stories the year
'round. Illustrated by Viví Escrivá.
Santillana/Loqueleo/Vista
<u>Books in Spanish</u>
Como nació el arco iris
Después de la tormenta
El papalote
El susto de los fantasmas
La hamaca de la vaca
La jaula dorada
La piñata vacía
La sorpresa de Mamá Coneja
No fui yo
¡No quiero derretirme!
¿Pavo para la Cena de Gracias?
Rosa alada

<u>Books in English</u>
A Rose with Wings
A Surprise for Mother Rabbit
After the Storm
How the Rainbow Came to Be
I Don't Want to Melt!
In the Cow's Backyard
It Wasn't Me
The Empty Piñata
The Golden Cage
The Kite
Turkey for Thanksgiving? No, thanks...
What are Ghosts Afraid Of?

Individual narrative titles
in Spanish

Allá donde florecen los framboyanes. Illust.
Antonio Martorell. Atheneum

Atentamente, Ricitos de Oro. Illust. Leslie Tryon.
Santillana/Loqueleo

Bajo las palmas reales. Atheneum
Pura Belpré Gold Medal [ALA]
Best Books of the Year 2000 [ALA]

Barquitos de papel. Illust. Pablo Torrecillas. Laredo

Barriletes. Illust. Pablo Torrecillas. Laredo

Con cariño, Amalia. Atheneum
Junior Literary Guild Selection
International Latino Book Award

Cristina y la rana. Frog Street.

Cucarachita Martina. American Reading Company

Días de circo. Illust. Pablo Torrecillas. Laredo

El gallo que fue a la boda de su tío. Putnam

El gallo que fue a la boda de su tío. Frog Street

El manto de plumas y otros cuentos. Illust. Viví
Escrivá Alfaguara

El pañuelo de seda. Illust. Viví Escrivá. Laredo

El reino de la geometría. Laredo

El secreto de Abuelita Benchmark

El unicornio del oeste. Atheneum

El vuelo de los colibríes. Laredo

En el barrio. Scholastic

En el mar.

En la playa. Hartcourt Brace

Encaje de piedra. Editorial Guadalupe. Buenos
Aires. Argentina
Marta Salotti International Award Gold Medal.
[Argentina]

Extra! Extra! Noticias del Bosque Escondido.
Illust. Leslie Tryon. Loqueleo

Había una vez en Dragolandia. Frog Street

La moneda de oro. Illust. Neil Waldman. Atheneum.
Christopher Award Medal

La tataranieta de Cucarachita Martina. Illust.
Scholastic

Los seis deseos de la jirafa. Hampton Brown

Lugares mágicos. Mariposa TES

Más poderoso que yo. Illust.Viví Escrivá.Hartcourt
Brace

Me encantan los Saturdays...y domingos. Illust.
Olivia Sabadier. Atheneum
Notable Book for a Global Society List

¡Me gusta...!

¡Me gusta jugar!

Me llamo María Isabel. Atheneum
Notable Book in the area of Social Studies
[NCSS and the Children's Book Council]
"Pick of the List" [American Booksellers Assoc.]

Mi madre siembra fresas. SRA

Nacer bailando Atheneum
Junior Literary Guild Selection

Olmo y la mariposa azul. Hartocurt Brace

Pin pin sarabín. Illust. Pablo Torrecillas. Laredo

Pregones. Illust. Pablo Torrecillas. Laredo

Querido Pedrín. Illust. Leslie Tryon. Atheneum.

¿Quién cuida al cocodrilo? Illust. Viví Escrivá.

Ratón Pérez. American Reading Company

Sale el oso. Hampton Brown

Tesoros de mi isla: Una niñez cubana. Atheneum
Incluye Bajo las Palmas Reales *[Premio Pura Belpré de ALA]* Allá donde florecen los framboyanes y Días en la Quinta Simoni

Una semilla nada más. Hampton Brown.

Under the Royal Palms
> *Pura Belpré Gold Medal* [American Library Association]
> *Best Books of the Year 2000* [American Library Association]

Individual narrative titles
in English

Abuelita's secret Benchmark 2019

Abuelita's secret. Reycraft. 2019.

Bernice the Barnacle. Harcourt Brace.

Dancing Home Atheneum
> *Junior Literary Guild Selection*
> *International Latino Book Award*

Dear Peter Rabbit Atheneum
> *Parents' Choice Honor Award*
> *"Pick of the List"* [American Booksellers   Assoc.]

Extra! Extra! Hidden Forest News. Atheneum.

Friend Frog. Hartcourt.

Giraffe's Sad Tale. Hampton Brown

Good News.

I Love Saturdays...   y domingos. Atheneum

In the Barrio. Scholastic

Island Treasures. Atheneum
Junior Literary Guild Selection
Americas Award Commended Title [Center for
Latin American Studies]
Jordi's Star. Putnam
Just One Seed. Hampton-Brown
Love, Amalia. Atheneum
Junior Literary Guild Selection
International Latino Literature Award
My Name is María Isabel. Atheneum
Notable Book in the area of Social Studies
[National Council of Social Studies and the
Children's Book Council]
"Pick of the List" [American Booksellers Assoc.]
My Mother Plants Strawberries. SRA
Olmo and the Blue Butterfly. Hartcourt Brace.
Once Upon a Time in Dragonland. Frog Street.
Serafina's Birthday. Atheneum
The Gold Coin. Illust. Neil Waldman. Atheneum
The Christopher Award
Notable Book in the area of Social Studies
[National Council of Social Studies and the
Children's Book Council]
"Pick of the List" [American Booksellers Assoc.]
The Great-grand daughter of Martina. Illust.
López Escrivá. Scholastic.
The Malaquite Palace. Illust. Leonid Gore.
Atheneum
The rooster who went to his uncle's wedding.
Illustr. Kathleen Kuchera. With and introduction
by Tomie DePaola. Putnam. 1993.
One of the Best Books of the Year [Bank Street
College]

The rooster who went to his uncle's wedding.
Illust. Claudia Legnazzi. Frog Street
The Three Golden Oranges. Illust. Reg Cartwright
Atheneum.
The Unicorn of the West. Illust. Abigail Pizer
Atheneum.
Where the Flametrees Bloom. Illust. Antonio
Martorell. Atheneum.
With Love, Little Red Hen. Illust. Leslie Tryon.
Atheneum.
Yours Truly Goldilocks. Illust. Leslie Tryon.
Atheneum.

Stories in Anthologies
In Spanish

Martina Martínez y el Ratón Pérez. In Jaime
Hernández Ed. **La Matadragones. Cuentos de
Latinoamérica**. Toon Graphics.
Serena In E. Pérez Díaz Ed. **Vestida de mar y
otros cantos de sirena**. La Habana, Cuba.
Ediciones Unión. 2010. págs. 150-160

In English

Choices. From *Under the Royal Palms.* In **Choices
and other stories from the Caribbean.** NY:
Friendship Press. 1993 pages 1-3
"Martina Martínez & Pérez the Mouse." In
The Dragon Slayer. Folktales Latin Am.
"*My Abuelita, My Paradise*" in Bonnie. Christensen.
Ed. **In My Grandmother's House. Award-
Winning Authors Tell Stories About Their
Grandmothers**. Harper-Collins, 2003, pages
175-185.

My Name is Maria Isabel. In *The Norton Anthology of Children's Literature*. Zipes, et al 2005

"Not a Piñata this Year" in Lois Metzger (ed.) **The Year We Missed My Birthday**. Eleven Birthday Stories. Scholastic. 2005. pages 29-37

Stories in Children's Magazines

In Spanish

"Aloha" [cuento] **Iguana. Revista para niños** Vol. 9, no. 2 May 2013 pps. 2-5

"Pina y los piratas" . In **Cuentaquetecuento** Costa Rica, Vol. III, no. 3, 1998

Stories in Educational Materials

In SPANISH

Atentamente, Ricitos de Oro SOLARES 4.1 Scholastic 2001

Barriletes ¡VAMOS DE FIESTA! Grado 4 Harcourt, 2000-2003

Cuando el sol desapareció LUNA, LUNERA 1 Macmillan/McGraw-Hill, 1993

Cuéntame un cuento. Todos Juntos 1-4 TROFEOS. Harcourt 2003

El desfile de las nubes ¡ARRIBA LA LECTURA! Libro 1 Grado 2 HMH 2019, págs. 41-58.

El color del agua ¡ARRIBA LA LECTURA! Libro 3 Grado 2 HMH 2019, págs. 178-181.

El gallo que fue a la boda de su tío. ABREMUNDOS Colección de lecturas, colección 2, libro 2. Silver Burdett Ginn, 1997

El gallo que fue a la boda de su tío. LECTURA. 2.2 Scott Foresman 2000

El gallo que fue a la boda de su tío. Antología para la lectura en voz alta, K. Harcourt 2000-2002

El niño de la armónica. ABREMUNDOS Colección de lecturas, colección 3, libro 2. Silver Burdett Ginn, 1997

El papalote. LECTURA 1.3 Scott Foresman 2000

El picnic.SOLARES, 1.1-1.3 Scholastic 2000

¡El temporal! LENGUAJE 6. Edición de Texas. Houghton Mifflin, 2001

El vuelo de los colibríes. Lejos y Cerca 5. ESTRELLAS DE LA LITERATURA. Harcourt Brace Jovanovich 1993

El vuelo de los colibríes. ABREMUNDOS Colección de lecturas, colección 5. Silver Burdett Ginn, 1997

La lagarita y el sol ¡VAMOS DE FIESTA! Velitas y fiestas 3-2 Harcourt 2000

La lagartija y el sol VILLA CUENTOS Listos para el despegue 2-2 Harcourt School Publishers 2009

La hamaca de la vaca, o un amigo más. LECTURA ¡Me gusta! 1.4. Scott Foresman 2000

La mascota de Rafa. TROFEOS Alcanza un sueño 1-2. Programa de lectura y artes del lenguaje de Harcourt. Harcourt 2003 [Luego publicado como libro: **Daniel y su mascota**]

La moneda de oro. Donde Digo Digo, 5 Macmillan/McGraw-Hill, 1993

La moneda de oro. ABREMUNDOS. Colección de lecturas, colección 4. Silver Burdett Ginn, 1997

La moneda del oro. LECTURA. Edición para Texas, 5. McGraw-Hill 2001

La moneda de oro. FORO ABIERTO PARA LA LECTURA 6 SRA/McGraw-Hill 2002

Me gustaría tener. ¡BUEN VIAJE! 1 Macmillan/McGraw-Hill, 1993

Me llamo Maria Isabel. LENGUAJE 4 Harcourt, 2002

Me llamo María Isabel. TROFEOS. Caminos
Abiertos 4. Harcourt 2003

Mediopollito. EXCURSIONES EN CALIFORNIA
Polvo de estrellas 3-2. Harcourt School
Publishers 2010

Mediopollito. SENDEROS 2.2 Houghton Mifflin
Harcourt, 2011

No fui yo. ABREMUNDOS. Colección de lecturas,
colección 1, libro 1. Silver Burdett Ginn, 1997

¿Quién cuida al cocodrilo? LECTURA
¿Te lo imaginas? 3.1 Scott Foresman 2000

¿Quién nacerá aquí? LUNA, LUNERA 1
Macmillan/McGraw-Hill, 1993

Tarjetas de Navidad. LITERATURA DE NUESTRO
MUNDO. Antología, grados 1 y2. Macmillan
McGraw-Hill, 1992

Un amigo más. [La hamaca de la vaca] VILLA
CUENTOS. Alcanza las estrellas 1-3
Harcourt School Publishers, 2009

Un amigo más. [La hamaca de la vaca]
EXCURSIONES EN CALIFORNIA
Tu Mejor Jugada 1-3
Harcourt School Publishers 2010

Una extraña visita, ¡BUEN VIAJE! 1
Macmillan/McGraw-Hill, 1993

Una extraña visita. ABREMUNDOS. Colección de
lecturas, colección 1, libro 2. Silver Burdett
Ginn, 1997

Una semilla nada más. LUNA, LUNERA 1
Macmillan/McGraw-Hill, 1993

Temporal de *Bajo las palmas reales*
LENGUAJE. Houghton Mifflin.2001

In ENGLISH

A Day at School. HOUGHTON MIFFLIN READING
Here we Go! 1.1 Houghton Mifflin 2005

After the Storm. TOOLS 3. English Language
Development, Richmond Publishing (Santillana),
1999

Christmas for All from *Under the Royal Palms.*
TRIUMPS, 6. Houghton Mifflin, 2003

Daniel's Mystery Egg. COLLECTIONS. Join In 1-2
Reading/Language Arts Program. Harcourt 2001

Dan's Pet. MOVING INTO ENGLISH 1.
Harcourt, 2005

Fiesta in San Antonio. In CELEBRATING LITTLE
THINGS, DLM Early Childhood Program. 1995.
Pages 83-85.

Friends TOOLS 1. English Language Development
Richmond Publishing (Santillana), 1999

Gilda, an autobiographical narrative from *Under
the Royal Palms.* LAUNCH INTO READING level 1
Heinle & Heinle Thomson Learning, 2002

Half-Chicken. HARCOURT LANGUAGE 3
Harcourt, 2002

I Don't Want to Melt. TOOLS 4 English Language
Development. Richmond Publishing (Santillana),
1999

It Wasn't Me TOOLS 1. English Language
Development, Teacher's Edition. Richmond
Publishing (Santillana), 1999

Mathematics from *Where the Flame Trees Bloom.* In
EDGE. Reading, Writing and Language.
Hampton-Brown/National Geographic. 2009
pages   133-139

My Name is Maria Isabel. SIGNATURES.
Wings 3-1. Harcourt Brace, 1997

My Name is Maria Isabel. COLLECTIONS 4
. Reading/Language Arts. Harcourt 2001

My Name is María Isabel. TROPHIES. Lead the
Way 4. Reading/Language Arts Program
Harcourt, 2003

My Name is Maria Isabel. TRADITIONS 4
Houghton Mifflin, 2003

Olmo and the Blue Butterfly. SIGNATURES
Picture Perfect 1-1. Harcourt Brace, 1997

Storm! From *Under the Royal Palms.* ENGLISH 6
Houghton Mifflin, 2001

Tell Me A Story. TROPHIES. Time Together
Harcourt Reading/Language Arts Program
Harcourt, 2003

Tell Me a Story. MOVING INTO ENGLISH 1
Harcourt, 2005

The Bats from *Under the Royal Palms.* In
TEACHER READ ALOUDS. Level 5. 2002
pages 1, 15-21
SRA/Open Court Readers

The Empty Piñata. TOOLS 3 – English
Language Development, Teacher's Edition
Richmond Publishing (Santillana), 1999

The Gold Coin. Don't Forget to Fly, 5
Macmillan/McGraw-Hill, 1993

The Gold Coin in JUST LIKE A HEROE. CELEBRATE
READING Scott Foresman. 1993 pages 30-47

The Gold Coin. SIGNATURES
In Search of a Dream 4. Harcourt Brace, 1997

The Gold Coin. SIGNATURES. Rare Finds 4
Harcourt Brace, 1997

The Gold Coin. OPEN COURT READING 6
SRA/McGraw-Hill 2002

Non-Fiction Pieces
included in Educational Materials
In Spanish

In English

Just Like a Hero CELEBRATE READING! 6F
Scott Foresman, 1993
Stand and Deliver: an interview with Jaime Escalante. DREAM A WORLD, 8
Macmillan/McGraw-Hill, 1993
Stories and Storytellers. MOVING INTO ENGLISH 3 Harcourt, 2005

Translations
included in Educational Materials

El dolor de muelas de Alberto. NARANJA DULCE, 2. Macmillan/McGraw-Hill, 1993
La cintura de Anansi. Míralo de cerca 1.2 LECTURA. Scott Foresman 2000
LonPoPo by Ed Young. Polvo de estrellas 3-2 EXCURSIONES EN CALIFORNIA. Harcourt School Publishers 2010
Los cazadores invisibles/The Invisible Hunters ¡A NAVEGAR! 3 Macmillan/McGraw-Hill, 1993
Salí de paseo. Míralo de cerca 1.2 LECTURA. Scott Foresman 2000

II
LITERATURE FOR CHILDREN

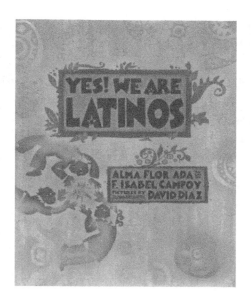

by Alma Flor Ada & F. Isabel Campoy

Poetry anthologies with F. Isabel Campoy
In Spanish

Colección Alegrías National Geographic/Cengage

Alegría. Poesía cada día. Teacher's Anthology
Alegría A. Oversized book
Alegría B. Oversized book
Alegría C. Oversized book

Colección Puertas al sol Santillana/Loqueleo/Vista
Libros
Antón Pirulero.
Chuchurumbé.
Mambrú
Pimpón.
Journals
Letras
Palabras
Poemas
Rimas

Colección La rama azul. Harcourt Brace
Dulce es la sal
El verde limón
Gorrión, gorrión
Huertos de coral
La rama azul
Nuevo día
Ríos de lava

Frog Street
Salta, saltarín 2010. Illustrated by Claudia Legnazzi.
Poemas con ton y son. 2020

Houghton Mifflin Harcourt
En los montes, monte soy

Bilingual oral folklore with F. Isabel Campoy

Mamá Goose
Merry Navidad
MuuMoo
   CCBC Choice [Cooperative Children Books Center]
Pío Peep
   Best Ten Books for Babies. [Beginning with Books.
      Center for Early Literacy]
   Best Book of the Year [Nick Jr. Magazine]
   Media Award [Parents' Guide to Children's Media]
   100 Titles for Reading and Sharing [NY Public
      Library]
   Books of the Year Award. [Parenting Mazagizes]
   2 X 2 Reading List [Texas Library Association]
   Starred Review [School Library Journal]
   Starred Review [Críticas. ALA]
Ten Little Puppies / Diez perritos
   Junior Library Guild Selection

Anthologies co- authored with F. Isabel Campoy
In English

Series *Gateways to the Sun.* Santillana/Loqueleo
Books
Dreaming Fish.
Flying Dragon.
   Laughing Crocodiles.
   Singing Horse.
   Journals
   Letters
   Poems
   Rhymes
   Words

COLECCIÓN LA RAMA AZUL

The poetry anthologies of this collection have been listed under Poetry Anthologies in Spanish

CULTURE

Ecos del pasado
Imágenes del pasado
Sigue la palabra

THEATER

Acto final
Actores y flores
Ensayo general
Escenas y alegrías
Primer acto
Risas y aplausos
Saludos al público

BOOKS CREATED BY PARENTS AND CHILDREN

Así pasaron muchos años
En un lugar muy lejano
Érase que se era
¿Quieres que te cuente...?
Y colorín colorado
Y fueron felices

COLECCIÓN MÚSICA AMIGA

The 10 books contain original poems by Alma Flor Ada and F. Isabel Campoy, some pieces from the folklore and a few poems by other authors. Illustrated by Ulises Wensell. The 10 CDs contain all poems with music and voice by Suni Paz.

Canción y alegría

Canta la letra

Caracolí

Con ton y son

Corre al coro Do, re, mi, ¡sí, sí!

El camino de tu risa

El son del sol

¡Qué rica la ronda!

Sigue la música

Colección Puertas al Sol /Gathering the Sun

The Poetry anthologies of this collection have been listed under Poetry Anthologies in Spanish and Poetry Anthologies in English

ARTE

Books English
   Artist's Easel
   Blue and Green
   Brush and Paint
   Canvas and Paper
Books Spanish
   Azul y verde
   Brocha y pincel
   Caballete
   Lienzo y papel
Journals English
   Colors

Crayons

Pencils

Watercolors

Journals Spanish

Acuarela

Colores

Crayones

Lápices

BIOGRAFÍA

Books English

Paths

Smiles

Steps

Voices

Libros Spanish

Caminos

Pasos

Sonrisas

Voces

Journals English

I Am

My Memories

My Stories

This is Me

Journals Spanish

Así soy

Mis Recuerdos

Mis relatos

Yo

CULTURA

Books English

Eyes of the Jaguar

On the Condor's Wings

The Quetzal's Journey

Books Spanish
> **El vuelo del quetzal**
> **En alas del cóndor**
> **Ojos del jaguar**

LENGUAJE

Books English
> **A New Home for the Seven Little Kids**
> **A New Job for Pérez the Mouse**
> **Happy Birthday, Little Red Riding Hood**
> **One, Two, Three. Who Can It Be?**

Books Spanish
> **El nuevo hogar de los siete cabritos**
> **Feliz cumpleaños, Caperucita Roja**
> **Ratoncito Pérez, cartero**
> **Uno, dos, tres. Dime ¿quién es?**

TEATRO

Books in English
> **Curtains Up!**
> **Rat-A-Tat-Cat**
> **Roll 'N' Role**
> **Top Hat**

Books in Spanish
> **Escenario de Polichinela**
> **Tablado de Doña Rosita**
> **Teatro del Gato Garabato**
> **Teatrín de Don Crispín**

TEACHER'S GUIDES/ ACTIVITIES/ ASSESMENT

Teachers' Guides
> Silver. English
> Gold. English
> Silver. Spanish
> Gold. Spanish

Activities and Assessment
    English
    Spanish
Teacher Training DVD
    Puertas al Sol/Gateway to the Sun

Colección Cuentos para Celebrar / Stories to Celebrate

Parallel Books in Spanish and English.
Combining a present-day realistic story and non-fiction information about the holidays described.
Published by Santillana/Loqueleo/Vista.

Celebra el día de Martin Luther King con la clase de la Sra. Park
Celebrate Martin Luther King, Jr. Day with Mrs. Park's class
Celebra el Año Nuevo Chino con la familia Fong
Celebrate Chinese New Year with the Fong Family
Celebra Mardi Gras, con Joaquín, arlequín
Celebrate Mardi Gras with Joaquin, Harlequin
Celebra el Día de San Patricio con Samantha y Lola
Celebrate St. Patrick's Day with Samantha and Lola
Celebra el Cinco de Mayo con un jarabe tapatío
Celebrate Cinco de Mayo with the Mexican Hat Dance
Celebra el Cuatro de julio con Champ, el campeón
Celebrate Fourth of July with Champ, the Scamp
Celebra un Powwow con Sandy Starbright
Celebrate a Powwow with Sandy Starbright
Celebra Halloween y el Día de Muertos con Cristina y su Conejito Azul

Celebrate Halloween and the day of the Death with
  Cristina and her Blue Bunny
Celebra el Día de Acción de Gracias con Beto y
  Gaby
Celebrate Thanksgiving Day with Beto and Gaby
Celebra Hanukkah con los cuentos de Bubbe
Celebrate Hanukkah with Bubbe's Tales
Celebra Kwanzaa con Botitas y sus gatitos
Celebrate Kwanzaa with Boots and her Kittens
Celebra Navidad y Reyes Magos con Pablo y
  Carlitos
Celebrate Christmas and Three Kings Day with
  Pablo and Carlitos

Narrative Titles with F. Isabel Campoy
In Spanish
Cuentos que contaban nuestras abuelas.
  Atheneum.
  Notable Book for a Global Society List
¡Sí! Somos latinos Charlesbridge
  First Price - International Latino Book Award
  Junior Literary Guild Selection
Una semana de pingüinos y más. Hartcourt
Una semilla de luz. Madrid: Alfaguara

In English
Tales Our Abuelitas Told. Atheneum
  Notable Book for a Global Society List
  Best Folklore in Best Books of the Year [Nick Jr.
    Family Magazine]
  Kirkus Best Books [Kirkus Review]
  A Parent's Choice Recommended Book
  Best Books of the Year [Books for a Global
    Society SIG/   American Library Association]
  Notable Book in the Area of Language Arts
The Picnic.   Hartcourt

Yes! We Are Latinos. Charlesbridge
First Price - International Latino Book Award
Junior Literary Guild Selection

Non-Fiction Pieces
included in Educational Materials
Co-authored by AFA and FIC

Antiguas culturas de las Américas
Bailes y Fiestas 4 ¡VAMOS DE FIESTA!
Harcourt Spanish Reading/Language Arts
Program. Harcourt 2002
El Caballo. Bailes y Fiestas 4. ¡VAMOS DE FIESTA!
Harcourt Spanish Reading/Language Arts
Program Harcourt 2002
Frida Kahlo ¡ARRIBA LA LECTURA! Mi Libro 3
Grado 2 HMH 2019, págs.. 41- 50.
¡Sí! Somos latinos ¡ARRIBA LA LECTURA! Mi
Libro 1 Grado 4 HMH 2019, págs. 45 - 54.

III
LITERATURE FOR ADULTS

by Alma Flor Ada

Memoirs

Cartas de Napoli [Mariposa]
Vivir en dos idiomas [Aguilar]
Vivir en dos idiomas [Mariposa]
Long Life Journey: Becoming a Teacher
   [Mariposa]

Novels

A pesar del amor [Alfaguara Miami]
A pesar del amor [Alfaguara Spain
A pesar del amor [Mariposa edition]
A pesar del amor [Acana, Cuba   ]
En clave de sol [Alfaguara Miami]
En clave de sol [Mariposa edition]

Poetry

Books

Cuando el amor vive en la mirada [Mariposa]
Minuto eterno [Mariposa]

Poems in Anthologies

"En la piel de tus hijas, Madre América" Na pele
   da tus filhas, Mae America" In **Mujeres Fuertes
   /Mulheres fortes**. Carlos Díez Polanco y Teresa
   Aguilar Larrucea Eds. Santillana. 2008.p. 14-15

Family and ancestry

Alma Flor Ada.

> **Casa de grandes arcos. Dos familias luminosas** [Mariposa]
> **Once There Were Four Children**
> **A orillas del Tínima. Antepasados de la familia Salvador Arias. I.** [Mariposa]

Modesto Ada

> **Sin temor de Dios. Hacer el bien por el bien mismo**

Alma Lafuente Salvador de Ada

> **Del ayer hasta el mañana** [Mariposa]
> **Manantial de sentimientos**
> **Mi vida.** [Mariposa]

Medardo Lafuente [author]

> **Jornadas líricas [2nd ed.]** [Mariposa]
> **Jornadas líricas [CD]**[Mariposa]
> **Mi cada vez más querida mía** [letters from Medardo Lafuente a Dolores Salvador] [Mariposa]
> **Páginas rescatadas [3rd ed.]** [Mariposa]

Dolores Salvador

> **Dolores Salvador: Maestra de maestras** [Mariposa]

Mireya Lafuente Salvador

> **Recuerdos de mi vida** [Mariposa]

Virginia Lafuente Salvador [author]

> **Palabras**

Rosalma Zubizarreta Ada

> **From Conflict to Creative Collaboration: La facilitación dinámica** [Mariposa]

Collette Zubizarreta

> **A Little Bit Creative / Un poquito creativo**

IV Academic & Professional Writing
by Alma Flor Ada

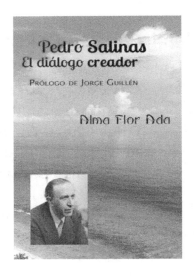

Books

A Magical Encounter. 1st Santillana. 1990.

A Magical Encounter. 2nd ed. Allyn & Bacon, 2002

A Magical Encounter. 3rd Mariposa.

Guía para padres y maestros [1st ed.] with Colin Baker

Guía para padres y maestros [1st ed.] with Colin Baker

Pedro Salinas: el diálogo creador Preface by Jorge Guillén.] Madrid, Gredos. 1969. [Pedro Salinas: The Creative Dialogue] Madrid. [The author's name appears as Alma de Zubizarreta]
Reviewed by: A. Debicki. **Books Abroad**. (Spring 1970. P. 273-7). D.H.Harris. **Bulletin of Hispanic Studies.** (Liverpool) (XLVIII,4,p.367-69).
 J.Palley.**Hispania**. (v. 53, 1970, p. 576-77). E. Zuleta. **Cuadernos de Filología**. (Mendoza, Argentina) (3, 1969, p. 176-77).

Pedro Salinas: el diálogo creador [Mariposa]

The Power of Two Languages with Josefina Tinajero Eds. Macmillan.

Chapters in Edited Books

2010 [Co-authored with F.Isabel Campoy] *Latino Literature for   Children and Adolescents.* In Lynn Atkinson & Ruth A. Oswald (Eds.) **Multicultural Literature and Response. Affirming Diverse Voices**. Libraries Unlimited.

2001 [Co-authored with F.Isabel Campoy & Rosa Zubizarreta.] *Assessing our work with parents on behalf of children's literacy.* In S. R. Hurley, & J. V. Tinajero (Eds.) **Literacy Assessment of Second Language Learners**. Boston, MA: Allyn & Bacon.

2001 [Co-authored with Rosa Zubizarreta] *Parent Narratives: The Cultural Bridge Between Latino Parents and Their Children.* In M. L. Reyes, & J.J. Halcón (Eds.) **The Best for Our Children. Critical Perspectives on Literacy for Latino Students**. New York: Teachers College Press.

1998 [Co-authored with Nancy Jean Smith] *Fostering the Home- School Connection for Latinos.* In María Luisa González, Ana Huerta-Macías and Josefina Villamil Tinajero (Eds.) **Educating Latino Students. A Guide to Succesful Practice**. Lancaster, PA: Technomic.

1997 Contemporary Trends in Children's Literature Written in Spain and Latin America. In: Josefina Villamil Tinajero and Alma Flor Ada (Eds.) **The Power of Two Languages**. New York. Macmillan/McGraw Hill

1997 *Mother Tongue Literacy as a Bridge Between Home and School Community* In Josefina Villamil Tinajero and lma Flor Ada (Eds.) **The Power of Two Languages**.New York. Macmillan/McGraw

1997 *Linguistic Human Rights and Education.* In Enid Lee, Deborah Menkart and Margo Okazawa Rey **Beyond Heroes and Holidays: A Practical Guide to K-12 Anti-Racist, Multicultural Education and Staff Development.** Washington,D.C. Network of Educators on the Americas

1996 *A Visionary Look at Spanish Language Arts in the Bilingual Classroom"*. In Catherine Walsh (Ed.) **Education Reform and Social Change. Multicultural Voices, Struggles, and Visions**. Mahwah, NJ: Lawrence Erlbaum

1996 *The Transformative Language Arts Classroom.* In L. Scott (Ed.) **Promising Practices. Unbearably Good, Teacher-Tested Ideas.** San Diego, CA: The Greater San Diego Council of Teachers of English. **pp. 5-10**

1995 *Fostering the Home-School Connection"* In Jean Frederickson (Ed.) **Reclaiming Our Voices. Bilingual Education, Critical Pedagogy and Praxis.** Ontario, CA: California Association for Bilingual Education.

1989 *Creative Reading: A Relevant Methodology for Language Minority Children.* In Catherine Walsh (Ed.). **Literacy as Praxis: Culture, Language and Pedagogy**. Norwood, NK:Ablex.

1988 *The Pájaro Valley Experience: Working with Spanish-speaking parents to develop children's reading and writing skills in the home through the use of children's literature.* In Tove Skutnabb-Kangas and J. Cummins (Eds.) **Minority education: From shame to struggle**. Clevedon, England: Multilingual Matters.

1987 *Creative Education for Bilingual Teachers.* In M. Ogazawa-Rey, J. Anderson, and R. Traver (Eds.) **Teachers, Teaching, and Teaching Education.** Cambridge, MA: Harvard Educational Review. Reprint Series No. 19, 57-65.

1987 *Creative Reading. A Relevant Methodology for Language Minority Children.* **Theory, Research and Appliciations. Selected Papers**. National Association for Bilingual Education.

1985 *La enseñanza bilingüe a la población hispánica de los Estados Unidos: Condiciones presentes, posibilidades futuras.* In Miguel Siguán (Ed.)

**Enseñanza en dos lenguas y resultados escolares.
IX Seminario sobre "Educación y lenguas."**
Universidad de Barcelona. pp. 73-84.

Journal Articles

A Lifetime of Learning to Teach. **Journal of Latinos
  and Education**. Vol 6, number 2, 2007, pp. 103-
  118

[in collaboration with Judith Berhard, Jim Cummins, F.
  Isabel Campoy, Adam Winsler and Charles Bleiker].
  *Identity Texts and Literacy Development Among
  Preschool English Language Learners: Enhancing
  Learning Opportunities for Children at   Rish for
  Learning Disabilities."* **Teachers College Record**.
  Volume 108, Number 11, November 2006, pp.
  2380-2405. Columbia University.

[with Jim Cummins and David Ramírez] *Speaking of
  Technology: Raising Voices, Linking Wisdom.* In
  **Virtual Power. Technology, Education and
  Community**. pps. 2-7 [Also in PSR*TEC web site]

Dear Teachers In **Voices from the Middle**. National
  Council of Teachers of English. Volume 9, Number
  2. December 2001

[with Isabel Campoy] *El nacimiento de una literatura
  infantil: La literatura infantil en los Estados
  Unidos.*In **Cuentaquetecuento. Revista
  latinoamericana de literatura infantil para niños
  y jóvenes**. Volume III,number 3,1988. pps. 89-100.

*Curtains Up! Contemporary Children's Plays in
  Spanish.* In **Tops of the News**. American Library
  Association Young Adults Services Division. Volume
  43, number 3, Spring 1987. pps. 279-285

The Challenges and Joys of Becoming Bilingual.
  CBC Features. Children Book Council. Vol. 52,
  Number 2. 1999

Book Prefaces

2016 Riojas Clark, Ellen et al. **Multicultural Literature for Latino Bilingual Children: Their Words, Their Worlds**. New York: Rowman & Littlefield.

2005 Eggers-Piérola, Costanza. **Connections and Commitments. Conexión y compromiso. Reflecting Latino Values in Early Childhood Programs.** Portsmouth, NH: Heineman

2001 Ramírez, Lettie & Olivia M. Gallardo. (2001). **Portraits of Teachers In Multicultural Settings. A Critical Literacy Approach**. Boston, MA: Allyn & Bacon.

2001 Steiner, Stanley F. **Promoting a Global Community Through Multicultural Children's Literature**.Englewood, CO: Teachers Ideas Press.

1995 Igoa, Cristina. **The Inner World of the Immigrant Child.** New York: St. Martin's Press.

1994 McCaleb, Sudía Paloma. **Building Communities of Learners. A Collaboration among Teachers, Students, Families, and Communities**. New York: St. Martin's Press.

1992 Fernández, Mayra. **Barrio Teacher.** Sandcastle Publishing.

1992 Pérez, Bertha & María E. Torres-Guzmán. **Learning in Two Worlds. An Integrated Spanish/English Biliteracy Approach**. New York: London.

1969 Bécquer, Gustavo Adolfo **Rimas y leyendas**. Lima, Perú. Editorial Universo. Colección Autores Clásicos. [Selección y prólogo Alma de Zubizarreta, pp. 3-19]

Contributions in Books

Dream Walkers by Ruth Culham. "*Exploring Latino Literature with a Writer's Eye*" pages 9-10

More than a Score. The New Uprising Against High-stakes Testing. Jesse Hagopian *Discovering a Deeper Meaning in Life...* In "*Đear President Obama, We Need Literature Over Test Prep...*" Ed. Hymarket Books. 2014. pages. 253-257.

Poems are teachers. How Studying Poetry Strengthen Writing. A. Ledwig Vanderwater.
"*Writing in 1st person   singular*" pages 59-62
"*End of one...*" pages 201 -203

V.
Pedagogical Writing

by Alma Flor Ada & F. Isabel Campoy

Books

Authors in the Classroom
Ayudando a nuestros hijos
Está linda la mar.   Santillana
Guía para padres y maestros [2nd ed.]
   with Colin Baker
Música amiga: Aprender cantando
Owning Meaning
Palabra amiga [book]
Palabra amiga [workbook]
Spanish Literacy
Strategies for Young Learners

Transformative Education Handbooks

Comprehensive Language Arts
Effective Language Acquisition
Home-School Interaction with Cultural or
   Language Diverse Families

VI.

Publications about
ALMA FLOR ADA

Books

Alma Flor Ada. An Author Kids Love
by M. Parker Rock

Alma Flor Ada from a family of storytellers
Scholastics

Alma Flor Ada and You   Volume I

Alma Flor Ada and You   Volume II

Articles in Books featuring Alma Flor Ada

In ENGLISH

In Sweet Company. Conversations with Extraordinary Women about Living a Spiritual Life by Margaret Wolff. Lotus Press. 2004. Pages 51-66

Dream Walkers. **Mentor Texts that Celebrate Latino Culture** by R.Culham. Stenhouse Publishers *Exploring Latino Literature with a Writer's Eye* pages   3-4, 9-10, 29, 31, 38-39, 54, 75-77

Hispanics in the US book. Santillana.

Hispanics in the US activity book. Santillana

Something About the Author Vol 222 [pages 3-30]

Something About the Author. Vol 43. Gale Research Co. 1996 pages 25-26   p. 59

Something About the Author. Vol 84. Gale Research Co. 1996 pages 1-7.

Something About the Author. Vol 143. Gale Research Co. pages 1-13

Something About the Author. *Featured Author.* Vol 222. Gale Research Co. pages 3-30

In SPANISH

De raíces y sueños. 50 libros para niños y jóvenes de autores latinos en los E. U. S. Andricaín, P. Cerrillo A. O. Rodríguez. p. 38

Diccionario de autores de la literatura infantil cubana. Tomo I.
R.L. Herrera Rojas y M. Estupiñán González. *Alma Flor Ada* pps 15-17

El fuego sagrado. Los escritores cubanos para niños se confiesan por Enrique Pérez Díaz.
Alimentar nuestra propia fe y nuestra esperanza" por A. F. Ada pages 40-44

La aventura de la palabra por Sergio Andricaín. Miami: Fundación Cuatrogatos. 2014 págs. 37-38, 77-78, 150-151, 187

Los que escriben para niños se confiesan por Enrique Pérez Díaz. *Alimentar nuestra propia fe y nuestra esperanza* por Alma Flor Ada p. 29-32

Hispanos en los EE UU

Hispanos en los EE UU activity book

VIII INSTRUCTIONAL MATERIALS

by Alma Flor Ada & F. Isabel Campoy

READING AND LANGUAGE ARTS SERIES – PUBLISHED BY HARCOURT & HMH

SOLE AUTHORS

Cielo abierto. *Lectura K-6.* 2000

PRIMARY AUTHORS IN A COMMITTEE OF AUTHORS

Arriba la lectura. *Lectura K-6.* 2019

Colecciones. *Lectura K-5.*

Excursiones en California. *Lectura K-6.*

Senderos. *Lectura K-5.*

Trofeos. *Lectura K-5.*

Vamos de fiesta. *Lectura K-6.*

ENGLISH AS A SECOND LANGUAGE

PARTICIPANTS IN A COMMITTEE OF AUTHORS

Moving Into English. *ESL Program K-6.* Harcourt. 2008.

PRE-K/KINDERGARTEN PROGRAMS

PARTICIPANTS IN A COMMITTEE OF AUTHORS

Frog Street Pre-K Program. 2010.

VIII
INSTRUCTIONAL
MATERIALS
by Alma Flor Ada

PRE-K/KINDERGARTEN

PROGRAMS - *Co-authored with Pam Schiller*

DLM Kindergarten Program

SRA Kindergarten Program

SPANISH READING PROGRAM

PARTICIPANTS IN A COMMITTEE OF AUTHORS

Villacuentos. *Lectura K-6. Macmillan-McGraw*

ENGLISH AS A FOREIGN LANGUAGE

PARTICIPANTS IN A COMMITTEE OF AUTHORS

Parade. *K-6.* Scott Foresman, 2005.

SPANISH LANGUAGE ARTS - HIGH SCHOOL

EDITORIAL ARICA/ EDITORIAL BRASA - [Lima, Perú]

SOLE AUTHORS

Iniciación Literaria

Oír y narrar

Ortografía y vocabulario

Ortografía práctica

Ver y describir

PRIMARY AUTHOR

Castellano I

Castellano II

Castellano III

HAGAMOS CAMINOS SPANISH READING SERIES
MC GRAW-HILL MÉXICO
SOLE AUTHOR

Books

Partimos

Andamos

Corremos

Volamos

Workbooks

Partimos *cursive*

Partimos *script*

Andamos *cursive*

Andamos *script*

Corremos *cursive*

Corremos *script*

Volamos *cursive*

Volamos *script*

IX
DVDs & CDs
by Alma Flor Ada
and F. Isabel Campoy

In Spanish
El encuentro mágico con el folklore infantil*

by Alma Flor Ada
In English
Creative Reading Methodology
Hagamos caminos. A Creative Reading Initial Literacy Program
Meeting and Author
My Journey as a Writer
Participatory Research – A Dialogue with Paulo Freire

In Spanish
La lectura creadora
El encuentro mágico con el folklore infantil*
Escribiendo desde el corazón

CDs
by Alma Flor Ada
Bilingual
The Gold Coin – La moneda de oro
In English
The Malachite Palace – The Unicorn of the West – Jordi Star
Stories the Year 'round

In Spanish
Cuentos para todo el año

CDs
by Alma Flor Ada & F. Isabel Campoy
In Spanish
Cuentos que contaban nuestras abuelas

Musical CDs
Text Alma Flor Ada Music and Voice Suni Paz
Aprender cantando
Abecedario
Arrullos de la sirena
Como una flor
Coral y espuma. Abecedario del mar
Cuéntame un cuento
Gathering the Sun
Todo es canción
Tres princesas

Libros para contar
Cuentos para todo el año

Text Alma Flor Ada Music and F. Isabel Campoy
Music and Voice Suni Paz
Cantarín [Frog Street]
Pío Peep [Mariposa]

Made in the USA
Monee, IL
23 January 2021